'One of the compulsive aspects of Boyt's book is that, as a reader, you get to listen in on her trying to make honest sense of events that go well beyond what any daughter might be expected to fathom. I ended up reading it in one sitting, well into the early hours of the following day' Tim Adams, *The Observer*

'I can't think of an art book with an opening page like it. Lines land like detonations . . . The writing is hypnotic and propulsive . . . It's so powerful, so horrible, the set-up compelling'
The Sunday Times

'The reader is invited into the innermost intimacies of a private life, not just the scandalous details and long-held secrets, but the long waking hours, the temporal chasms between the more gossip-worthy parts of Boyt's existence . . . *Naked Portrait* is a hall of mirrors with the young Boyt at its centre, surveyed from above by her now-66-year-old self . . . A portrait of Freud that's even more revealing than his nude depiction of Rose' *The Telegraph*

'Boyt's stories of her father and her relations with him are dramatic and often shocking' *i*

'The unexpected miracle of the book is its emotional complexity'
Claire Dederer, *The Guardian*

Naked Portrait

Rose Boyt was born in London and as a child lived on a cargo ship trading in the Baltic and beyond. She emigrated to the Caribbean with her mother and siblings, but the family was repatriated. She left home when she was fifteen and in the seventies began to take photographs and had a Saturday job at the punk shop Seditionaries. In the eighties, she worked as a DJ and on the door of the Café de Paris. She is the author of three novels.

Naked Portrait

A Memoir of Lucian Freud

ROSE BOYT

PICADOR

First published 2024 by Picador

This edition first published 2025 by Picador
an imprint of Pan Macmillan
The Smithson, 6 Briset Street, London EC1M 5NR
EU representative: Macmillan Publishers Ireland Ltd, 1st Floor,
The Liffey Trust Centre, 117–126 Sheriff Street Upper,
Dublin 1, D01 YC43
Associated companies throughout the world
www.panmacmillan.com

ISBN 978-1-0350-2492-6

1 3 5 7 9 8 6 4 2

A CIP catalogue record for this book is available from the British Library.

Typeset in Janson Text by Jouve (UK), Milton Keynes
Printed and bound by CPI Group (UK) Ltd, Croydon, CR0 4YY

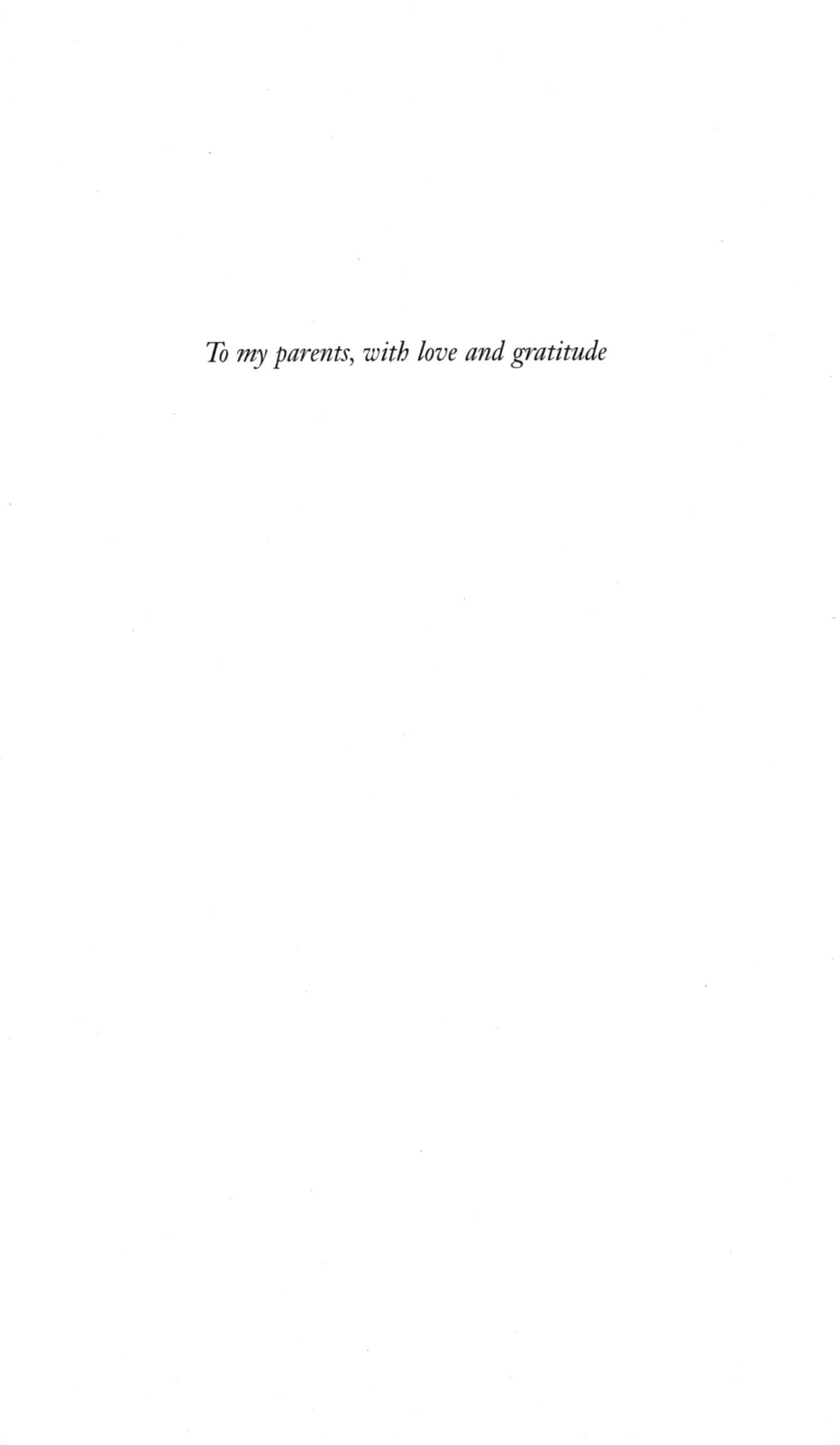

To my parents, with love and gratitude

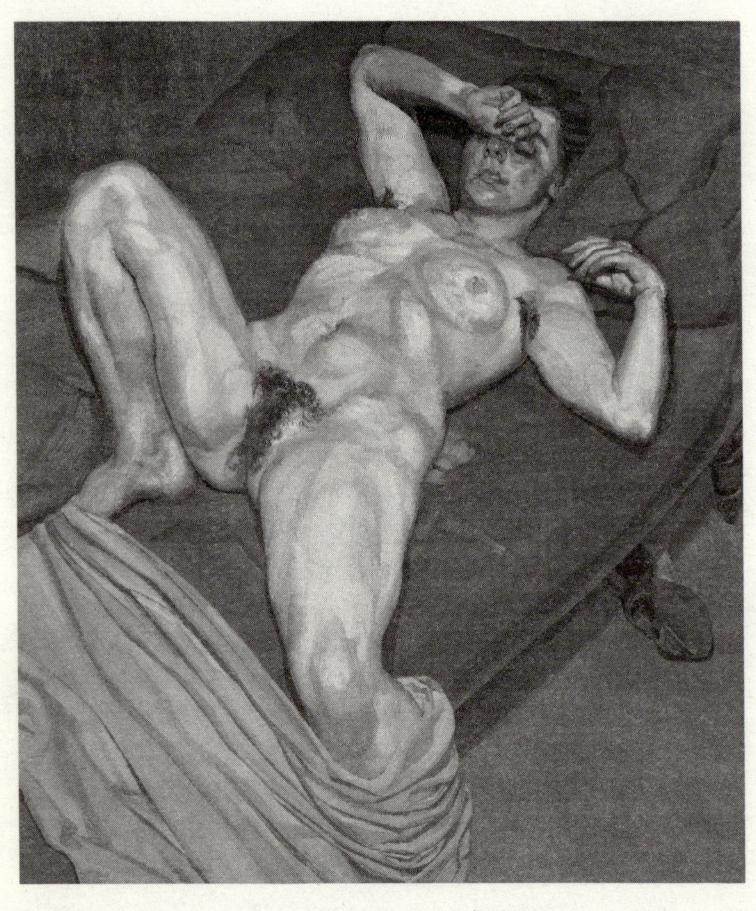

Rose (1977–8)

LUCIAN FREUD

ONE

Nothing had been discussed, I just assumed I would be naked. I got undressed and asked him what he would like me to do. He said it was up to me. I lay down on the sofa and shielded my eyes, the big ceiling lights in the studio working on full power. I lay down, but I didn't want to look obedient in my portrait, I didn't feel obedient. I wanted my father to paint me but not like the others – there was some kind of battle going on, unacknowledged but expressed in the muscles of my bent leg – I was alert, prepared to spring up at any moment. I asked him not to paint in my hairy legs. He said it was not like that. We talked about make-up. He didn't like to paint it, but I was not going to take off my mascara. In the end he decided it was part of me. That was a small victory.

I wanted to know if he was happy with the pose. He thought it was spectacular, but showed some concern. I'm not sure whether he was worried about my ability to keep going until the end of the painting with so much tension in my body or if he was uneasy about the level of exposure I had unwittingly chosen to inflict on myself; I was unaware of how much he could see from his vantage point. I think I understand now he wanted my permission to use what he could see, to shift the responsibility onto me and take advantage of my generosity, even if I didn't know what I was doing, didn't know what he was asking for. I was shocked when I looked at the canvas and saw what he saw.

This was a night picture. I sat three or four times a week, starting when it got dark, often until dawn. We were collaborators, but he always wanted to work way longer than I wanted to work – I didn't know how to make him stop, how to stick up for myself. He groaned in disappointment if I needed a stretch or to go to the bathroom, the urgency of his resolve a trial of my courage. After a long session I didn't always go home; I slept in the studio if I was aching, wide awake but too tired to get up off the sofa – he chucked a blanket over me and gave me a big glass of port to knock me out, for which I was grateful. I started at Central School of Art a few months into the painting, on the foundation course, and after a couple of hours I would have to get up and go in. Sometimes he offered me one of the little blue pills that he kept in his bathroom cupboard next to the bottle of Mandrax, prescription drugs he obtained from his doctor to help him work harder and unwind at bedtime if he was too wired to stop. He told me the blue ones were called Purple Hearts, and that they had been used by fighter pilots during the war to keep going on overnight missions, associating himself in my mind with those heroes who had dropped bombs on Nazi Germany, the home from which he had fled with his family when he was nine. He worked heroically and I wanted to be like him. The pills woke me up and ruined my appetite. I went to art school in his shirts, his old jackets.

It upset me when the picture went badly and he stabbed himself in the leg with the end of his paintbrush. I just had to lie there while he shouted and hurt himself. When it went well he conjured a marvellous excitement under the bright lights, all the stories he told me, his escapades with aristocrats and villains in London, of his nurse and the legendary glimpse of Hitler in Berlin before he came over, the songs he sang to keep me entertained. He knew by heart Hilaire Belloc's *Cautionary Tales*, 'Prufrock' and Shakespeare's best sonnet, 'My Mistress' Eyes Are Nothing Like the Sun', a poem he recited so many times it stuck in my head and is still there to sustain me when I need to sleep and I can't sleep. I never got tired of listening to it, even the times he rewrote the last couplet off the top of his head for his own reasons without even knowing it; I shared his pleasure in the celebration of the unpoetical attributes of the beloved mistress even as I cringed in mild embarrassment – she was so rough and yet so adored. Although there was a poem he recited once too often as I lay there with my eyes half hidden under his scrutiny, by the Earl of Rochester, called 'Written Under Nelly's Picture', about Nell Gwyn. It went something like this:

She was so exquisite a whore
That in the belly of her mother
She placed her cunt so right before
Her father fucked them both together.

He loved Flaubert above all other writers, and was drawn to his letters in particular, as well as the letters and diaries of Kafka, the stories of Maupassant, 'Prufrock' and other Eliot poems, Nietzsche (after Francis Bacon) and the Eadweard Muybridge books of photographs, another enthusiasm that came through Francis. He told me that there were absolutes in art, nothing was relative, and loathed the idea of self-expression. He referred to Sigmund as 'MY GRANDFATHER' and knew some of the jokes out of *Jokes and Their Relation to The Unconscious*, but was not himself conscious of Freud's theory about Oedipus. He thought a person ought to be medically trained to perform psychoanalysis, that it took no heed of the lifespan and was shameful if you found yourself on the receiving end of it. I used to leave the studio after work and descend the stairs with so much stuff buzzing in my head I could hardly contain myself. I have forgotten any confusion or upset I might have experienced – as I remember my descent I was always elated, senses heightened, ready to take on anything under his influence.

The studio, on the fifth floor of a converted house in Holland Park, felt almost too private, the unusual arrangement of the doors into the flat adding to the sense of a closed world. The doors, two featureless panels of wood covered in fawn-coloured baize, were hung back to back in the doorway at the top of the communal staircase and hinged at opposite sides of the opening, a defensive system designed by my father to double his privacy and keep himself safe, the muffled panels pressed together when locked, no more than the thickness of a sheet of paper between them.

Often I had the feeling I had just missed somebody as I arrived or that another person would turn up on my departure, the day models and night models scheduled not to cross over because everything was secret and everybody must be kept apart. Sometimes there were clues – an unfamiliar blouse over the back of the bathroom chair, a cigarette stubbed out on a plate in the kitchen. Once the doors were locked nobody could get in – nobody had a spare key. I rather wished somebody might bang on the outer door during a sitting just to stir things up and relieve the tension.

When Häagen-Dazs first arrived in the shops from America he loved the strawberry flavour and used to stand by the freezer in the kitchen, spoon in hand, digging the ice cream out of the pint carton like a teenager. At work his concentration was complete, I had the luxury and pain of his full attention in the studio, but suddenly he would break off in the middle of a brushstroke, leave me on my own and go into the boiler room to make a personal phone call or place a bet, urgent activities that seemed to pull him away from the painting in the same way as the ice cream, wasting his time and my own.

Apart from the racing he never watched the small telly he kept in the boiler room, a rejection of the mundane I thought was part of the whole superman thing he got out of Nietzsche, ideas about the will and power that I half embraced and half rejected as too adolescent even for me. In a break we might go out and get something to eat locally – to an Athenian restaurant off Queensway or to A Taste of Honey in Notting Hill Gate, a place he frequented because the woman who ran it was like the mum or sister he never had, bringing him home-cooked food, being lovely to look at, loving him without complications and asking for nothing in return, married to somebody else but caught up with him.

One evening when I was not sitting I went back to North London to visit my mum. I owed her money for some reason, I can't remember exactly, and as I had no cash on me I wrote her a cheque, perhaps hoping she might not cash it, debt cancelled, the ordinary thoughts of a teenager reluctant to pay what was owed to a parent. I handed it over and she examined it forensically, her slow smile betraying grief and inflicting it; she claimed to be astonished by the signature – my bank account was in the name of Rose Boyt but my mum said she thought I called myself Freud now, since I lived near my dad and had gone over to his side. I tried to reassure her, offering comfort even though I felt hurt by her accusation, but she would not give it up; although she knew she was wrong she said she really believed I called myself Freud, and held on to her grievance no matter what I said to convince her, nursing the wound and reluctant to relinquish it.

On my birth certificate I have no surname at all, although both my parents are named, each registered at a different address, my father at 20 Delamere Terrace, Paddington and my mum at 357 Liverpool Road, a house in Islington that belonged to an actor called Norman Bowler, once married to Henrietta Moraes, who sat not only for my father but also for Francis. The house was full already, no spare bedrooms, but Norman was kind enough to put us up anyway, my mum on the floor of the sitting room with my brother Alexander tucked in beside her, until I came along and he had to move over. He was her first child, later known as Ali, not much more than eighteen months old when I was born, still small enough to ride in our pram. In my earliest memory we are parked out front in the pram to get some fresh air and look after ourselves for a while, I am propped up at the foot end under a thick blanket to keep warm and he is sitting in shadow under the grey braided fringe of the hood, wearing some kind of leather safety harness to restrain him in case he tried to climb out. Peace and quiet for Mum, who was upstairs; I hope she was painting.

She was a wonderful painter and believed in the importance of painting but not with such fierce zeal as my father, for whom it mattered beyond anything; when life got too hard for her to go on with that type of work she made other things, numberless manifestations of her creativity she didn't value highly enough, everything domestic and not attracting much acclaim, nobody sacrificed in the process, the thought she was making art never occurring to her or anybody else at the time.

We attended the register office on the eighth of January, better late than never, a good seven weeks after my birth. Dad accompanied us or met us there – a family outing – but Mum must have been too diffident and grand to insist on helping herself to his name on my behalf, let alone for her own sake; that was her style, her personality, no slight whatsoever implied towards anybody who might have been less backward at coming forward in the same circumstances. My guess is that Mum sensed she would do better not to claim anything from him, she wished to behave without rapaciousness and avoid any awkward scenes, always super cool when he was around and hiding her feelings because she didn't want to make him feel tied down. Everything was so precarious. But who knows what was really going on.

I am unable even to imagine a conversation between them about naming me, although it is not impossible they did talk about it, if only in a jokey way and way too late, my father rattling coins nervously in his pocket by the window of the register office and my mother holding the plaited handles of the Moses basket in one hand in front of the shiny desk, Alexander wedged on the opposite hip, the registrar, name of Gladys Tice, sat poised with her fountain pen over the red and white certificate, waiting for instructions from one or other of them. Lucky we were tame children, me so small and good still in my straw basket, swaddled in a white shawl, and my brother wearing a little white baby dress under his fawn woollen coat, garments handed down to me once he had grown out of them. The registrar wrote my name in the register, all four letters of it, and my mother's face would have been all smiles, obviously longing for more from my father but taking it nice and easy because she was not about to drive him away by insisting too bravely on the connection between us.

Still, they must have said something, my parents, even just to answer the registrar's questions, my mother's sweet fluting lightness of voice floating over my brother's head but witnessed by Gladys Tice, my father uneasy because he hated submitting to authority, almost furtive in his demeanour, reluctant even to give the address of his home as if disclosure of his whereabouts might lead to undesirable consequences. It was 1959, Gladys must have been thinking her own thoughts about the pair of them, my father prepared to show himself at the register office but not offering his name and my mother too smiley and unsure of her status to say anything, although perhaps Miss Tice had seen it all before, just doing her job, not paid to judge or hold anybody to account. At least he put in an appearance. They didn't talk, they talked, somebody decided to call me Rose, they left it at that.

Rose was the name of both the midwives who delivered me. My father was not in attendance at the birth, not unusual in those days, but turned up at Liverpool Road an hour or two after I was dragged out with forceps, two days late for my mum's birthday but just in time for my own. He brought two live lobsters as a birthday gift, and my mum had to get up and cook them on the stove in Norman's kitchen, the nappy bucket the only vessel capacious enough to contain them. They screamed when she dropped them into the boiling water and she was allergic to shellfish.

I didn't get my father's name, which has cut both ways with me, although my mother, rather than asking the registrar to write Boyt in the box instead, must have told Gladys Tice to leave the space blank, perhaps hedging her bets in case there was any change in circumstances, living in secret hope.

In her old-fashioned handwriting Gladys has written the word *Painter* under *Occupation of Father*, no space on the certificate for *Occupation of Mother*, it just went without saying the answer was motherhood. My parents met at the Slade, student and visiting teacher, Mum was just up from the country. She won prizes for painting, but had received no sex education as a child, not from her governess, not at school, not a word from her parents. She hated to talk about sex but told me the first she heard of intercourse she was actually having it. That must have been a horrible shock. He told me he took the Slade job to get girls. The authorities overlooked the birth of her first child but when her second pregnancy manifested itself they asked her to leave. She was expelled, but my father kept his job – nobody challenged him about his behaviour.

Mum described to me the short scene that occurred when she and her sister Bulie went down to Enford in Wiltshire to visit their mother, both sisters finding themselves required to impart news much too important to be delivered by letter or telephone. I don't know how Mum addressed her mother, but Bulie, recently married, still called her Mama, the *a* of the second syllable drawn out to rhyme with *bra*, an Edwardian pronunciation that in 1956 must already have seemed archaic, pushing their mother back into the past and maintaining the distance of the formal maternal relationship. I think of my grandmother by her maiden name, Linda Stevens, although her physical heft in my childhood I am able to recall only through a faint smudge of loss, my memory of her almost entirely wiped out now, just a dark narrow sleeve.

I imagine her seated at her spindly desk in the morning room when the sisters arrived at their childhood home, still in her dressing gown, hair in a turban of peach silk that looked a bit grubby round her pale face, the fabric in need of a wash – she wasn't very good at looking after herself in spite or perhaps because of her selfishness. She half-rose to acknowledge the arrival of her daughters then sank back down into her chair in the languid but slightly aggressive way in which she was accustomed to communicate her exhaustion and sadness, Bulie robust enough in her status as new bride to repel the influence of Linda's mood but my mum already beginning to feel diminished. Bulie's new girth was obscured under a dress and coat of brown tweed, and my mum was squeezed into the boys' Levi's she used to buy from the children's department of Jones Brothers on the Holloway Road, gaping at the waist because she was no longer able to fasten the button, a man's jersey worn over the top like a smock.

Bulie took off her coat and Linda turned in her chair to face the yellow sofa, raising her eyebrows interrogatively. The two sisters were seated side by side, Mum's feet in tatty black ballet shoes on the Aubusson and Bulie wearing stout brogues, her ankles already a bit puffy. Bulie made her announcement first and Linda expressed delight in her slightly off-hand way, reached for her cigarette case and offered it first to Bulie and then to my mum, neither of whom wanted to smoke right at that moment. Linda lit up, inhaled and exhaled in a long plume, and my mother told her that she too was pregnant. Linda's response was unforgettable.

'But darling,' she declared, 'I don't remember you having been married!'

Mum had to explain that she had had sex with a man to whom she was not even engaged, and Linda was utterly baffled, not only lacking the imagination to understand why any woman would submit to intercourse if she wasn't obliged to submit under matrimonial contract, but seeming to believe that sex outside marriage was a physical impossibility. She just could not take on board what she was hearing. I don't know whether my mum mentioned that the father of her unborn child was a painter, her teacher, already twice divorced, an immigrant, a Jew, nor if Linda would have been impressed or horrified by the connection to Sigmund, should that information have been proffered. Linda rang the bell for the maid and while they waited for her to enter with the tea things on a giant tray my grandmother had a brainwave. She decided to pretend in the neighbourhood that her daughter was dead, rather than subject herself and her husband to the embarrassment of having to explain away the irregularity of her circumstances. I thought this meant that my mum could never go back – she never spoke of a subsequent visit – but I was wrong. Going through the boxes of papers in my father's basement after his death I came across a letter from her addressed to him, written from Enford, where she was staying for a while with her new baby.

I was astounded. Linda must have been able to accept what had happened after all, unable to resist the lure of her new grandson or just curious to meet him, Mum only remembering the initial pain of her banishment, not the subsequent change of heart. Or maybe Linda stuck to her original idea and only allowed her daughter to come home under cover of darkness, the house itself quite remote from the village and surrounded by substantial grounds, the servants sworn to secrecy, Mum feeling the equivocation of Linda's mother love in the constrained logistics of the visit but ready to keep her head down and play her part in the deception. She may well have been in urgent need of some postnatal support, obliged to avail herself of any kindness Linda might have been able to spare, however intermittent and laced with unsolicited advice, her milk supply boosted by the substantial meals that appeared three times a day in the dining room whether or not Linda could muster any appetite, the linen sheets on the bed in which my mum slept so smooth, so beautifully laundered. Maybe she just chose not to tell me that part of the story, exaggerating Linda's cruelty and by omission the distance between herself and her mother, casting herself adrift in my mind from her family, her home, or perhaps the visit had been too hideous to mention.

In the letter she tells my father one of her dreams and suggests he might like to come and stay, so much eager romantic hope and so little expectation of his acquiescence evident in the phrasing of the invitation I think she must have known in her heart that the prospect of him actually showing up at her family home with a suitcase and box of painting materials was as dreamlike as the surreal nocturnal vision she described in her letter to him, her little boy floating up to the ornate ceiling of the drawing room like a balloon, connected to her only by a long piece of string.

Dad and I talked about Mum sometimes. He told me how she cooked eggs for us when we were children, the touching way she held the boiled eggs under the tap to cool them as quickly as possible and using a small spoon basted the yolks of the fried eggs in the pan with such delicate carefulness it made him smile in a dreamy way to describe it. He spoke lovingly of her, mostly with utter respect, but when I asked him if he had been in love with her he paused, trying to think, and gazed past the top of his easel and up at the ceiling of the studio for a few moments, averting his eyes from the moon that beamed down at us through the big skylight – he hated the moon – and said no, not really. His denial distressed me and made me feel guilty for having asked – I just wanted to understand what went on between them – but I know now his answer only meant she was available and he had no opportunity to yearn for her in desperation over what he couldn't get. He also said he thought she didn't like him all that much, she never showed him much affection, a plea made not complainingly but in self-defence, to justify himself, although there may have been some sadness and hurt in his voice. I can still remember her marvelling over what had happened to her. She said it was so strange how things worked out, she hadn't even been all that keen on him in the first place. Then she had fallen for him. Even though he wasn't really her type.

Francis Bacon was still pretty much my father's best friend at the time of the painting, although it was Frank Auerbach he trusted to stand beside him in front of a picture while the paint was still wet, Frank's task to help him decide whether or not it was finished. Francis, whom my father adored but who was perhaps more competitive, was showing some new work at the Galerie Claude Bernard in Paris and Dad wanted to go over on the boat with Katie McEwen, his young girlfriend, to pay tribute at the opening, which was a big deal as he disliked leaving London. Katie was reluctant to travel alone with him so I was invited along as a sort of buffer between them. She was the same age as me.

The trip took place in early 1977, not long before I started to sit, although since he'd met Katie I was seeing my father really quite frequently outside the studio, Dad inviting her along when he took me out and counting me in on their dates to encourage her to meet with him, time spent with his girlfriend plus his daughter the gooseberry better than no time at all in her presence, me just tagging along when Katie felt too shy or hostile to see him alone.

I had never been on holiday with him before, and it was mildly excruciating to witness him try and negotiate his hunger at the counter of the floating cafeteria, a wide room below deck cluttered with patio furniture, the staff wearing hairnets – he was more used to dining at Wheeler's – but I needn't have worried. He ordered fish, chips and peas three times, wolfed down his lunch and told us that frozen peas are not real peas, just little jackets of a plastic-like material injected with pea mash and additives, made in the Bird's Eye factory, a fiction he really seemed to believe and that made me question my own knowledge. Katie ate almost nothing.

We stayed at the Hôtel des Saints Pères, a hotel my father favoured and at which Miss Beston from the Marlborough Gallery was also resident for the duration of the festivities – she was in Paris to look after Francis. We attended various fancy parties and a couple of small dinners in oppressively claustrophobic private apartments, Katie and I wearing the home-made dresses I had run up back in London out of some striped shirting from Berwick Street, and lunched at all the famous brasseries, my father utterly au fait with the menus, nothing much having changed in those places since he had been in Paris after the war. As well as the oysters and grilled lobster he loved so much I remember him ordering poitrine d'agneau Sainte-Menehould, lamb's breast in breadcrumbs, a dish I had read about in *French Provincial Cooking*, and that turned out to taste unaccountably delicious.

One morning, after hot chocolate in bed, I went down to the foyer with Katie and my father and as we made for the door (some outing that never happened) my name was called out by the concierge – 'Mademoiselle Boyt, Mademoiselle Boyt.' Nobody had ever called me that before. I thought there must be some mistake – I knew nobody in Paris – but the concierge handed me a fat envelope containing hundreds of francs in large bills and a note from Miss Beston – she was returning to London and wondered if I might make use of her spare cash. Katie and I, in possession of our own funds, were no longer tied to my father, and so we abandoned him immediately, which feels pretty mean now, looking back, although I am sure he took it on the chin. Katie and I were too young to know any better.

We had so much money we did not know what to do with ourselves. We didn't go shopping because neither of us were interested in Paris fashion, and we didn't want to buy books – too heavy to cart around – so we went to the Louvre to look at *The Raft of the Medusa*, and afterwards to a cafe. Having drunk some wine, eaten chips and paid the bill, we sat at the table together, smoking Gitanes and chatting, the envelope of cash on the table between us. After about fifteen minutes a team of waiters skipped out from behind the service doors, closed in on us, took up the four corners of the tablecloth like some horrible conjuring trick and made everything on the table disappear, including Miss Beston's cash. The waiters shrugged and feigned incomprehension when I remonstrated with them in my school French, the theft of the money returning Katie and me to my father as emphatically as if he had orchestrated the whole thing. We meandered back to the hotel, downhearted and a little shamefaced after our loss, and waited for Dad, I for one secretly hoping he might offer to return to the cafe with us to seek justice in a fatherly way once we had told him our story, but that was too much to expect.

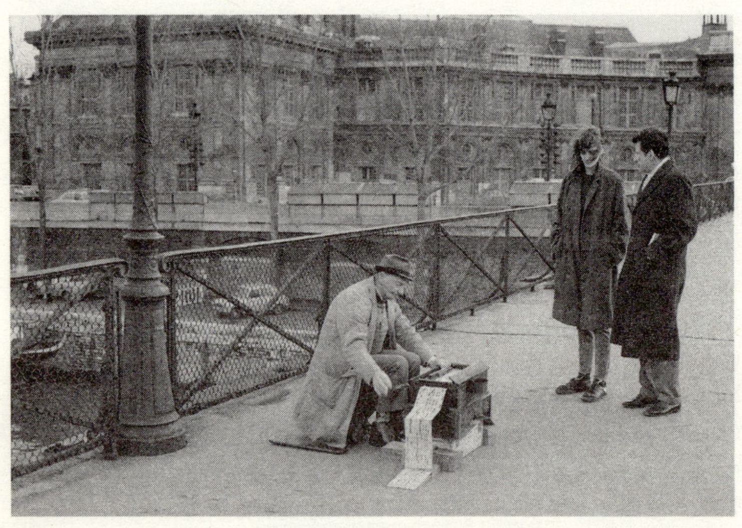

My father and Katie McEwen in Paris (1977)
ROSE BOYT

He loathed the smell of Imperial Leather and told me he was shocked to find tablets of it in all the bathrooms at Marchmont, the big house in Scotland where Katie had been brought up; he was taken aback by the unshowy parsimony by which Katie's mother was guided in some of her housekeeping decisions.

The first time I went there I was so innocent I thought Katie was playing a trick on me when the station taxi careered up the drive and deposited us on the gravel. I looked up at the rows of long windows, the mossy stone balustrades and double sweep of elegant steps and thought she must have decided to stop off at a stately home on the way to her parents' house for some reason, perhaps to genuflect under a frescoed ceiling or ogle a collection of paintings pillaged by somebody's ancestor on the grand tour. I protested because I was tired and just wanted to curl up somewhere warm and have a cup of tea or a few beers, but she told me the house was her home. I thought only the royal family still lived like that.

I remember on that visit I understood for the first time that it was possible to hate your own brothers and sisters, a discovery that unsettled me even though I had heard my father describe both Stephen and Clement with repetitive malevolence; perhaps I thought that he was an exception because his brothers were particularly loathsome, at least in the anecdotes he told me about them. Katie and her brother James adored one another but openly despised not all but one or two of their other siblings, dividing them into the loved and unloved and feeling totally justified in the persecution of their older sister in particular and expressing not just hostility but hatred towards her whenever they felt like it, no holding back to protect her from their mad spite. The physical disparity between the siblings was so marked it was hard to believe they all shared the same parents, not that anybody's paternity was in question, but the real shock was in the disparity of status between them, Katie stuck on the top rung of some imaginary ladder, James allowed to take his place beside her and everybody else positioned in descending order not of age but of beauty and personality, height even, each sibling fixed non-negotiably in relation to his or her brothers and sisters to the detriment of the whole family.

I loved them both too, maybe not as much as they loved each other but almost, and James loved me back, or perhaps I just assumed he did – he certainly wrote to me often, and I still have all the letters he sent me when I was in London and he was in Scotland or at school, all beautifully illustrated.

Before James and I got together the three of us crashed out one night in Katie's room, fully clothed, James and I on either side of the large bed and Katie in the middle, huddled together under the heavy covers because of the cold. The housekeeper came in before breakfast to open the curtains, was witness to our sleeping arrangements and although she made no comment at the time she reported us to Bridget, Katie's mother, who was very put out. She said our behaviour didn't show well, the first and only time I ever heard anybody use that expression.

It wasn't easy to work out how I was supposed to behave. Katie smoked in the dining room, turned her nose up at the food and painted on the walls of the flat, a wing of the house she used as a studio. At supper one night in the kitchen when the servants were off duty I had an argument with her father about Catholicism. To my amazement he became so angry he shouted at me, jumped up from the table and crashed out of the door, his face flaming red and his hands shaking. Nobody told me it was forbidden to question the existence of God, although I might have guessed; every year a priest moved into the house for the festive season, took all his meals with the family and celebrated Mass daily in the house chapel.

Katie insisted that she and her family were practically middle class, her father only a baronet, a classification that meant nothing to me, although my father was an expert on titles and courtesy titles, how it all worked. She and James were very friendly with the housekeeper's sons, and like them supported Glasgow Rangers, the Protestant football team, instead of Celtic, the team supported by Catholics. James tried to teach me to drive and took me out shooting, and his mother asked one of the women who worked in the big kitchens to show me how to pluck pheasants, as if to domesticate me in case I was required to become domesticated at some point in the future, for example if James and I got married and I replaced his mother as the lady of the house on the death of her husband. Not that I wanted any of that – I was in love with James but I was a teenager still, loved London and was not very aspirational. He felt that the house was more important than himself, his happiness, and his belief in maintaining it and the estate exerted great pressure on him. I wanted to be with him but had no desire to relocate.

Bridget said I had neat ankles, the only time she remarked on my appearance, but every time we went to a big party to dance reels at the home of some kilted duke or earl, travelling by minibus because there were so many of us, she persuaded me to accept the loan of a maxi skirt in the McEwen tartan, blue and green, fully lined in silk, which looked sharp enough with my leather jacket and cropped hair.

One Christmas Eve, the night of a huge dinner to be served in the servants' hall for friends and family, Katie and I dressed James as a girl, an experiment I had no idea would be contentious in that setting. The pale beaded flapper dress we found in a wardrobe in one of the unused bedrooms fitted him perfectly, we tied a long silk scarf round his head and applied vivid make-up. The effect was surprisingly feminine, but when we made our entrance at the dinner Bridget was scandalized in front of her numerous guests, rose up in her seat and shooed us out, properly shocked and upset, and I was genuinely unable to understand her problem.

I was never at Marchmont at the same time as my father and can only imagine he behaved as James behaved, sneaking about in the night and making sure he was back in his own bed by morning. We never crossed over but I can see how it must have been, the adults helping themselves to kippers or whatever from under the silver cloches in the dining room, Bridget buttering a triangle of cold toast with serene grace while Katie scowled, smoked and kicked James under the table, my father beside her eating kidneys with grilled tomatoes and bacon as he talked about painting or entertained her parents with one of his amusing anecdotes, his hand squeezing Katie's long thigh under the ample folds of the tablecloth.

I don't know how Katie's parents viewed my father's passionate love for their teenage daughter, how they accepted it and allowed him to stay under their roof, a middle-aged man with two ex-wives and numerous children, his reputation far from untarnished. Of course they were put in separate bedrooms, my father accommodated in a style befitting a celebrity guest, no suggestion of any open impropriety. Perhaps Robin and Bridget had been expecting him to propose to their daughter. Or maybe everybody just pretended their love was platonic, artist and muse, the parents so detached from their children and so dazzled by my father's achievements they turned a blind eye to their daughter's misery, hoping that he might educate her or open doors for her in the art world.

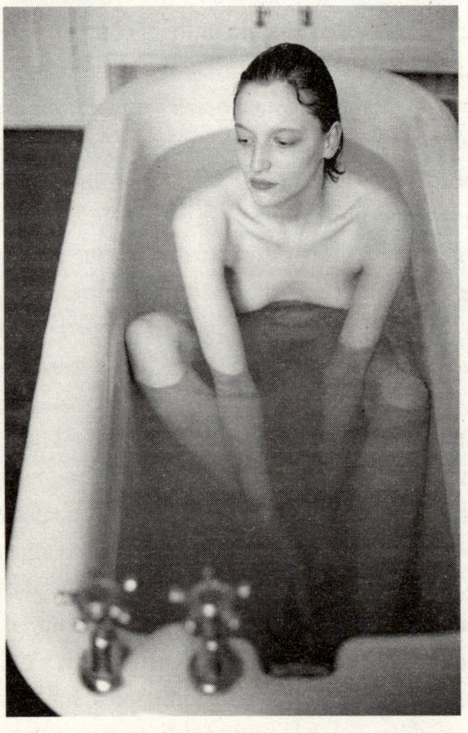

Katie at Marchmont

ROSE BOYT

Katie and James both died very young, James first, by his own hand – he shot himself with one of the many shotguns in the gun-room at Marchmont – then Katie, who drowned in mysterious circumstances off the coast of Africa, her clothes found in a pile on the beach, the thought of which wastage still brings me much pain.

I started a Saturday job at Vivienne Westwood's punk shop Seditionaries on the King's Road maybe a year after the Paris trip, and my father and Francis Bacon admired my bondage trousers. Dad was having a show at a gallery in New York and didn't want to go so he sent me, even though that meant he wouldn't be able to work on my picture again until my return, which must have been annoying for him. Standing in front of a pale nude the day after the private view, a woman engaged me in conversation – she said she was the painter's cousin, the daughter of his mother's sister, and had attended Central School of Art at the same time as him. I raised her on that, and she embraced me. He had never spoken to me of his cousin Jo Kaufmann who lived in New York, and she had never heard of me. She wrote down her address in my notebook, gave me the spare keys she carried in her shoulder bag and invited me to stay – she had spare rooms in her apartment, her children were away at university. I checked out of my hotel, paid my bill and moved in with her, delighted to have been rescued – Dad had arranged safe accommodation for me for the first four nights but expected me to be able to fend for myself after that, not having given me enough money to stay put for any length of time in the hotel he had chosen for me, on 58th Street and Madison, the upper corridor full of college girls eating Chinese food out of white cartons and brushing each other's hair.

The trip might have been a short one and my financial position less acute had I not been persuaded by a British Airways representative to sign up to a flexible travel deal, the return flight announced at the last minute, the ticket I was allocated not valid for travel home until eighteen days after my arrival in America. Talk about false economy. Not that I am saying my father wasn't generous – he gave me cash to buy clothes from work in advance of my trip, recognizing that clothes were important to me, but the discrepancy between his calculations and the reality of my stay hit me as I sat on my hotel bed on my first night. I looked quite tough in my new bondage dress, determined to live up to his expectations, but his confidence in my survival skills made me feel dizzy, wistful about his care and lack of care, the ambivalence of his attitude. New York was legendarily dangerous in the seventies and I couldn't help wishing he had revised his sketchy plan once I had told him how long I would be away. Had he miscalculated or run out of cash? He had been kind enough not to bemoan the unexpectedly long disruption to his painting – if he was angry he didn't say anything – but I don't think he was angry. I could do no wrong in his eyes most of the time, and am sure I would have been able to find some other way to take care of myself had I not bumped into his cousin. I tried to open the window in my hotel bedroom to get some air but it was impossible. I wanted to buy a toothbrush and some toothpaste but I was not even sure it was safe to walk the streets after dark. The phone rang, I reached across the bed and answered it, feeling sure it could not be for me. Anthony d'Offay on the other end of the line, in town for the show – he was my father's dealer at that time. Yes, my father had given him my number. Was I at a loose end? Would I like to go out?

Dad had forgotten about Jo, his New York cousin, but had given me the telephone number of Catherine Guinness, a friend of his who was working with Andy Warhol at the Factory. I called Catherine, introduced myself as Lucian's daughter and was invited to lunch. I met Andy and a few other slightly exhausted people, and was photographed for *Interview* magazine in my punk clothes. Andy took me to Studio 54, introduced me to the bouncer and asked him to let me in anytime I wanted to party in future, which made a real difference to my stay. I don't know whether or not any money changed hands.

Andy didn't make a big impression on me personality-wise. He was very kind but seemed to operate without desire for intimacy with anybody, emotional or otherwise, corralling people around him in a way that felt completely unthreatening. His voice was very flat – I thought perhaps he was depressed – but I didn't turn him down when he asked me to marry him; I was delighted, fully aware the proposal didn't mean anything was going to happen. He drew a ring on my finger with an indelible marker and signed it *AW*. At the top of the World Trade Center I took my own photograph in a Polaroid photo booth, holding my ringed hand up to the camera. I still have that picture somewhere.

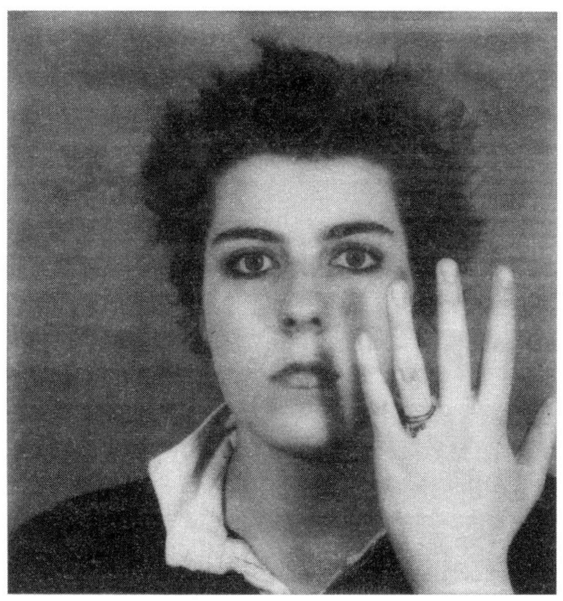

Self-portrait with Ring by Andy Warhol
ROSE BOYT

My father and Anthony d'Offay were good friends for a while before they fell out, and to celebrate Anthony's marriage Dad invited him and his new wife to lunch. On the morning of the wedding I went to Acton in a black cab to collect a pound of caviar from an Iranian caviar dealer, ordered a cake from Maison Sagne, dispatched another cab to collect the cake and bought four pounds of peas in their shells to make pea soup from one of the cookery books my father had given me for my eighteenth birthday and from which I was learning to cook. Anthony and Anne arrived straight from the ceremony in their wedding clothes and we all sat round the kitchen table, shelling peas and eating caviar out of the jar. I can't remember what else we had to eat. I made the soup and can still hear the bossy voice of Elizabeth David telling me to stew the peas in four ounces of butter. Yes, four ounces.

My mother told me that when she was young she believed that one day my father would marry her, or at least they would be together properly, living under the same roof, but that never happened. She received a marriage proposal from Tim Behrens, a fellow student at the Slade, and wrote to Dad to tell him, adding that my father was the only man she wanted to marry, but he failed to react. She had high hopes, although there was a teaspoon of hesitancy in her assertion because their relationship was so irregular. She never felt entitled to claim any connection to him unless through us, her children, his children; when he came up in conversation with people outside the family she called him 'the children's father', very self-consciously, as if even to speak his name might seem presumptuous, too ostentatious, maybe because he was famous and she didn't want to show off. She never called him 'my ex', not wishing to imply they were more solid together than they were in reality – I am not sure he ever stayed the night, I can't remember waking up in the morning to find him in my mum's bed, although he may well have slept over and slipped out early to get on with his work – and nothing was ever quite finished between them. But she must have felt loved at the beginning, when everything was marvellous, which makes me feel less sad about her subsequent unhappiness.

She was so lovable. We talked often towards the end of her life. I am thinking particularly of one time in her kitchen, she was seated at the table wearing a soft grey cashmere cardigan with pearl buttons (a present from my sister Susie) and I was almost out of the door, standing above her; she looked very small and was almost unable to smile. I could see in her eyes she was suffering breakthrough pain despite the morphine but still hoping to be cured, or at least expecting to feel better soon. It had not really hit me that she might die.

Her paints and brushes were on the countertop, a blue and grey palette by the sink, still wet, and a canvas turned to the wall – she was still working. Get Well Soon cards from her grandchildren had accumulated at one end of the kitchen table, and flowers everywhere, five bunches of flowers, one from each of us, although she was looking back at her life with sorrow and self-blame. I endeavoured to undercut the desperation of her mood with slightly forced cheerfulness before I left so I could walk home peacefully and not have to think about her too much until my next slot on the rota, countering her agitation with reassurance before I headed off – I reminded her she had single-handedly raised five children, we were all doing OK these days and that was a wonderful achievement. When I had finished I smiled and she blinked up at me, eyes pinned, and I could see she was trying to believe me, trying to hold onto something, although in my clumsy attempt to reassure her about her achievements I had failed to mention her painting or any other aspect of her creativity. I wish I had mentioned her painting and not just gone on about motherhood. Motherhood is not everything.

The hurt of her past was still so strong it was hard for her to talk about it, her eyes filled with tears even to look back. I sat down again and she began to talk about my father suddenly, trying to cheer me up, neither of us wishing my visit to end on a low note. She dried her eyes and laughed and told me that they almost bought a house once. She remembered standing with him and Alexander and me outside an elegant house in Fitzroy Square, she was pregnant again, with Isobel, I can see her looking up at the long windows and dreaming of love and happiness. She said he was only a few hundred pounds short of the asking price, he had the cash in his pocket but everything just slipped through their fingers – he went off to get some more money, lost everything and they missed their moment.

She believed that if she had been beautiful everything would have been different. She actually said that. She was beautiful, but that was not the point; she was slow to recognize he was not cut out for domesticity. She would rather blame herself, although she must have known he had tried for it once or twice before he met her, and it had not gone well for anybody. I don't know if she was angry with him in her secret heart – she used to cry often, with frightening abandon, and smash crockery, but not once during my whole childhood did she make even one disparaging remark about him, never uttered even one reproachful word, which was wonderfully elegant and admirable of her but very bewildering for me. I can't speak for my brothers and sisters.

I have just remembered one damning thing she did say – when she was pregnant with me we went on holiday with my father to the Scilly Isles, a romantic break she was almost too big even to contemplate, perhaps leaving Ali behind with a babysitter – I don't recall her telling me she was pushing a pram. They had one suitcase between them, an unthinkable level of domestic intimacy for my parents, the heavy piece of luggage containing my father's paints and brushes as well as their clothes, and Mum had to carry it, my father not keen to exert himself perhaps because his shoulder ached or he was reluctant to burden himself. He had to feel free.

I hate it when people go on about beauty, the most highly prized of all possible womanly qualities, and I seek to deny its power over me; both my parents were moved very strongly by appearance, not only their own but that of everybody else, including their children, and I don't want to follow in their footsteps. The conscious and unconscious bias they manifested towards certain physical types without questioning themselves about the impact of such prejudice was one of the things they had in common beyond painting and horses – my mother had ridden as a child, and told me that she loved her pony way more than she loved either of her parents.

But she was beautiful, the evidence undeniable, captured in the photographs Harry Diamond took of her; he didn't make her feel self-conscious, perhaps because she didn't care what he thought of her, and so she was able to shine.

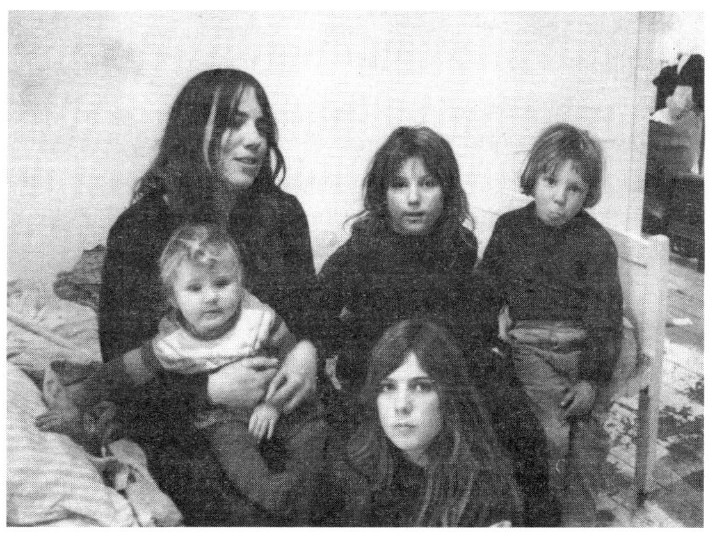

Suzy Boyt and four of her five children (1969)

HARRY DIAMOND

Harry photographed us at 17 Lonsdale Square, Islington, one of two houses in the same square that my mother bought with her inheritance after Linda's early death. Susie is such a sweet baby in the photographs, sitting on Mum's knee, so I must have been ten or eleven then, although I look older; the age gap between us is ten years. I recognize the khaki shirt I am wearing, the uniform of a communist youth movement based in Zagreb, in the former Eastern bloc – I exchanged it for my Woodcraft shirt with one of their delegates, a Yugoslavian boy I met on a two-week summer camp in Wales, the last year of primary school. I was a communist; I admired Lenin and made a life-size portrait of his bearded head to illustrate my school project about him; the world was unfair and I was angry about it, and not afraid to voice my opinion.

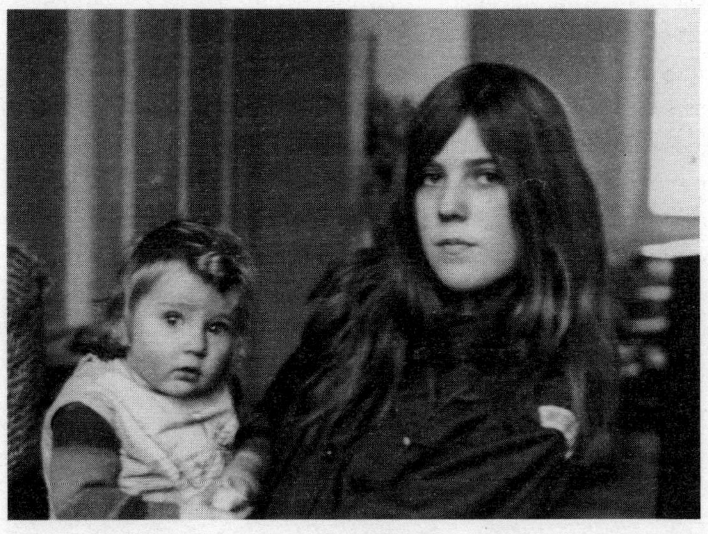

Little Susie and Rose when she was a communist (1969)

HARRY DIAMOND

People called me a tomboy. Mum told me I would have to tone myself down a bit and make the most of myself while I was still young if I ever wanted to get married. She was advising me to diminish myself, body and soul, to become smaller and quieter, more feminine, but I chose to ignore the warning about my personality because I wanted to stay true to myself and my convictions whatever the cost matrimonially. I knew Mum was wrong to say what she said but I felt uneasy suddenly about my physical self, her eyes on my hips and thighs, my stomach; she was weighing me up and found me too much, wanting in the lean allure she thought I should cultivate. Twice when she was near the end she told me she had wanted all her life to be thin, but it was not much fun now it had happened. She was genuinely disappointed.

I have no memory of how those photographs came about. I would like to think the whole thing was my father's idea, that he sent Harry as an emissary to photograph us because Harry was his friend and we were important to him, but Harry may well have turned up unbidden, just knocked on the door and asked Mum if he could come in. Mum is so alive in the photographs, radiating love and happiness, but when we looked at the pictures together during her last illness she didn't comment on her appearance, her own beauty and all of us blooming into our own personalities, she just said, 'Don't we look poor!' We were not rich for long after the death of her mother; she spent the money fast, perhaps deliberately ridding herself of any connection to the source of it and denying herself any stability.

A few years later Harry photographed me again, when I was fifteen or sixteen, this time with Dad and my brother Ali, and Ali's lovely girlfriend Dolly, who had been my best friend at school, our friendship the one thing that made the boredom of school bearable.

I wish I had never invited her home with me. Ali was hanging around in the kitchen when we got back after netball, they clocked each other and went upstairs almost immediately, not before the kettle had boiled but soon after, holding on momentarily for my sake but unable to restrain themselves long enough even to finish their tea. At the time I thought she was mildly embarrassed by her instantaneous submission to sexual desire, his and her own, although I might have misread her sheepish expression. I can still picture the impatient hilarity of their getaway, Ali running and Dolly scrambling after him, her hand in his, the laugh she tossed over her shoulder almost apologetic as she glanced back. I grinned and waved farewell through the banisters with just enough good grace not to disgrace myself as he pulled her up the stairs, the force he exerted no more than a slight tug against any compunction she might have felt for my sake, the abandoned friend, or any instinct for self-preservation that his haste might have awakened in her, not that I am saying I would have been much better at protecting myself in similar circumstances. She had changed out of her games skirt after netball and was wearing some kind of loose duster coat over her V-necked jumper and corduroy trousers, pushing back the floppy wings of her blonde hair with her spare hand, a gesture she made frequently and that until that moment I had not read as flirty or found irritating. The desire to fuck and get fucked was so urgent between them I felt helpless to remonstrate and just sat alone at the kitchen table, lit a cigarette and finished my tea, knowing my friendship with Dolly was finished now and there was nothing I could do about it.

The later photographs were taken at 9 Thorngate Road; Dad occupied two rooms on the top floor of a modest house, his bed in the smaller room at the back and his easel in the front, in a room with two windows overlooking the adventure playground, a sink and stove against the wall opposite the fireplace. He is dressed immaculately; I wonder if he was just about to rush off to lunch at Wheeler's or to meet Francis at Muriel's or whether he put on a suit and clean shirt and silk scarf especially for the photographs. I am wearing a luxurious 1920s black coat with a fur collar, a present from my mum. You can tell not just from the coat but by the mournful tilt of my head I am no longer a communist.

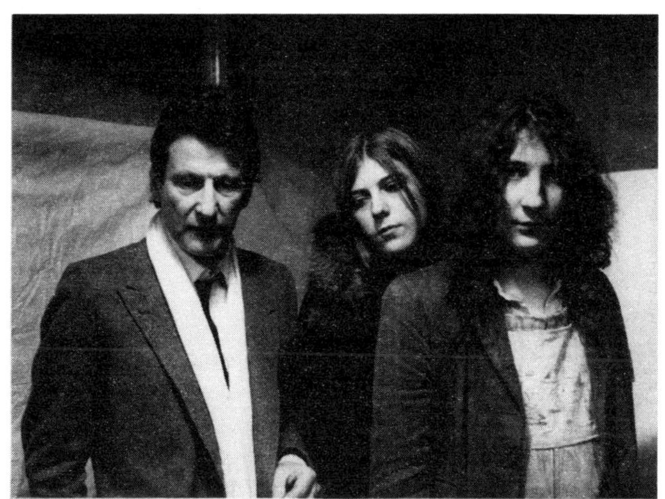

Lucian with Ali and Rose at Thorngate Road
HARRY DIAMOND

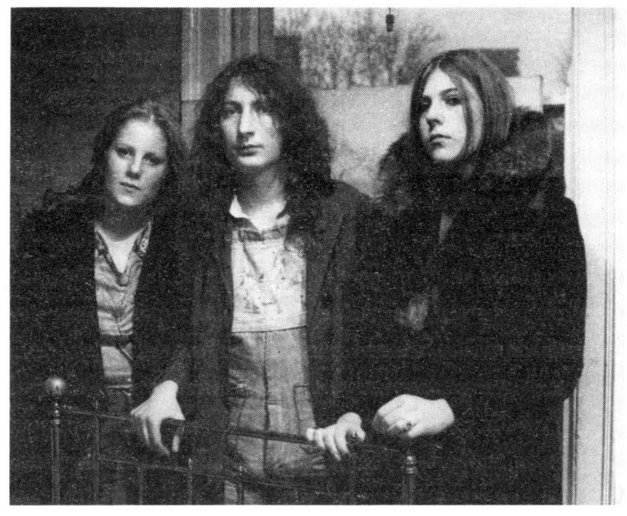

Ali's girlfriend, Ali and Rose at Thorngate Road
HARRY DIAMOND

I left home when I was fifteen and am living with my boyfriend in Elgin Avenue, round the corner from my father; to convince the landlady to rent us the flat we had to pretend to be married. Her name was Mrs Kolk, and I was frightened of her, the power she had over us. Dad used to visit quite often after I got home from school and before my boyfriend came home from his factory job, and I would make him a cup of tea and a fried egg on toast – he always seemed to be hungry. Something has happened to me since the earlier photographs. There is glamour and bravado in the black coat but I have lost some of my former self-assurance.

I was always conscientious and reliable in relation to my father but I let him down one evening because I had the flu and could barely manage to stagger to the nearest public telephone, a payphone in the dry cleaners, to tell him that I was unable to sit. I was wearing a coat over my nightdress, aching in my bones and running a high temperature, but he didn't believe me and was so furious he lowered his voice and spoke to me as if out of the corner of his mouth in a menacing way, like a villain in a Hollywood film, trying to keep a lid on his rage. He said that there would always be parties, I had made a commitment to him and must always prioritize sitting over and above everything. What amazed me was his assumption that I loved parties so much. He hardly knew me. I would never have stood him up to go out and enjoy myself. His authoritarian stance was all wrong, and made him sound pompous, a bit stupid.

Another thing made me uneasy during the course of the sittings; Katie, taking a short walk into Soho from her studio on Shaftesbury Avenue, looked in the window of a sex shop and saw one of those 3D slide viewers with a naked picture of me illuminated in the viewfinder. A couple of years earlier I had been living in a squat in Islington and had answered an advert for nude models in the back of a newspaper. The chaperone who attended the photo shoot patted down my hair (it was cropped then, shorter than in the painting) and applied blue eyeshadow and pearly lipstick, trying to make me more girlish. The photographer gave me a half bottle of vodka to help me relax and told me the photographs were for his own use and nobody would ever find out. Katie bought the slide viewer and showed the slides to my father.

I tried not to envisage the pair of them giggling over the view-finder, my face flushed and my mouth open to reveal the tip of my tongue as instructed by the chaperone, the outline of my body blurred and haloed in technicolour, my edges almost transparent like a tropical fish. The chaperone said I was supposed to try and look like I was enjoying myself. I lacked the capacity to work out how bad it was for my father to have seen me like that. It wasn't as if he hadn't seen me naked before. I did not know how to name what I felt and employed subterfuge even in relation to myself not to feel any worse.

I can't think why they didn't keep quiet about Katie's discovery. I knew I was stupid to have been deceived by the photographer and was angry with him in an impersonal way because he had humiliated me, but Katie had behaved with no regard for the protection of our shared teenage womanhood, not on my account nor on her own. I reprimanded her lightly just to say something to her about her behaviour, suppressing the full force of my disgust in case I upset anyone, but she brushed off my feelings, turning away like she was bored and I was making a fuss. Dad placed the slide viewer on the seat of a high stool in the studio and asserted his professional interest in it as a painter to make me feel better, telling me that having studied me in 3D really helped him understand how I was made.

Anthony d'Offay commissioned me to take an informal portrait of my father to display on a small easel in the window of the D'Offay Gallery in Dering Street and to use as a frontispiece in the catalogue of the forthcoming show of recent work – I had taken dozens of pictures in Paris and New York and was getting quite good. When I arrived at the studio a model called Raymond was already there, naked and larking around with his rat, a choice of pet that was quite popular in those days; Katie had one too, and a pet monkey. My father would not keep still. He didn't like to be photographed, and would not take seriously my need to capture him for posterity. I had one roll of film, and it was running out. In the end I persuaded him to sit down in a chair on his own just long enough for me to take one shot. This of course was the photograph Anthony chose. In the background you can see the plants that were such a big feature of the studio. My father was working on *Two Plants*, now in the Tate – every time I sat I could see the progress he was making, each leaf a small portrait.

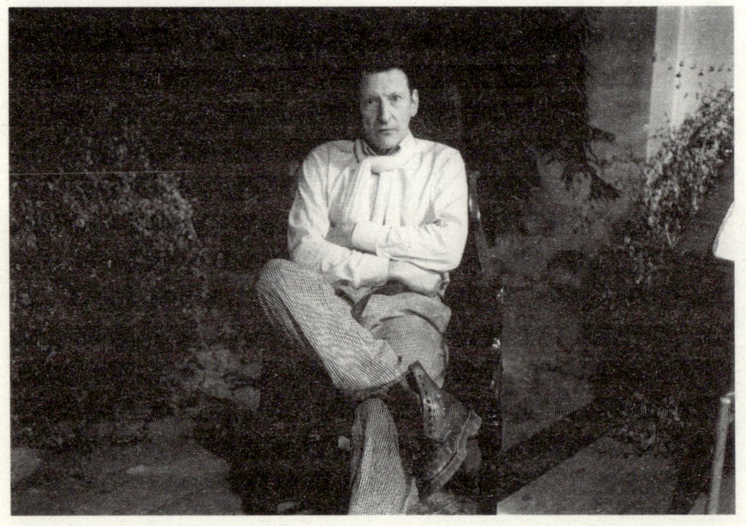

In The Studio 1 (1977)

ROSE BOYT

Dad was also painting his mother at that time; sometimes we were allowed to overlap. In the back of a parked taxi with Helena, Katie's younger sister, the old lady engaged us in stilted conversation while we waited outside the bank or the betting shop for my father to emerge and take us to breakfast. She asked Helena if she was Lucian's daughter. Helena said no. 'I think you are,' said his mother. Then she asked me. I said yes. 'I don't think so,' she said.

It was clear to me towards the end I was too big to fit on the canvas – my leg was going to be chopped off above the ankle. I thought the end of the limb would look too stumpy and awkward at the bottom edge of the picture so I suggested bandaging it with one of the unused paint rags that were always to hand in the studio, old hotel sheets that came via Mum from Ratzker's, a rag yard in Brick Lane. He arranged the piece of cloth and it looked better than I expected, something of its former life insinuating itself into the atmosphere of the finished painting.

How did I feel about sitting? Angry and exhilarated, outraged by the terms and conditions, honoured to have been chosen. Just to spend time with him was inspirational. I loved him. He influenced my reading. I learnt what work looked like, how to be punctual and dependable, and how to stick up for myself a little bit. I wanted to learn how to cook, to be lovable, but was trying to become my own person. He was planning to call the picture *The Artist's Daughter* but I said he should call it *Rose*. His title would make anybody think about incest. Mine is better, less misleading.

My sister Annie phoned recently and asked me what I was working on. She is a poet and Dad's eldest child, her mother Kitty Garman, an artist in her own right. I told Annie I had just begun something mild about Dad, sitting for Dad, how he had been inspirational in my life and that I loved him, and I heard in the constraint of her breath down the phone how adeptly she dealt with that information, how instantaneously she forgave me for flaunting the success so far of my work to resolve my feelings about him. At his expense and our own we laughed over the impossible simplicity of my position, not uproariously but with some solidarity as sisters, as daughters, and she said it was such a relief she no longer felt obliged to say he was inspirational, she was glad she no longer felt she had to say she loved him. I thought about the equivocality of her poetry and how I might forgive myself if I contradict myself as I work out what I think and feel.

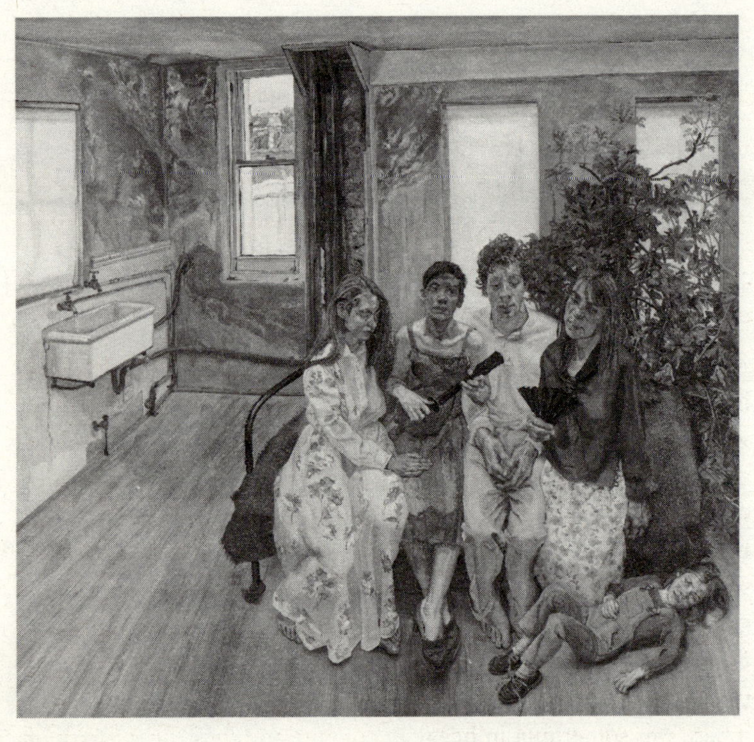

Large Interior W11 (after Watteau) (1981–3)
LUCIAN FREUD

TWO

A few years after the completion of the naked portrait my father began a very ambitious painting with a painful story contained within it. *Large Interior, W11 (after Watteau)* portrays Celia Paul, soon to become the mother of my brother Frank, my sister Bella playing the mandolin, my brother Kai and a child called Star, the little sister of Ali's girlfriend Susie Foley, as well as my mum, who was happy to be asked to sit again. My father had not painted her since *Woman Smiling* in 1958–9, a loving and intimate portrait interrupted temporarily by my birth – she was twenty-three and the mother of two babies by the time the picture was finished. There was something in her wild courage and the vulnerability of her young motherhood in relation to him that drove him to try a new way to articulate his excitement about her, his response to the complexity of her contradictions necessitating a change of brushes from sable to hogshair, the start of a much looser and more risky way of working.

The models came together in the studio for the first sitting of *After Watteau*, four seated adults squeezed together on a single bed, little Star on the floor at my mother's feet a later addition. Once my father was happy with the composition he used charcoal to establish everybody on the canvas in preparation for the painting, Celia at one end of the bed and my mum at the other, the initial session the one and only time they crossed over in the studio during the whole process. They were kept apart once the preparatory drawing was complete, although Celia says my mum telephoned her one night in frustration because after months of sitting Lucian had just totally wiped her out of the painting. Celia says my mum was upset because she had given so much of her time, but of course she returned to the studio and the painting continued. In the end Dad felt he had got it right, Mum's 'wild woodland head' surrounded by foliage, although Dad told Sophie de Stempel (another young woman painter who was sitting at that time) that Mum thought the black fan he asked her to hold was too funerary. And Sophie told me. Bella is wearing brass-studded shoes from Manolo Blahnik. Mum supplied the rest of the costumes from her shop on Northwold Road in Upper Clapton, a treasure trove of old-fashioned clothes. Celia says she always loved my mum and felt especially close to her 'maybe to do with the Slade and that we were both painters with children.' She was a student there just like my mum, also taught by my father.

At the time everything just happened according to the demands of the painting, Mum and Celia brought together in the studio, fixed in position then kept apart, Dad hoping to make it all work, but looking back at the painting now the choice of sitters seems unnecessarily provocative, the composition hinting at trouble autobiographically and then causing it, Celia under false pretences and Mum's feelings not taken into consideration even for one second. I remember she once referred to a book of my father's work as 'Bluebeard's Catalogue', and at the big show at Tate Britain in 2002, surrounded by the flesh of naked women, she told me she preferred the paintings with no people in them.

Large Interior, W11 (after Watteau) went on and on. Mum got all messed up again with Dad, a reversion that destabilized her and made her very unhappy, and I was destabilized by her desperate unhappiness, freaking out on a family holiday to Lake Garda in Italy at the end of my second year at university, overwhelmed by sorrow and terror on the plane on the way out; a few nights before we left she told me about Dad and said she was so stupid to have gone back she felt like killing herself, which was not a threat – she just wanted me to know how bad she was feeling.

In the box that contained the surprise letter from Enford I found some postcards and letters from me to my father, childish messages posted from ports in Denmark and Germany, Sweden and Norway and Finland, when we lived on *Inga*, a three-masted schooner, one of two leaky old cargo ships my mum bought with the proceeds of selling our home, having fallen in love with a German sea captain called Uwe, neither of the vessels insured because they were not reliably seaworthy. I wonder how my father felt, receiving my postcards, knowing his children were at sea, out of reach, another man in charge of their well-being.

Black Rose sank first, almost immediately, before we had even sailed in her, then *Inga*, but not for a while – Mum took Ali and me out of school when I was seven and we lived on board for a year and a half and went everywhere she went, taking cargoes round the Baltic, my mum encouraging Ali and me to write every day in our diaries, the two little ones too little to be educated, Isobel not even five yet and Kai only a baby.

As well as keeping the diary I was supposed to keep our toys tidy on deck and take care of Kai while Mum prepared food in the galley. The first time I lost him I found him hanging from his fingertips over the mouth of the hold, a sheer drop of thirty feet, and had to haul him to safety. The second time he had gone overboard, on his back in the sea, his big blue eyes still open although he had been knocked unconscious on impact. Mum and Uwe jumped over the gunwale and fished him out of the freezing water, and Mum carried him into the main cabin and cuddled him back to life, although a few days later he was diagnosed with pneumonia. I remember Uwe paid the doctor in tobacco and alcohol for Kai's medicine, the cartons of cigarettes and bottles of spirits kept

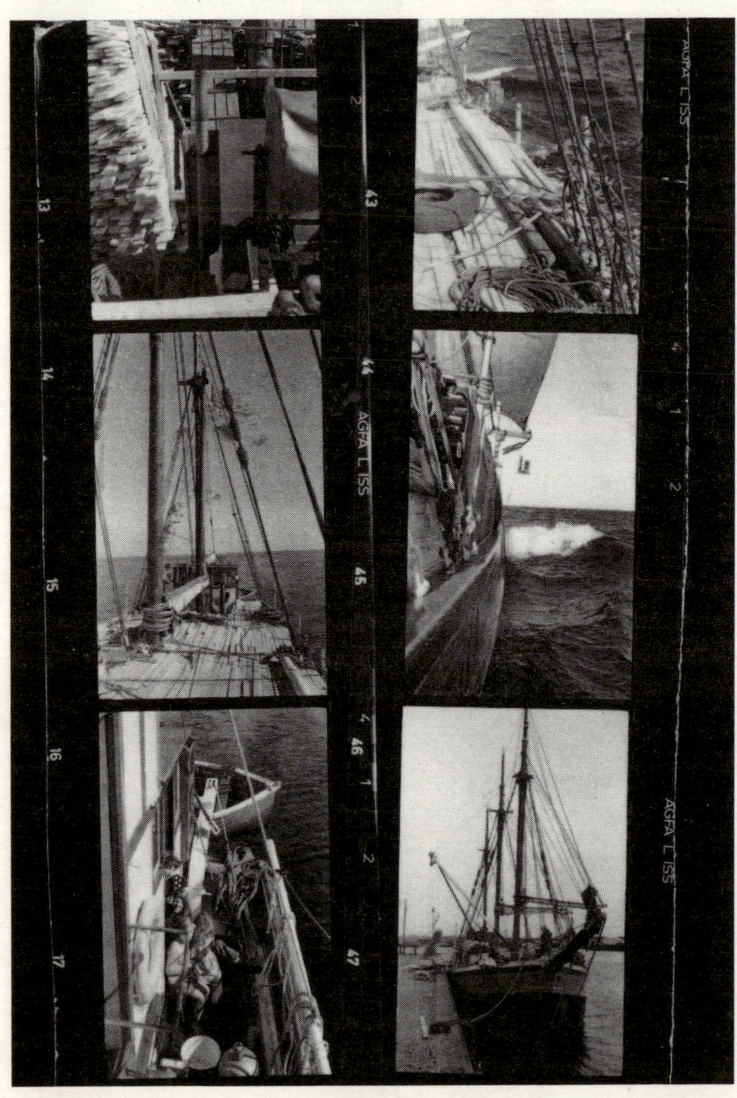

Inga
Photographer Unknown

in a secret stash in the back of the revolving airing cupboard, one of my other jobs to ensure that when the customs inspector came on board for a random check the contraband was out of sight so we didn't have to pay duty on it.

I heard a song on the bosun's transistor that spoke to me because it was about life on a ship. I remember the drunkenness of the crew on the sloop *John B*, a line about not being able to reach the captain because he was ashore, then the endless refrain of a homesick sailor with whom I felt no conscious identification but whose plaintive words came out of my mouth over and over again as I went about my business on board, Kai on my hip or toddling beside me on his little legs – *let me go home, let me go home, I want to go home, let me go home, why don't you let me go home, I feel so broke up, man, I want to go home, please let me go home.*

I wrote also from Trinidad – *Dear Daddy, Love Rosie.* None of us called him Daddy, not even when we were babies, I don't know what I was thinking. We travelled to the Caribbean by passenger ship while Uwe navigated *Inga* from Denmark with a small crew, a journey I am glad to say my mother forbade us. We rented a house outside Port of Spain and he ferried cargoes between the islands, setting sail without us every time he set sail, even the short distances, the loads of quicklime and other unstable chemicals stashed in strong sacks in the hold but still liable to get damp and break up the ship.

Every time he came back he brought gifts, unfamiliar sweets in bright wrappers and silk pyjamas from China – not really from China, he was only pretending. I loved my pyjamas wherever they came from, petals of camellia in every shade of pink from pale shell to deepest rose embroidered on navy silk, and the jacket fitted me perfectly because he was quite a good judge of me in that way, which feels overfamiliar to me now just as it felt at the time, accepting his present and loving it while he nauseated me with all his sentimentality and heavy breathing.

The jacket was roomy enough, the mandarin collar and button placket piped in yellow silk, a row of knotted toggles fastening in rouleaux loops of the same fabric, but a sensation of discomfort halfway between a memory and a persistent stain in my mind of the way he regarded me comes back to me now when I think of his gift – the pyjama bottoms cut me in half longitudinally when I got into bed and I had to tug the French seam out of my crack.

China was a joke, he never went very far, the ship too frail for another long voyage. Even so he was away often, either at sea or I don't know where he went otherwise, maybe carousing in port with the mate and the bosun, not that I missed him, although now I am safe I suspect the longer he was gone the more deeply my mum must have feared he might never return. She must have asked herself in the night if he had taken the ship and abandoned us with nothing apart from the food that grew in the yard, the hands of bananas and the root of the cassava tree we learnt to dig up and boil hard for an hour not to poison ourselves. I imagine she would have felt almost unbearably vulnerable, night and day, no cash to buy rice or to send us to school and no idea what to do next, although she was always too proud and brave to acknowledge that something was wrong. I am grateful to her for her fortitude in difficult circumstances, the stories she told to soothe and contain us, having only recently begun to question her version of events and my own memories.

I thought Uwe loved me but I learnt not to feel safe in his presence because I was not safe. I can't remember dreading his return when he was away but I must have dreaded it, in spite of the promise of sweets and my mother's relief if she was not too angry with him to feel anything, too angry to speak. I must have dreaded it because he terrorized me when he was around me, first in the Baltic and then in Trinidad, and I never thought to tell either of my real parents at the time, although my mum knew something, she must have noticed him trying to hold himself back. I don't know what Dad could or would have done if I had written to him about it.

What happened is hazy now but I remember quite clearly one time on the ship I screamed until my mum came to the rescue. I must have been eight, I was on my back under the covers in my high bunk, wearing only my nightie, no knickers, wondering if I had something coming to me because I had angered Uwe earlier on in the day and knew there was unfinished business between us. I held onto the blankets when he entered my cabin but he snatched them away, he grabbed my ankles and pulled them over my head. My bare bottom was exposed to his face at eye level, front and back, his other hand raised to spank me because of what I had done earlier, some pretext for the assault, although it was not straightforward because I did feel guilty about being naughty. Mum heard my screams and pushed open the door. He was unable to react quickly enough, transfixed in plain sight with his hand raised to me, his broad palm and thick fingers, and did not let go of my ankles until she shouted at him. He came back to himself and let go of my ankles, my legs snapped back and I hurried to cover myself, glad to hear my mother was on my side, although she was telling him off for trying to smack me, as if it was his rough parenting that was the problem, not him feasting his eyes on me, his nose almost in my vagina.

In Trinidad I slept in my own room, in a double bed, the darkness a substance of such opacity and warmth I had to learn how to sleep under it when it came down. Everybody else was asleep, the nocturnal noises of the house creatures, friendly and unfriendly, audible in my dreams. I woke to the soft *thud thud* of Uwe's head against the polished stone wall just inside the door of my bedroom. I heard him breathing in and out of his mouth and knew he was thinking about me inside the bridal whiteness of my mosquito net. He was headbanging but too gently to hurt himself, thinking about traversing the distance between us. The bed was so wide the empty expanse behind me made me feel easy prey. I thought I could help him resist if I held my breath. I was pretending to be dead, not wishing to be dead, wishing he was dead, unable to scream, not even able to think about screaming. He muttered something in German and went out, leaving the door ajar, but I was too frightened to sleep in case he came back. I heard the flush of the cistern, the slap of his bare feet on the floor tiles. The sky was light abruptly. I came out of my room but he was just outside, naked on the hall chair, legs spread and penis erect, as if he had been there all night. He encircled my wrist with his hand as I passed him, preventing me from making my way to the bathroom. He may or may not have tried to get me to sit on his lap.

I was relieved when *Inga* sank, and would not have been sorry if the captain had gone down with the ship. He did not go down, but sent us a postcard from somewhere – *SHIP SUNK, GO HOME* – and we were repatriated, no longer welcome in Trinidad with no means of support, the British government impounding our passports until we paid back our travel expenses. I don't know what happened to Uwe, Mum didn't say anything, perhaps he met somebody else or returned to Germany. He just disappeared, not that I am complaining about it.

We travelled tourist class, a journey of four weeks, our bunks stacked deep in the hold of an Italian liner, the cabin shared with seven or eight other passengers – in those days travelling by ship was much cheaper than flying. An old man from the Islands occupied the bunk below mine, and I remember the ladders in his stringy brown cardigan, the questions he asked me about England, a land he had never seen. It felt strange to me then that I knew things he didn't know although I was only a child. I was afraid his expectations were too high.

A canary in a cage hung from an elbow of pipe in the dank corridor outside our cabin, the bird pecking the bars in a futile bid to escape. I assumed it was a pet but my brother told me it had been deployed to fall off its perch when the air ran out. I thought he was kidding me.

In the tourist-class dining room a mural of Picasso's *Guernica* stretched the full length of the back wall, passengers at the communal tables groaning and throwing up into the stew, gravy and vomit splattering over the paper tablecloths. I still hate that painting.

A smell of limes emanated from the vents in the window of the ship's barbershop, the plump red chairs behind plate glass and the angled mirrors reflecting to infinity. I made friends with the son of the barber, a boy who knew his way around but spoke only Italian, a language with which I was entirely unfamiliar. He led me up forbidden staircases, the looped banisters of red rope and the carpet like double cream, treads rising from the twinkling darkness into the sunlight. On the top deck, out of bounds to the tourist class, he took my hand under a canopy of potted palms and from behind the lush foliage we watched the first-class people lounge round the mosaic pool in their swimwear, water spouting from the mouths of mermaids and dolphins.

His hand was very soft, the same size as my own. He climbed on the grand piano in the empty ballroom after dark, careful not to snag his delicate cardigan or displace the puzzling bow tie he had chosen to wear for the occasion, and gestured for me to join him. I scrambled up, he liberated the white instrument from its moorings and we rode it backwards and forwards across the sprung floor as the ship lurched across the Atlantic, stars visible through the glass roof, the strings generating strange music.

Mum gave me a strong pill every morning to deal with my seasickness, a drug that caused me not to feel too acutely the fear I might have felt otherwise as we headed back into the unknown, unsure where or how we would live. I looked forward to that pill, and my friendship with the young Italian was part of that dreamy feeling, the alien glisten of his pomade, love that didn't mean anything.

Many years later, when I told my daughter about this journey, she compared the displacement of the old man in our cabin to that of my father when he came to England at nine years old, the same age I was when we were repatriated. She said my father used to sing her sea shanties. I had never thought of that before, his flight from the Nazis by sea, him sharing the old man's hope of a warm welcome.

That family holiday on the shores of Lake Garda after Mum started seeing Dad again we sunbathed and smoked cigarettes and grilled fish on a fire in the orchard of the beautiful house that belonged to my sister Annie on her mother's side of the family. We tried to have holiday fun, Annie and her young daughter May, my mum and Susie, my friend Pam from university and her baby, and I took some good photographs, but I was horribly anxious the whole time, day and night, and at the end of our stay I had to take Valium prescribed by the local doctor and drink grappa even to get on the plane.

The entire holiday I had assumed that once I was back home I would feel better automatically, but that didn't happen. I was referred to the Hackney Hospital, hoping that some lovely doctor or kind nurse could help me to stabilize myself, but after enduring an interminable wait for my appointment in the waiting room of the outpatients department, trying to keep hope alive, I sat in a little office with a bewildered and threadbare woman psychiatrist, who blinked ineffectually when I told her my story and offered me a bed upstairs. The offer was made in a spirit of almost complete ambivalence and made me feel even more frightened – she said I was welcome to a bed, but added that it might not help me in the long run, because the psychiatric ward was like prison, not that you were locked in necessarily but in her experience most patients develop recidivistic tendencies – they keep on coming back, they can't help themselves.

I fled while I still had my freedom, and in the corridor on the way to the exit I stepped round a gathering of barefoot Rastafarians, men clothed in loincloths and blankets, some sitting and some standing near the radiator, the tallest nodding his burdened head under the trunk and branches of his hair and making wordless deep music in his throat, knocking rhythm out of the gloopy pipes with his rod of correction. I was heartened by the sight of these peaceful people but disbelieving of my own eyes in my fragile state and in want of an explanation, so I turned round and went back in, I went back to reception and asked what was happening. The receptionist had just started her shift and had not seen me waiting in extreme agitation for my appointment with the psychiatrist, she knew nothing about me, I could have been anybody. I leant over her desk to make myself heard without raising my voice over the noisy remonstrations of the other outpatients in the waiting area, trying to act normal, but she was alarmed all the same, I could feel it, because I was too scary, my questions inadvertently disrespecting patient confidentiality. She smiled and closed her eyes for a moment, maybe to shut me out, but I thought if I kept on I could talk her round until she let go of her initial misgivings and capitulated. So I kept on asking questions and I was right, in the end she gave in, she told me that the dreads lived in the corridor full-time, sleeping under their blankets – she said they were clean and kept themselves to themselves, not making trouble or disturbing the staff or other patients.

I was so grateful, calmed by her trust and surprised once she got going how she continued to flow. Her outlook was generous and I felt her change her opinion of me in response to my receptive listening and my voice, each word carefully annunciated, my compassion and display of equanimity I hoped making her wonder if I was a trainee social worker or concerned student anthropologist, in spite of my multilayered outfit and my hair, which had become unruly, betraying my own struggle to look after myself. She told me a couple of the Rastas were inpatients upstairs, but most had been discharged too soon from the psychiatric ward and didn't feel ready to go back out into the community; it was safer for them in the hospital, and they had been joined by some of their friends taking refuge from the outside world, all harmless men of faith who worshipped as God incarnate His Imperial Majesty Haile Selassie, Emperor of Ethiopia, who had died five years earlier. The hospital authorities turned a blind eye.

On my way home to Clapton, smiling but way too anxious to take the bus, I thought fondly of the Rastafarians in the hospital corridor, and also of Linda Stevens, my grandmother, the wayward protagonist or heroine perpetrator of the stories my mum told us in Trinidad, once we were old enough. We used to sit out on the verandah overlooking the yard during the long evenings before the abrupt fall of darkness, all the unfamiliar tropical noises just a buzz in the distance, the whole world almost silenced by the grave sweetness of my mum's voice. I was completely caught up in her childhood, that other world so far away both geographically and historically, and loved to hear about Linda's cruelty to servants, the false accusations, dismissals and other thrillingly condemnable misdemeanours, shocked by the impact of her behaviour on her household but too young even to consider the impact of her unkindness on my own mum. Although nothing was simple or straight in my mind about how things worked out between mothers and daughters. I was puzzled because my mum was always sympathetic towards Linda in spite of everything and never expressed any anger towards her, never condemned her however badly she behaved; my grandmother was not a witch in a fairy story, and sometimes my mum offset the principal version of her with an alternative version, another side of the story, the unforgettable Linda who defied the rule of the ferocious governess, and on one occasion even rescued her little daughter from a horrible punishment.

I can't remember the exact details of the offence she described to us as night fell and the bullfrogs squawked over the road, the mongoose eating a snake or whatever, all the munching sounds in the darkness, Uwe out there somewhere battling a storm on his way to Jamaica. The offence is forgotten, but I remember the punishment. The governess, to whom Linda and my grandfather had outsourced my mother's care, washed out the mouth of her little charge with soap and put her on the floor in the attic corridor and left her there on her own with her guilt and shameful thoughts to shiver in fright in the cold and the pitch black. My mother was terrified, and cried out, not expecting to be heard, but Linda heard, Linda came, Linda scooped her up behind the back of the governess, put her into bed in the nursery and fed her bread and milk to comfort her and take away the taste of the Imperial Leather.

Everything was so confusing, so far from home, and as I walked down Homerton High Street on my way back from the hospital, my best coat over my second-best coat over my suit jacket to insulate myself from the weather and to look smart in case people thought I was mad, my blouse washed and ironed and mended to within an inch of its life, what came to mind about my mother in her state of extreme unhappiness about my father were her stories about Linda's brothers, Uncle Ron and Uncle Bee, who lived together in a big house near my mother's childhood home and were never unkind to anybody.

Their house was called Walcot Hall, and my mother stayed with them often in childhood, having a wonderful time, although she was chased by the wild cranes and bullocks that roamed the estate, climbing trees to escape their unwanted attentions. The uncles were passionate about birds and kept waterfowl on a lake, at first unsuccessfully then successfully, many rare species, and entertained various local landowners and grandees of the neighbourhood at their home, including Haile Selassie, at that time living in exile in the West Country with his large entourage, said to be of approximately twenty-five people.

This God incarnate and recipient of fervent adoration from the Rastafarians in the hospital was a frequent visitor to the uncles, and perhaps because of this ancestral friendship I felt a certain proprietorial connection or kinship with his worshippers, respect and love and commonality I may not have felt otherwise, not only towards those who made healing music in the corridor of the outpatients department but respect and love towards all the others I passed in the street on the way back to Clapton, love flowing through the too-permeable two-way membrane of my self towards

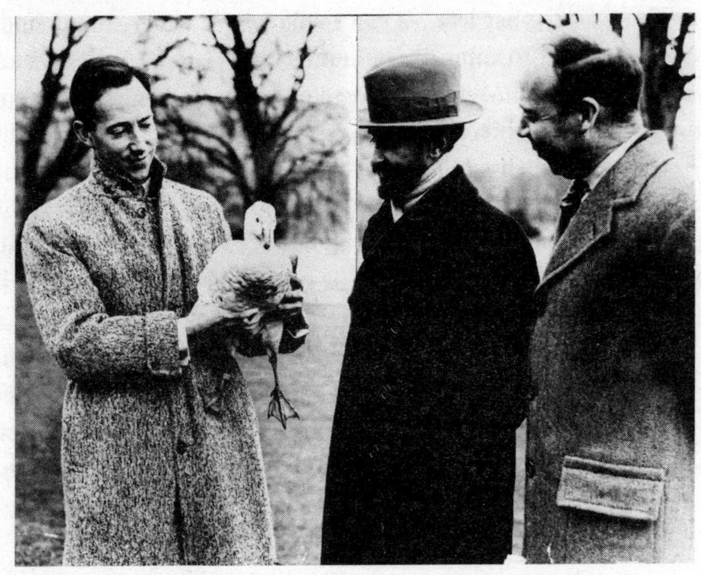

Uncle Bee with Haile Selassie and Uncle Ron
Photographer Unknown

everybody who struggled and suffered persecution, anybody who was just going about their business in their own way, trying to keep going as I was trying to keep going. I was brimful of love but my anxiety was overwhelming me at the same time, in part because I was implicated in my mother's suicidal unhappiness.

I had become a bit friendly with Celia – I met her through my father just as I had met Katie through him – and had developed a close friendship with Sophie de Stempel. It was different with Sophie, much worse, because he met her through me, or maybe through Bella, which seemed to come to the same thing. Sophie and I had collided at a Bow Wow Wow roller disco on New Year's Eve 1980, literally, ending up in a heap on the floor, neither of us very good at roller-skating. She was wonderful, she met Dad, he wanted to paint her and one thing led to another or the other way round, I don't know and I'm not going to ask her; we do talk about him but not in that level of detail. But she was my friend, and I had wanted her to come on our family holiday to Italy. Everything was all right until Mum started seeing Dad again. Mum asked me not to invite Sophie, which even I could see was the right thing for everybody. I should have known better than to have put Mum through that, but I was unable to feel what was and what wasn't endurable for any of us. If I had not been so numb and conditioned to acceptance, beyond outrage, I may well have been outraged by Sophie's disloyalty to me, a betrayal of friendship that neither of us registered at the time, and by my father, whose behaviour I failed even to question. He saw Sophie was young and lovely and was right in there, not thinking to protect her from himself in any way, and I just tried to keep going, not finding fault with either of them.

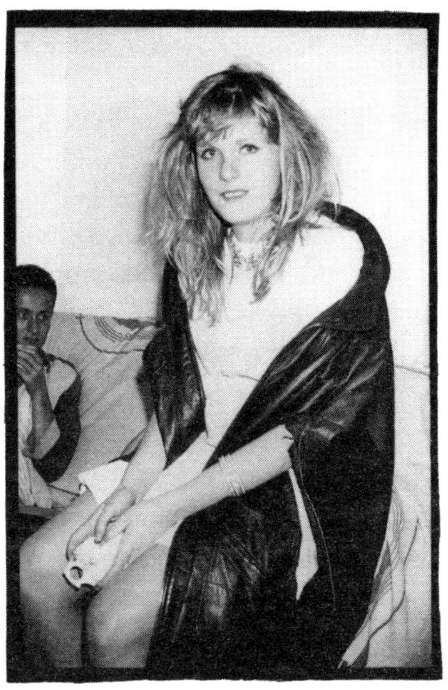

Sophie de Stempel at Northwold Road, 1981
ROSE BOYT

Uwe reappeared when I was fourteen, and I recognized him immediately, the heavy blonde thatch of his hair clearly visible through the side window of a white estate car parked up on the unmade road outside 9 Barnsbury Terrace, opposite the mica factory, the last house I lived in before I left home. Terror inhabited me as soon as I saw him, melting me from the inside, my legs trembling under my weight, the intensity of fear revealing to me how much danger I had learnt to live with the first time round. He was wearing some kind of pretentious neck-scarf or bandana and a coat of brown leather with epaulettes like a Gestapo officer, staring at nothing through the dirty glass of the windscreen to avoid catching my eye. I am sure he saw me but he was pretending he was invisible, tuning out the noise in his head, as self-conscious as a teenage boy. I mounted the steps to our front door as if I had not seen him, his eyes on my back. I was wearing a thin skirt and a T-shirt with short sleeves, the strap of my school bag slung across my chest. He must have been wondering whether the little child he had loved could have turned into this big schoolgirl. I could barely fit my key in the lock because my hands were shaking so violently.

My mum was baking a cake as if she knew he was coming. I told her he was out there and waited to see what she would do. She asked me to keep an eye on the cake and the other children, went out and talked to him through the car window. I don't know what he said to persuade her, if she needed persuading. I don't think she was expecting him. I took the cake out of the oven.

She served him a large slice, still warm, split and sandwiched with jam, but he ate with no joy, only back in our lives for five minutes and already employing the tricks he used on the ship to deny my mum any pleasure in pleasing him. I couldn't look at either of them. The motive for his return was unclear. I was so happy when he put on his coat and went out again, hoping that was it, he was gone again, but he came back about an hour later, pleased with himself, carrying a bottle of vodka and a giant red and white bucket of Kentucky Fried Chicken.

Of course he was hoping to curry favour, and I was always hungry even for school dinners. The hot sweaty smell of the chicken was unfamiliar in the house, new to me, not just because my mother was too skint to splash out on takeaway food but because fried chicken was not for us, not something she would bring home, never mind how much spare cash she had in her pocket. The skimpy leg meat on the small brittle bone was halfway between disgusting and delicious, too greasy but nice and salty, everybody shiny round the mouth apart from Mum, who had no appetite and would not eat Kentucky Fried Chicken if it was the last food on earth.

It didn't take him long to get his boots under the table, even though it was perfectly obvious there was something the matter with him. In front of my mum and my four-year-old sister he coerced me to confess to the loss of my virginity and made me admit I was on the pill, information I had kept to myself because it was private and I didn't think my mum would be able to cope with it. He said he was surprised the boys hanging round me weren't turned off by my tummy. He made a cupping gesture with his hand, palm and fingers curved to fit me, and I tried to hide myself behind the yellow piano in the hall. He didn't say whether or not he was turned off himself but looking back I think he implied without really implicating himself that he might be prepared to overlook any physical defect I had developed since puberty, even if younger men were not so forgiving, maybe in the hope that if he destroyed my confidence I would turn to him as a last resort.

Back then nobody cared if you were too young to drink and dance in the bar of a licensed premises. He must have followed me to the pub, I could feel him right behind me, glass in hand, his eyes on the back of my neck. I loved to dance, 'Use Me' by Bill Withers and the Staple Singers' 'I'll Take You There' on repeat on the jukebox, maybe some early seventies band playing live on a small stage in the basement. He would never smile to acknowledge me, never said a word to justify himself. I had to tone it down in case he thought my moves were for his benefit. I don't know if he was playing cat and mouse, biding his time, or what he was up to, breaking me down, but in the end he pushed me too far.

Since his return my mum had moved out of her bedroom on the first floor, presumably to put some distance between her and her children, and was sleeping with him on a mattress on the ground floor in what used to be our sitting room, the room repurposed but only in an incomplete way, the telly still in the corner. I was having a lie-down on their bed when he came in but was not very frightened because he was fully clothed, disabled by alcohol, and both of us were aware that my mum was downstairs making the supper. I warned him I would scream if he didn't get off me, he didn't get off so I screamed, and my mum came running up the stairs with a wooden spoon in her hand, not to use as a weapon but because she had been stirring something on the stove. He lumbered up off the mattress and crashed out of the door. I gave her an ultimatum and she got rid of him, she chose me over him.

He threw himself off Tower Bridge a few weeks after this incident, the misery of his rejection perhaps taking some time to hit home, even assuming his suicide bid was connected to what happened between me, him and my mum. He hoisted himself over the parapet and fell into the water but was pulled out by the River Police and came to no harm. I rolled my eyes in disgust at his antics when she told me what had happened, expressing regret only that he had not drowned, not holding back because I felt justified in hurting her. She was moved and excited by the failed grandeur of his gesture, caught up in the drama, and said I was cruel and heartless not to care. Her failure to understand or accept my refusal to share with her the sympathy she thought he deserved in his unhappiness did not surprise me because she was never really prepared to understand or accept the harm he caused me. She got rid of him for my sake, but never condemned him or his behaviour.

She enjoyed talking to me about him, not very often but often enough, smiling albeit a little tentatively and looking at me to gauge my reaction as she introduced him into the conversation. I always picked up too much playful fondness in her voice when she brought him up, like he was Captain Haddock or the benign naval officer serving fishfingers in the Bird's Eye advert. One time I remember she was excited to have received information from his first wife that he might sail up the Thames in some new boat he had acquired, wondering if we should line the banks and wave as he sailed past – she said they might even open Tower Bridge for him, which would be marvellous – and was crestfallen when I knocked her back with a few disparaging words. She seemed to assume I must have forgotten what he was like or at least forgiven him, challenging me with her eyes to contradict her in her defiance of the truth, unconsciously rubbing my nose in what really happened. I found any mention of him infuriatingly painful, and when she got old and needed my care I asked her to stop it. She said she was surprised I still found it too hard to talk about him, implying that I had not been efficient enough at putting the past behind me. I said I was happy to talk about him truthfully, but not listen to her whitewash. She said I got off lightly, he had gone all the way with one of his own daughters. I was sickened, but that was the end of it; she never mentioned him again.

I feel only love for her now. It was her birthday recently. I stopped work and went with Kai to visit her grave. We cleared all the dead leaves away and Kai pointed out the shoots of snowdrops breaking through the rich soil of her plot. I don't know why I didn't spot them myself, maybe because they were unexpectedly early. I planted the snowdrops last year, in the green, and was so happy to see they had come back. Once we had tidied up and said goodbye we walked to the grave of my father, which is close but not too close as she requested, just the right distance. I find it very satisfactory that we have safely stowed both of them in the same cemetery, almost a miracle, like having two parents under the same roof.

THREE

My father didn't want to work from me again after the completion of the naked portrait. I think he had done all he could – the painting said everything – and I was adamant I didn't want to sit again anyway, whether he asked me or didn't ask me. I wanted to get on with my own work and was not prepared to subject myself any time soon to a repeat of that level of intensity.

That didn't mean I was reluctant to see him. We went out together when he wanted to go out, just the two of us or with Bella or one or two of my other brothers and sisters, and sometimes he turned up at the Hot Sty, a club in the West End I ran with a couple of friends, to dance when he was in an exuberant mood or watch Fab 5 Freddy spin on his head in front of the DJ booth, but he also liked to see me to some purpose.

Dust collected at Holland Park, loose white threads from the rags and other debris he tolerated until it began to annoy him, and although he had a regular cleaner her job didn't extend beyond the domestic parts of the flat and so I took on the task of cleaning the studio, one way for me to make myself useful. I liked the smell of the wet floorboards and was always keen to see what he was working on, happy to enjoy a sneak preview and inhale the wet paint, although I was always careful not to gush or sound too worshipful; I am unsure even now if it could have been possible he would have welcomed a few more words of encouragement from me, his energy and sheer talent so great it is hard to remember he was ever troubled by doubts over his work.

My reluctance did nothing to discourage him once he was ready for me to sit again, his enthusiasm intensified perhaps by my lack of enthusiasm. I remember feeling humble and picturesque in my bare feet with the mop and bucket between the unfinished canvasses, hoping to please him with my willing demeanour as well as the perfection of the floor, which really mattered to him, when suddenly he jumped up in his unlaced boots from the armchair in which he was resting and said he HAD to do another picture of me. It was more than ten years since I had last sat for him, and not the first time he had asked me in the interim. He knew I didn't want to sit and I felt steamrollered by his disregard for my feelings, anxious because it was so hard to say no, even though I was delighted he wanted to paint me – he only painted the people he loved or at least liked very much, or in whom he took a special interest. I squeezed out the mop in the bucket and continued to wash the floor, grimacing comically to show him I was still disinclined to cooperate. He smiled like I was joking, picked up a tiny canvas that was propped against the skirting board as if in readiness for us to begin again, and showed it to me in an encouraging way.

'Look,' he said. 'It's OK. It need only be a little one. Like this!'

I grew up in the belief that nothing was possible for me, everything desirable out of my reach as though I were cursed. I wrote poetry until I was eleven and confessed as a teenager I might like to direct films, but Dad scoffed and told me that everyone wanted to do that. I loved to write but I remember I envied him that in paint he didn't have to commit himself one way or the other as I was struggling to do – he never had to say anything definitive or reveal himself in a direct way.

He had company nearly the whole time when he was working, someone to talk to, the sitter always required to turn up and pose even when my father was painting the view out of the window, although all but the most assiduous of us might slack off a little under those circumstances, eyes shut against the light, fidgeting more frequently when not skewered under his direct gaze. We were required not only to exert bodily pressure on the furniture and even the walls, to keep them back, but to maintain the heightened atmosphere in the studio and just be there as he toiled, to keep up his spirits and share soothing tea in the breaks if he began to flag, no improvisation necessary in the clearly defined roles of both parties. He loved his working relationships, his vitality intensified by the imposed inactivity of his sitters, everybody stilled for his sake as he worked, how we made everything possible for him, and it may have been a projection of this symbiosis that caused him to tell me, when I was starting tentatively to write a book in longhand two weeks after I left university, that he was worried I couldn't be a writer because I was too sociable, I wouldn't enjoy spending all day on my own, I had the wrong type of personality. He was genuinely concerned I would be too lonely.

I believed in him but kept going all the same, and it turned out he was wrong about me – I am happy to work on my own, although writing is painful for other reasons. I began to take photographs when I was seventeen, and have always found photography much easier, loving the consolation without having to explain myself in the capture of everything I was unwilling to lose. My wordless attempts to allay loss allowed me to disown what I might have been thinking or feeling without depriving myself of a point of view. I didn't know what I might or might not say in writing about anything, how far I could go, and until quite recently had a horror of going back down memory lane, unable to think straight about my father, afraid to feel everything.

Towards the end of the summer of 2016, clearing out of our house to make way for builders, I found an old diary in a cardboard box, hundreds of typed pages, many covered on both sides, the first dated 9 September 1989. I put the diary away without reading it; I had lost my father, my mother had died only four months earlier, and moving out of my home with my husband and children into temporary accommodation was very anxiety-provoking for me in my grief; it was not the right time to think about anything. I was heartbroken.

As I remembered it the diary was about sitting again, an easy portrait this time, fully clothed, the manuscript mainly a record of my father's remarkable stories. Everything was less lopsided between us by then, although the canvas he chose was not nearly as small as the one he had shown me to persuade me to sit again. I wore my best skirt, although it can't be seen in the painting, and carried a folded sheet of paper concealed in a pocket between the broad pleats, also one of those stunted pens you can pick up off the pavement outside any betting shop, or else a short stub of pencil, well sharpened. He talked and I listened, and I made surreptitious notes in the bathroom during the breaks, scribbling down everything he told me out of fear I might forget, protecting myself from that loss and preserving something of him for the future while he immortalized me. My best friend Lucy reminded me recently that I knew at the time the diary would be an important document. Soon after each sitting I typed up my notes, his words still fresh in my mind. Looking at the enormous typescript as I packed up the house I imagined all the stories he told me were amusing, uncontentious, but even if that had been true I still would not have been ready.

The building work took more than a year. Once we were back home and I felt settled enough I opened the box and was surprised to discover not only that I had started keeping the diary a few months before the sittings even began but also that I kept it going long after the painting was finished. In the beginning I describe my life as it was unfolding, maybe in the knowledge that sooner or later I would agree to sit again, unable to resist, my father sure to come out on top in any battle of wills between us.

In 2019 at Ordovas, a gallery in Savile Row in London, I showed thirteen of the photographs I had taken in the studio when I was a teenager, my work displayed on a wall adjacent to the naked portrait of me, which can be seen unfinished in some of the images.

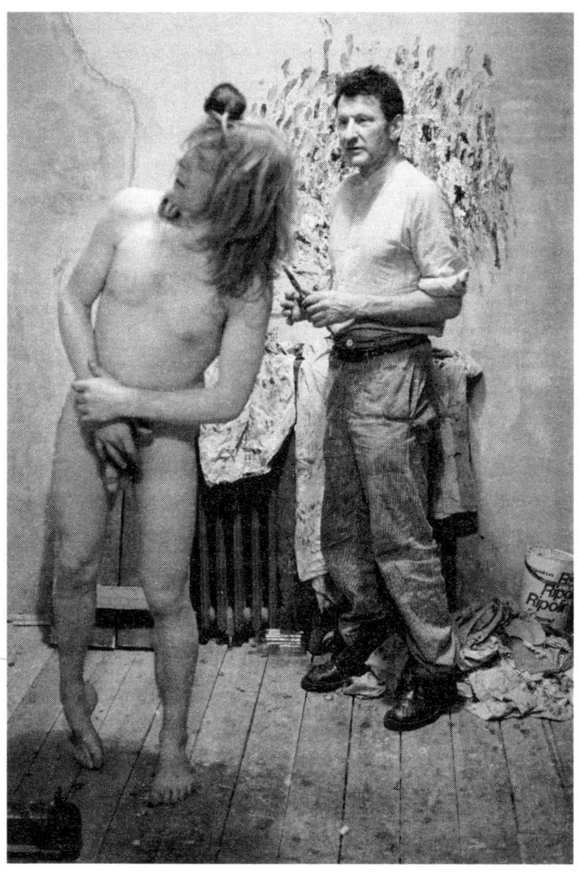

In The Studio 3 (1977)
ROSE BOYT

I was left in the gallery with the painting for a few moments when Pilar Ordovas took a call in the office at the back, shortly after the work had been unpacked from its crate, quite pleased on balance that none of the art handlers clocked that the naked woman in the portrait was me. I was transfixed, full of love for my father and his version of me, and amazed to find myself thinking about writing about sitting for him, something I had never wanted to do before, out of respect for his privacy, fear of what might come out, my own tender feelings.

Pilar suggested an essay for the catalogue and although I didn't feel free to write completely openly I found a voice that sounded honest enough, not wishing to embarrass Pilar, shame my father or bring shame on myself. I hadn't considered the photographs anything much until I saw them framed on the wall of the gallery. My father had always insisted that photographs were ephemeral and should not be shown in that way, like they were art, an attitude that I embraced without question, not prepared to make claims for photography perhaps because it wasn't as painful as writing, at least for me, and certainly wasn't as important or hard as what he was doing.

I was thrilled by the success of my essay in the Ordovas catalogue and in spite of my reluctance to commit myself any further on the same subject I began to wonder about expanding the essay as well as extracting my father's stories from the diary, believing I had the starting point for a quiet book about sitting. I thought I might make a record of his anecdotes and touch lightly on my feelings, not sure anybody would be interested in my feelings, whether recorded at the time or triggered in hindsight, but it turns out that it is impossible to separate his anecdotes from the rest of the diary material – he was too central in everything that was happening in the rest of my life.

I would not have been able even to read the diary let alone work from it without the help of my psychotherapist, a woman I had started to see only a few weeks before embarking on this enterprise. Without her at my shoulder the journey backwards would have been too much, although had I anticipated the level of pain I was to encounter I may well have swerved the whole thing. I am not saying I sought help only because I needed support with my book, and it was not like I hadn't had psychotherapy before, as you will discover. I was still having difficulties, and at my preliminary psychological assessment was stunned to be told I was suffering from childhood trauma and would require intense treatment. I was almost numb to things that had occurred by which I am now horrified. To admit that I was traumatized is a giant step. I have always felt I had no right to mind anything that happened to me, but now I feel different.

This was not my first diary. I had filled bundles of notebooks in my time and put them out with the rubbish whenever I moved house or even spring-cleaned, as if ridding myself of the contents might facilitate my new start without the past spilling over into the present, unwilling ever to go back over what I had written because I wrote mainly in misery, hoping to alleviate it or work it out of my system, always too happy to keep a record of my days and nights in the happy times.

And before that, on the ship, it was easy in port to find something to describe and illustrate, an old schooner like ours called the *Selma* in dry dock, the *Selma* on the slips, swans on the frozen harbour, the trek with my mum back from the fishmonger with a giant cod that fought for its life as we carted it back to the galley, but at sea I was too bored or seasick to write very much, trying to think of something to say when nothing much happened worth writing about, every day the same, calm or storm, nothing to see. I couldn't be bothered to unfasten and fasten the tiny heart padlock that was supplied with the diary, and mislaid it with the inevitability I was already beginning to anticipate from my experience of how things just disappeared, the loss or theft annoying but not problematic on a practical level because I regarded the entries like schoolwork, I was not about to write down my secrets, my handwriting deceptively open and childish. I wonder what happened to that diary. I left it behind when I left home. Mum lost it and with it the evidence of harms, however obliquely I must have expressed myself not to alarm anybody, and the sitting diary possesses some of the same obliquity.

The vitriol I express at the beginning against the sexism of Frank Auerbach needs to be counterbalanced in advance. I have always felt very warm-hearted towards him, his wife Julia and their son Jake, whom I have known all my life and consider a dear friend. I am very surprised by the tone of what I have written but I was fucking angry and Frank takes the brunt of it here. That's how I felt back then. With love and hope for forgiveness.

FOUR

Saturday, 9 September 1989

In bed after an evening at Dad's. Frank and Julia, (my sister) Esther, Angus and me. Grouse very raw, not sure if the flesh is supposed to be so bloody, the cavity full of lukewarm organs. I had to spit out a mouthful of the meat into the palm of my hand and leave it on the side of my plate. Angus was the cook. He tried to say NEW YORK REVIEW OF BOOKS but was nervous, too drunk. Frank, Julia and Dad were still at the theatre when I arrived, a play called MEIN KAMPF – a farce with Esther in it – I had come early to help Angus with the preparations.

Dad and Frank appeared before Julia, who showed up a few minutes later, perhaps because she was parking the car. Or maybe she drove Frank to the theatre, Dad met them there in his car, and after the show they made Julia drive back on her own so they could travel together. Dad and Frank slagged off the play but agreed that Esther was LOVELY in it, Dad said it first then Frank repeated the word, almost killing it off for me. Angus kept on opening the oven door to prod the grouse, anxious not to overcook it. Apparently Esther was naked on stage, wearing a long blonde wig.

The way Dad and Frank said LOVELY led me to believe her character was purely ornamental, not required to speak, but that was a mistake on my part.

Dinner was served. Dad and Frank took turns delivering judgements on subjects such as the late work of Van Gogh – 'I HATE the Town Hall at Arles painting' (Dad) – and making pronouncements – 'Painting is like housework' (Frank.) It's not that their conversation was uninteresting but I got the feeling everything they said over dinner had been said before – they were just quoting themselves. Frank was the worst, Dad's chivalry touching and inoffensive compared to Frank's seeming belief that women are by nature without the capacity for judgement or intelligent thought. I have never heard one-sided bickering before – it's usually a case of sniping received and returned – but Julia sat patiently in Frank's line of fire without flinching or retaliating. Everything she said Frank corrected or contradicted, and Dad joined in once or twice, which surprised and upset me; the disparagement seemed to be catching. I imagined Frank on his hands and knees on the kitchen floor with a bucket of suds and a scrubbing brush, Julia having locked herself away in the studio to get on with her own work, a DO NOT DISTURB notice on the door. I wonder if he even knows what housework feels like.

Then talk of famous actors I'd never heard of. I had a conversation with Julia about SEXUAL INTERCOURSE (my first novel, recently published.) She said the book got under her skin and made her feel uneasy. I was glad. Frank joined in. He said my book was good. The way he judged it/me was like GOD. I hoped he would ask me some questions about writing so I could hold forth but the only thing he asked me was whether I had sold my paperback rights yet. He began to make some derogatory remarks about word processors but gave it up when I explained how useful I found mine – hours of typing and retyping saved, particularly if you can't type properly. Then he used the word INTIMACY to describe a writer's closeness with HIS own writing. He felt that the word processor would interfere with this in some way.

A naked etching of Angus hangs over the fireplace in my office, the sofa he is reclining on the same one that can be seen in the teenage portrait of me.

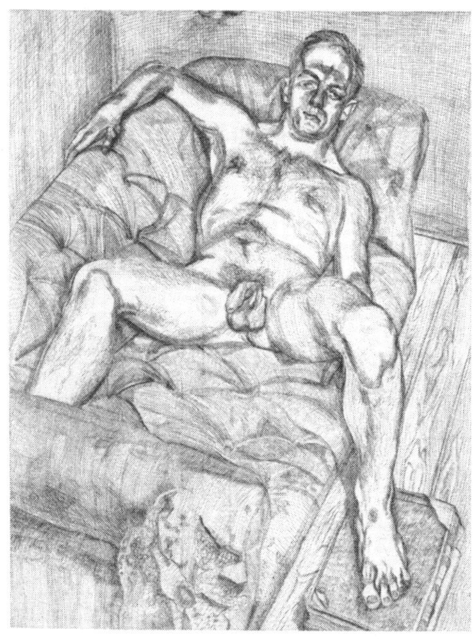

Man Posing (1985)
LUCIAN FREUD

He came from Campbeltown in Scotland and was my friend first, my earliest memory of him at UCL in 1979, Mr Needham's weekly Anglo-Saxon seminar, Old English Poetry and Prose a compulsory element of the English course in the first term – we were translating and discussing 'The Battle of Maldon', an almost surreal insider pursuit, pleasurable only in the grapple to understand the language and the complete contrast it provided to real life at 95 Graham Road in Dalston, where I lived in a small bedsit on the ground floor of a house that was miserably scary and cold.

Angus was sitting near Mr Needham's desk and I was a bit further away from the centre of activity, quite near the door of the narrow room, all the hard wooden chairs between us occupied by other students. Taking advantage of Mr Needham's complete focus on the explication of the poem Angus handed a note to the student next to him and asked her to pass it on down the line. The note travelled from hand to hand until it reached me. I unfolded the scrap of paper and read the message – *I LOVE YOU*. Angus was smiling at me when I looked at him, his cheeks mottled pink, and I was reminded of Valentine's Day my last year at primary school, two boys in my class gave me cards and I walked home on air, not that I fancied either of them.

Angus came out to me not long after his declaration of love, which was no big surprise in hindsight; I pretended I already knew, to avoid humiliation and not wishing him to think I might hold it against him; I suspected he was afraid he had disappointed me, any romantic hopes his note might have ignited dashed by his disclosure. Not that I had hopes, nor did it occur to me to wonder about his motivation. He wanted to be friends, and was just making mischief in the Anglo-Saxon class, toying with me to while away the time until we were released, perhaps having heard about my illustrious antecedents and drawn to me in part by the allure of all that, and who can blame him? He sat for Celia first, then for my father, not that I minded, although the more he became involved with my father the harder it was on our friendship.

He was living near the British Museum at the time of the diary, in the flats just over the road from me, with his boyfriend, the artist Cerith Wyn Evans, and Celia lived just round the corner. Angus and Cerith are the subject of one of her best ever paintings, so full of mournful tenderness, the paint embodying Celia's love for them as well as their love for each other.

I was new to the area, recently moved from Notting Hill, where my landlord had been giving me problems. He was a friend of Sophie de Stempel's, easy-going and generous most of the time, and happy to rent me the top floor of his house for twenty-five pounds a week, share of kitchen and bathroom, the informal tenancy arranged for me by Sophie, who had occupied the two rooms previously. The landlord lived below me, above the shop, and although he never complained about me and my friends coming and going at all hours – he liked it – he used to play Segun Adewale and His Superstars International and The Jesus and Mary Chain at full volume at four in the morning when I was trying to sleep, and shouted at me if I asked him to turn it down because he owned the house and I didn't. So I was moaning to my father after a bad night, no conscious agenda on my part, and he offered to buy me a flat. I was amazed, and felt so grateful I told him he was off the hook for anything he might have done wrong so far in my life, and in fact at that time I did feel I was able to forgive him for everything, including and particularly the poverty of my very early childhood and the years of want after we were repatriated from the Caribbean, the contrast between the life he led and my mother's struggle to pay the bills and put food on the table, not that he was entirely to blame for her losses. The flat made it all better.

I began to look in the windows of estate agents, high on excitement and gratitude, although when I went inside I was unable to disclose the size of my budget, the first question they asked me, because my father hadn't put any limits on his wonderful offer. He was relying on me not to deny myself in the modesty of my aspirations nor to become too rapacious and eager for inappropriate magnificence under the heady thrill of his gift, so I had to be careful, not only to do myself proud but also not to skin him alive in the defenceless vulnerability of his generosity, half-conscious as I was that he was compensating me for the privations of the past. My choice of property was an opportunity for security and also a test of my personality and how I saw myself, how I might pitch myself regarding the number of bedrooms, the status of my chosen neighbourhood. I had to protect him but also to intuit to what extent I was worthy, imagining what he might think I deserved, feeling undeserving because I was used to the humiliation of poverty and over-deserving for the same reason, determined above all else not to seem greedy and importunate.

I know people roll their eyes and glaze over as the dreamer describes the antics of their night, impatient for something more real, itching to evade the inevitable boredom and embarrassment induced by the inconsequentiality of the action, the lack of proper structure, but at least the following extracts are brief and reveal with relative economy my other states of mind at the start of the diary, anger not my only emotion.

Sunday, 10 September 1989

Three significant dreams in one night. I dreamt I was pregnant and happy. The dream made me realize I could be pregnant and happy. That is something I have always feared might never happen. Also about fullness.

The second dream was about sitting for Dad. I was lying on a sofa in the studio. He went to a Vivienne Westwood fashion show with Bella and I discovered I could find a comfortable position in which to sit. I could be myself on the sofa and Dad would still be able to paint me, to want to paint me. I did not have to contort myself.

It's not that he wanted me to contort myself, I just assumed with some certainty that he didn't want me to show or even to have suffered any anger or sorrow about anything even remotely connected to him, which must have felt to me at the time like the same thing. In the dream he goes off with Bella and the shameful secret of my jealousy is revealed, so what if I was learning how to be myself. My jealousy back then is hard to own up to even now, the teenage torture intensified by the depth of my shame.

I must have been eighteen when he turned up one afternoon at the flat he had borrowed for me from one of his friends, at Clarendon Gardens in Maida Vale, a maisonette with two bedrooms, way safer and more substantial than any of the other places I had ended up since I left home. The naked portrait of me was not yet a possibility for either of us, but he was agitated, something on his mind, it was obvious, so I just waited until he was ready to tell me. We stood in the sitting room, neither of us said anything, then he coughed and told me it was bad I had neglected to throw out a bunch of flowers that had died a few days ago, the stale water actually a danger to me. We both looked at the dead flowers and I knew he was making up the threat to my health because he disapproved of my slovenly housekeeping or was reminded of Mum, who used to keep flowers and enjoy them once they were faded and dry.

We moved into the kitchen to get away from the humiliation of his criticism, I made him some tea, and he began to talk about Bella, who was still living at home with Esther and their mother Bernadine, and Bernadine's new family. Bella hated her home in the country. She wanted to take A levels at sixth-form college in London. She wanted to move.

I hardly knew Bella, but I knew what he wanted from me – he

was so keen for her to be happy. I said it would be fine if she moved in with me. He thought that was marvellous, although Bernadine was making difficulties, which he found very irritating. So I wrote to her, eager to make myself indispensable. I offered to write, but Dad should have saved me from myself – not from my jealousy, which was inevitable, but from my fantasy that I would be able to take care of my young sister. He forgot to consider the impact on me of the arrangement.

I can still feel the mad pleasure I took in writing that letter, a sheet of creamy white paper torn out of a drawing book and five or six big inky sentences composed so persuasively and with such delusional self-confidence to please Dad it was impossible that Bernadine would not roll over. Bernadine was reassured, I was delighted, and a couple of weeks later I found myself in loco parentis to an almost complete stranger, having assumed foolishly Bella would resemble me in some fundamental way rather than being her own person, a child coming into my home with too much sexual allure, too much ruthless desire for excitement and danger. She left sixth-form college almost before it had begun, had to be fed because she didn't want to waste her money on food, and realized her ambition to get stuck into everything cool and dangerous as soon as possible, with hardly a care for herself or for me.

I had a short crop like a boy and her waist-length hair was gorgeously lush, the colour of black treacle, falling in soft waves round her sweet face, but she wanted to chop it off like mine, a significant act I tried to dissuade her from because I knew if she went ahead she would enter my world with the recklessness I lacked and the comparison between us would be even more obvious. But she went ahead and looked even more devastating, her head a beautiful shape, and everybody fancied her more than they fancied me, the pain just one more bad thing about myself I had to learn to hide or try and ignore. She had that alluring shine and still possesses it, although when you look at photos of us together when we were flatmates for the first time you can see we looked like sisters then, not all that different. You can also see we loved each other, and I have been wondering recently if I could ask her about how she felt in those days, if she was even aware of my jealousy, thinking how horrible it must have been for her if she knew. It also crossed my mind it's not out of the question she might have experienced similar feelings in relation to me.

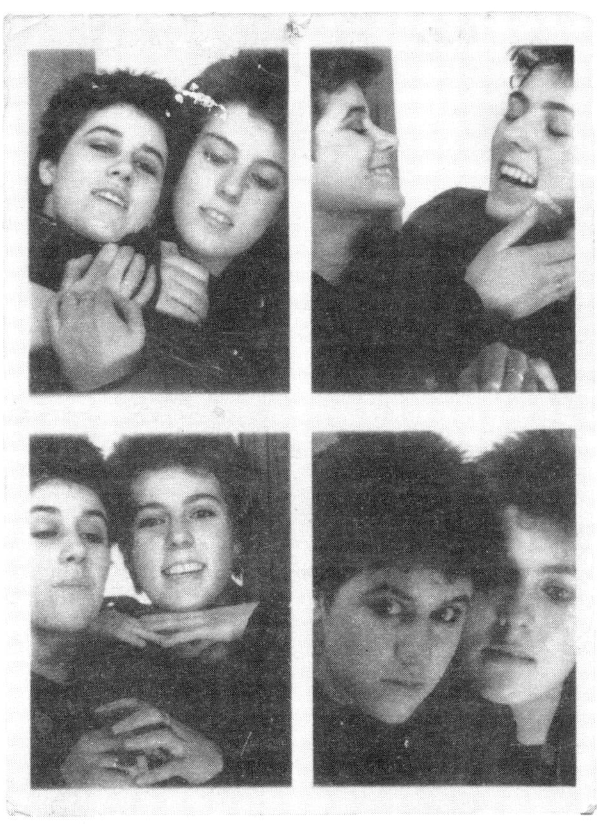

Bella and me (1977)

The point is, I had no influence over her and was unable to keep her safe, although I am ashamed to say that I loved her more as she went downhill because she was less of a threat. When I moaned to Dad about the impact of her behaviour on me he dismissed my concerns and told me that everything I held against her was just more fuel to my fire, an accusation I found very hurtful under the circumstances. I was overwhelmed by love for her and the burden of the responsibility I had taken on without knowing what I was letting myself in for, and our father was implying that my objections said more about me than about her, meaning I was just too angry and jealous and spiteful. I was silenced by the criticism implied in his response, and no longer felt free to talk to him about my sister, even though I was almost unbearably worried about her.

I had always believed I was the sensible one, terribly sensible but only when compared to my other family members, the parameters of what was possible drawn fairly loosely not only by our various parents but by ourselves, none of us too cautious when it came down to it, all of us lucky to be alive. I remember two of my siblings smoking heroin in the kitchen at Clarendon Gardens, and my conviction when they offered me the tinfoil that I might try it with no harm to myself, which is probably what most addicts think when they get started. I tried it on two separate occasions then decided enough was enough, the seductive release from all feeling too compelling not to resist.

Sunday, 10 September 1989, cont.

The third dream was rebirth. Writing in it, the writing in words and pictures, good because it was clear. I prepared a family meal but I was angry because somebody dished it up before it was ready and everybody began to eat. I was getting younger and younger, becoming an angry child in my behaviour, and then Mum suffered pain, terrible pain I inflicted on her. I knew I was reborn because I read the writing I had written and it said so. It described a kind man with hands he placed one on each side of my waist to help the birth, a bearded man I saw clearly through the writing, flowering thyme, also to help me. When I woke up I felt quite different – detached, separate, I let go. Reborn.

I am struck by my dream belief in the veracity of my own writing, when in reality I was struggling with the novel I was working on, the fiction that was true and not true, and the pain it might inflict on my family. And I am shocked by the blithe and obtuse tone I use in this diary entry to describe the pain I inflicted on my mum as if I felt she deserved it, too angry until recently to recognize my own cruelty.

Monday, 11 September 1989

Johnnie's third birthday. Pam and Steve gave him a real car he can sit in and drive on the pavement. It runs on batteries and cost £400. Pam bought a train cake from Marks and Spencer and we all sat on the floor and watched Johnnie hack up the iced sponge with a bread knife. Lola sat on my knee. Pam had the idea of trying to sell SEXUAL INTERCOURSE to Channel Four for £12,000. If that works out all my problems (financial ones) will be over.

I had seen Pam in the English common room and the library at UCL a few times before I got to know her, always with Angus, the two of them whispering together and sharing private jokes even though, like the rest of us, they had only just met. She was seventeen at the start of the course, visibly pregnant, wearing punk clothes, and I was older than her by three or four years, and felt more experienced, perhaps because she was from out of town. And I understood how to take care of babies.

She told me she was going back to Basingstoke to give birth in the Christmas holidays but was not allowed home – some woman her mum knew from church was putting her up because her parents were concerned what the neighbours might think when she went off in the ambulance, her mum unable to face the shame when she came home. I asked her how she was going to cope. She shrugged and smiled, and my heart was suffused with love for her suddenly, and for her unborn child, not as if the baby was my own but more like it was me again. I said I would be available any time she needed me, I was good with babies and would like to help out.

The second week of the new term I saw her in a lecture on Milton, feeding her daughter under her big black-and-red striped mohair jumper, head down because she was not sure if she would be called out, still able to take notes on disobedience in *Paradise Lost* with her spare hand. She took me up on my offer of help and I was delighted. The baby was called Laura.

Who knows if I was conscious at the time of the parallel between her situation and that of my mum when she was a student at the Slade, which is part of UCL, if I wished my mum had had someone like me to give her encouragement and practical assistance, but I was drawn to Pam and her baby with such determination to make myself useful I suspect I must have been motivated unconsciously by the similarity of their circumstances, hoping to make it up to my mum through Pam for her struggle. Anthony, the father of Pam's child, wanted to be with her, to move up to London from their hometown and embrace fatherhood at close proximity, but she had other ideas. With Angus we started our own little family, to take care of Laura and each other, then after university Pam married a man called Steve and had two children with him, Lola and Johnnie, and at the time of the diary was living just round the corner from me, right opposite Angus and Cerith.

Monday, 11 September 1989, Cont.

After John's birthday tea I went to see my sister Susie at Belgrave Mews North. She is very sad about Robert's death. They really loved each other and were planning to get married. For supper we had some salad and a carton of chicken soup from Tyler's. I felt very close to her. She lay down on the floor and I stroked her head and rubbed her feet and we did some deep breathing. I gave her a few drops of Rescue Remedy.

To bed about twelve and didn't wake up until ten. I don't know why I'm so tired. The effort of having such vivid dreams and the energy I use up on all the big revelations and new leaves I keep on turning over. Still, I went for a swim and here I am.

Finished reading my new book. I am really very pleased with it, although the middle part could use more fantasy of men in general and memory of Uwe in particular, inc. the real terror of catching a glimpse of him from the top deck of a bus every now and again in the present, the shock of him, his thick golden hair, me looking down at the top of his head even though it is never quite him in reality, like seeing a friend in the street from a distance you remember suddenly you forgot they were dead. Although Uwe is still alive in real life as far as I know, not that I have seen him since before I left home.

Tuesday, 12 September 1989

Rang the LONDON REVIEW OF BOOKS and gave my proof marks over the phone for my piece on Acid House. Typed out the diary notes I wrote on Saturday night with elaborations and amendments. Managed to read most of my new book again. Some of it seems good, other parts a bit weak, but at least I can tell the difference. I keep forgetting. I keep forgetting I can do something about it if I don't like it.

Thinking about Dexter and Maya. How long have I been with him? Maybe since Maya was six. I am worried about her. I'm scared of being on my own but I feel lonely in spite of him. I don't want him to stop loving me. Each time I decide to break up with him I change my mind a little bit less each time I change my mind about him.

Thursday, 14 September 1989

Debbie's birthday paella was delicious.

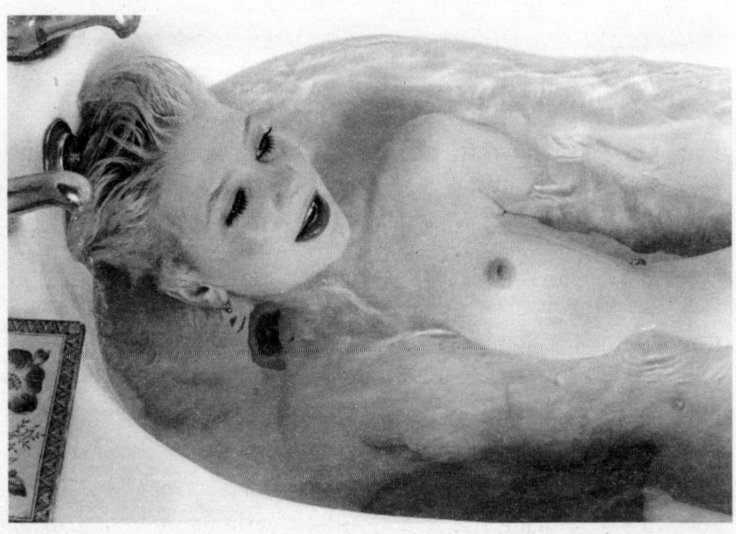

Debbie, an old friend since the punk days. She used to go out with Johnny Rotten, then made a career for herself in film production.

ROSE BOYT

For her party Cerith was wearing a kilt, Pam a tartan jacket, Dexter a pair of plaid trousers. Susie turned up unexpectedly. Invited Mum at the last minute. She was lovely. Angus and Cerith played with Maya's Barbie dolls. The cake took the biscuit. Played old singles. 'Silly Games', 'Brand New Key'.

Everybody went home apart from Debbie and Dexter. I was lying next to him on the floor, my face buried in his shoulder, suddenly overcome by doomy feelings brought on by late-night drinking and my loneliness. Debbie went to bed in the spare room and I joined Dexter in my bed. Some comfort in his arms. Alert to signs of love fading away. On Wednesday night I dreamed he left me before I had a chance to leave him. I kicked myself for letting things get so painful. He fell asleep and I read a couple of chapters of THE COURTSHIP OF ELIZABETH BARRETT AND ROBERT BROWNING by Danny Karlin.

Danny Karlin taught us at UCL. Not long after his arrival he gave a seminar on the poetry of Emily Dickinson, a memorable event during which he read out various poems and asked us to separate the good from the bad, a sort of show trial not only of the poet but also of ourselves, his students – we were required not just to note down in private which poem fitted into which category but to speak the verdict out loud if we thought we knew. He stood in judgement at the front of the room, straight from Cambridge and not much older than the rest of us, a huge fan of Bruce Springsteen but very clever and good-looking, inadvertently humiliating anybody who made the wrong choice without intending to big himself up or make us feel stupid or insensitive, even those of us unable to hear in one of Dickinson's slighter or more subtle verses the shocking sharp truth of her genius.

I reminded him of this seminar a few years ago when I met him at the funeral of one of our other beloved professors, and he apologized to me as if I were calling him out on a crime perpetrated against my student self. I had not intended to embarrass him, and insisted that there was no need to apologize, but he was genuinely ashamed. I regretted having said anything, and in an attempt to reassure him I told him I had learnt much from him in the seminar and had not questioned his teaching method at the time because it was so familiar to me, the incontrovertible authority of his opinions on the poetry just like the absolutes of my father. I adore Degas and Rodin and Cézanne, Courbet and Ingres and Velázquez amongst others, all his favourites, but there has never been any question for example of liking Renoir or Henry Moore, because he didn't like them, although these lessons were unspoken. I remember when my mother said Cézanne wasn't really much good I laughed in admiration of her courage to say what she felt, and was genuinely shocked by her disavowal. It was only after my father died I felt free to love more widely.

Friday, 15 September 1989

Spent the morning clearing up the party mess of last night. Writing this diary alleviates the dread I have of muddle, loss of memory, confusion. Since I have begun it my head feels much clearer.

Postcard from Emma Tennant asking me for a short story for a collection she is putting together. Also a letter from the clinical psychologist at the Middlesex Hospital offering me an appointment in October – I have applied for help with my travel phobia. I am looking forward to Bridges coming back from holiday – not long now.

Bridges was my psychotherapist at the time. He interviewed me at the Tavistock Clinic when I was struggling with anxiety in my early twenties and asked me if I thought I could work with anybody I had met so far in the assessment process. I chose him, was offered three sessions a week and accepted with gratitude. The only other thing I can recall clearly about the assessment process was some other male therapist or analyst asking me if my sexual fantasies were violent. I said no, although I am not sure I would have been brave enough to give a straight answer if the truth had been otherwise. I thought at the time that this question was some type of deal-breaker, like the man was trying to work out whether I was neurotic but worthy of psychotherapy on the NHS or some psychotic sex maniac who was beyond help.

Friday, 15 September 1989, cont.

Just found a piece of paper on which I recorded the rebirth dream so here we go again.

Rooms, people. The food I had cooked was served up before I was ready. More people were arriving. Some brought their own food, pre-prepared. I was angry with Mum because when I came back into the room everybody was eating. I was trying to choose a jersey to wear, getting angrier, becoming more and more childish. Then Mum had to experience terrible pain on my behalf – I inflicted it on her. Afterwards I knew I had been reborn. I saw it written on a piece of paper in my handwriting. I called it 'yelding'. A man was involved, lessening the pain, holding her/my sides. And some herbs, the words on the piece of paper replaced by the objects themselves. Garlic, flowering thyme, honey. They all helped me. When I woke up I knew it was a dream and yet I felt released from my anger against Mum. Also today I have been writing about her, saying bad things about her in my new book.

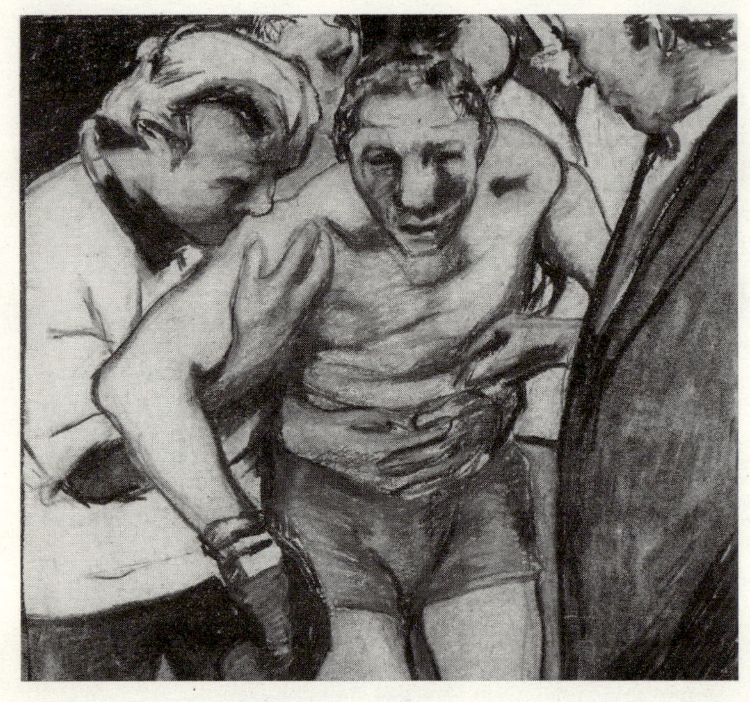

Dave 'Boy' Green (1977)

KATIE McEWEN

FIVE

Saturday, 16 September 1989

Long telephone conversation with a solicitor at Goodman Derrick about the closure of The Colville Rose – I am still trying to extricate myself after all this time. I remain unpaid, a fact that diminishes to nothing compared to the disaster of the guarantee. If Lord Goodman can't save me from the jaws of the bank then nobody can.

The Colville Rose was a Notting Hill bar and club I set up early in 1989 in an old Courage pub and first-floor function room with seven tall windows, the new interior designed by architects Catrina Beevor and Robert Mull. I decided to leave suddenly, having taken legal advice because I overheard the money men talking about the VAT fraud they were perpetrating behind my back, and the business collapsed, not that it wouldn't have gone down the pan anyway, one of the partners threatening to burn down my flat if I said anything to anybody. I remember having tea in Dad's kitchen and feeling sad after he had arranged for me to consult his solicitors, devastated I would have to abandon everything I had worked so hard to organize. His girlfriend Susanna was there, smoking at the kitchen table and looking concerned but not in a motherly way – she had her own children to worry about – and my father asking me why I was so upset, his puzzlement over my distress a puzzle in itself, as if the failure of my endeavour should have glanced off me and not hurt me at all. I began to cry quietly to myself and told him that twenty people would lose their jobs, as though it were less embarrassing to cry for them than for myself, not that I wasn't distressed about letting everybody down, and he and Susanna smiled at each other over my head because they thought my concern for all those people was too sweet.

Saturday, 16 September 1989, cont.

Dexter shouting at Maya when they turned up at lunchtime. It is pointless making children bend to your will because it is your will and for no other reason. I told Dexter he should apologize to Maya for losing his temper but he denied losing his temper. This is still unsettled between us but sorting it out doesn't matter anymore because I have decided to break up with him anyway. Time he is supposed to spend with his daughter he gets a job and leaves her with me.

Maya had a good cry then played Barbies with Lola and Frances. They built a camp in the sitting room out of the clothes airer, blankets, towels and cushions. Maya went home with Lola.

Frances is my adored niece, daughter of my sister Isobel. My father had two daughters born in the same year, both named Isobel, one he referred to as Ib and one he called Bella. Ib arrived at motherhood in her mid-twenties, although she never made me feel bad she got there before me. I used to look after Frances almost every Saturday while Ib and her partner Pat were at work, which was delightful, and I also took care of Pam's children and Maya, who was not very good at enjoying herself when she was with me. Dexter loved his daughter with all his heart but when he smoked weed and lost focus his nurture of her went so far and no further. Defending Maya was complicated, and of course I identified with her, although I never felt overwhelmed, because taking care of children was what I did and have always done, the ache of my childlessness lessened as well as exacerbated by those important connections. Not that I was ready for motherhood at that point in my life, not that I wanted to have children with Dexter, I just wanted to know that one day I would meet a man I could trust with my life before it was too late. Being uncommitted felt shameful and precarious because of the intensity of my desire for the opposite, my longing for a conventional version of happiness a reaction to my mother's struggle, as though marriage and children might heal everything. My early thirties would have been much less fraught had I known how things would turn out. I remember going to parties and meeting men who were afraid of me because I was single and childless.

And my mum's attitude was not very encouraging. I was twenty-eight when she told me it was such a shame I never had children. She had given birth for the fifth time when she was not much older than me and seemed to regard my childlessness as some sort of affront to her integrity. We were at her house in Medina Road, near the Rainbow in Finsbury Park, the first time I had been round since her alcoholic drug-addict boyfriend Tom had moved in, and I remember I was unexpectedly deeply depressed during my visit by the alterations she had made to the basement sitting room, even before she started on me. The lacy textiles and old chintz, in faded shades of pale roses, threadbare but perfectly clean and smelling of Lux flakes, had been sold or packed away, Tom's grungy carpets and floor cushions everywhere like an opium den and a new dirty smell from his things that I found almost unbearable.

Tom was out by some lucky chance, Mum said he had gone to the pub. The concern in her voice for my happiness was halting as she tried to take me down, poking me with a stick to see if I would retaliate but worried about herself, worried she was too mean. I can see now that her assumption I had left it too late was her depression expressing itself. Perhaps she thought Tom would save her. I felt she doomed me to childlessness and other major life dissatisfactions because she didn't have the self-belief to teach me to believe in myself, and I was not at all sure I would ever meet anybody worthy of my trust, not sure I was lovable enough. Her smile was sweet and sad, extremely provocative. I turned on her bitterly and said I was still trying to recover from my own childhood.

Saturday, 16 September 1989, cont.

Collected Maya from Pam's, drove Frances home and hung round at Ib's for a while. Maya played nicely with Frances. Mum was there too, staying over because she had had an intruder at her house – she woke up in the night and there he was at the end of her bed in the moonlight, just standing there looking at her. She gave him a fiver to get rid of him and he went, but she was still very shaken. Plan to sell her house and buy a flat near Ib's. I must stop her from accepting too little, don't want her to end up in a dump.

My assumption that I ought to interfere in my mother's finances must have been hard for her to take, or perhaps she felt glad I was concerned for her well-being. I am reminded of the time my father gave me some money to get her some clothes, partly for my sake, because she was going through a bad patch and I could not bear her to look like a bag lady. I asked him for help, kept the cash in my own pocket on the shopping trip and dipped into it to pay for her purchases – she chose a beautiful narrow skirt from Agnès b. amongst other things, and looked very good in it, elegant and severe. My failure to relinquish the money he gave me for her still troubles me now, how I demeaned myself and my mum by interceding between them and prolonging the intercession until we spent everything apart from a handful of change, an inexcusable lack of respect on my part, although I suspect my motivation wasn't all bad; I knew she wouldn't have spent the money on herself had I handed it over.

Saturday, 16 September 1989, cont.

Left Maya at Ib's for a sleepover and went straight from there to Annie Freud's for supper. Had a horrible time. Aggro from Annie I didn't need, I was feeling too delicate. Also she lives quite near Northwold Road – such a difficult time for me when Bella and I shared the flat behind and above Mum's shop. Had difficulty driving home – welling loneliness and the discomfort of being stuck in this thing with Dexter when I have had enough. Reading Philip Roth in bed.

I didn't meet Annie, my father's eldest child, until I was a teenager, although I was vaguely aware of her existence and that of Annabel, her sister, whom my father called Ama. I came as a complete shock to both of them when we first met, Dad having chosen not to tell them he had other children. They were both born in wedlock, and Annie at least had a more conventional start than the rest of us, Dad and Kitty only splitting up after Annabel was born, the two girls raised by their maternal grandmother until Kitty married again and was able to give them a home. Even after the divorce they used to stay with our grandparents at Walberswick, a Suffolk coastal village that reminded Ernst and Lucie Freud of the island in the Baltic where they used to spend every summer before they left Germany. Annie says there were so many of us suddenly after we met she didn't know where to draw the line, convinced that not only Bella and I but some of the other young women we hung around with were not just more punks but more sisters.

Monday, 18 September 1989

Today I will see Bridges for the first time in five weeks. My decision to end it with Dexter has coincided with Bridges' return not by chance but by the design of my unconscious mind. Very nervous about seeing him again.

He smiled at me and said hello. I was less cowed than I am normally. Such a relief he is back. Arranged to meet Dexter on Wednesday evening. Can't believe I am ending something after a lifetime of leeching and clinging on. I am hoping Dexter will still want to be friends with me. And of course there is Maya to think about.

Wednesday, 20 September 1989

Yesterday made some progress with part five of the new book then psychotherapy again. Subject mother inevitably. Rang her when I got home, for a chat. Afterwards went round the corner to Celia's, drank two or three large glasses of champagne and talked about men. Angus and Cerith's for supper. They are planning a literary party for October. I want to meet HH from the LONDON REVIEW OF BOOKS.

In the post this morning received the LONDON REVIEW OF BOOKS with my Acid House article in it. Rubbing shoulders with Frank Kermode and John Sutherland.

I was so proud of myself. Angus had helped me to edit the article. We sat side by side in the pub with the typescript between us, Angus wielding a red pencil. He was helpful and incisive but decimated me. The process was very humiliating.

Wednesday, 20 September 1989, cont.

Head full of anticipation of this evening, seeing Dexter and ending it. More time on my hands once we have split. I'm looking forward to the clarity I hope will come once I am out of this. Tomorrow tomorrow. And yet I know I will be miserable because he is lovely. Senate House is a good place to mourn, to read, and write notes. And Dexter and I are going to a wedding tomorrow like some awful romantic comedy.

Saturday, 23 September 1989

Have been unable to write anything since Wednesday when Dexter came over as planned and I said what I had to say. He was marvellous about it. We were both very sad. Went to bed together afterwards for the last time. At the wedding everybody kept asking us when we were going to get married. I said NEVER. Took some photographs.

Reading ZUCKERMAN UNBOUND. Good to know I am not the only writer tortured by the fear of doing a dirty on my family. Zuckerman's father on his deathbed calls Zuckerman a bastard then dies.

Bridges on Friday morning talk of loss and mother, the strength of the voice in me that wants to pretend that everything is all right between me and Dexter, everything will be all right between us, just like Mum pretends things are all right when they are all wrong.

After my session I went to Ib's and played with Frances.

Sunday, 24 September 1989

In the morning went swimming, a lovely day, then Dad's at four to clean the studio.

Cleaning the studio made me feel special, downtrodden and loved for all the wrong reasons. The floor was marked with a brush and thinned paint to establish the exact position of any furniture that was in use, the painted hieroglyphics of no particular colour but indelible so that everything could be repositioned and put back between sittings according to which painting he was working on, my eye always caught by the self-conscious way he performed the marks, nothing weak or meaningless, all the functional lines alive and purposeful like his handwriting. The beds, chairs and easels stood on castors that made it possible to drag even the heaviest items across the room without too much difficulty, although I hardly ever moved anything when I was cleaning up, preferring to wash under the bed or the sofa on my hands and knees just in case I did any damage. The floorboards round the easels were scattered with the small pointed pellets of cotton wool he compressed between his fingers and used to remove paint from his canvas when he made a mistake. I stooped to collect the discarded pellets and the scraps and threads of cotton shed from the rags, having decided at the start against using the broom or vacuum cleaner in case I raised dust that might adhere to the surface of a work in progress and ruin it, a catastrophe I intended to avoid at all costs. Also, I hated the noise of the vacuum cleaner, and was glad of an excuse not to take it out of the boiler room.

He relied on me not to interfere with the heaped rags until he had finished with them, not to examine with too much interest the pictures turned with their face to the wall, some of which he might never complete. I was very careful not to poke anything with the stick end of the mop as had happened one time on the shift of an artist friend of mine called Brian who worked for my father for a while. He was mopping between the easels and inadvertently impaled a half-finished portrait from behind his own back with the mop handle. Brian says he was mortified.

My father brought Andrew Parker Bowles into the studio once while I was cleaning it, the brigadier wearing a fawn jersey and tweed jacket and not the regimental uniform in which he is portrayed in the spectacular portrait of him. Dad introduced us then left us alone together almost immediately because he had to make an urgent telephone call. Andrew strolled round the room to see what was happening in the absence of his host, taking in the unfinished paintings on the easels, the mop bucket and the daughter of the great artist on her knees with a wet cloth, and told me that everybody knew I was the boss of my father if anybody wanted anything from him, trying to make me feel important in case I was humiliated by my servitude. He whistled and examined the floorboards I had already washed, the distinctive brown patina they had acquired where they were most used, and advised me that washing the floor was a losing game, there was nothing I could do to make any difference. He thought I was failing to make it sparkle, not understanding I was engaged in something quite different.

Sunday, 24 September 1989

Beautiful painting of Angus finished, a small nude, also Jacob Rothschild portrait.

Dad said he had to do a portrait of me. I grimaced comically and he showed me a tiny canvas, saying encouragingly 'It need only be a little one, like this.'

Went through piles of letters together over the big bin in the boiler room, talking companionably and throwing things away. To amuse me he read out some bits from an old diary of his, just names and appointments – ST BERNARD'S, DAVE 'BOY' GREEN.

Nothing of any significance came to mind about St Bernard's when I read the above so I phoned Susie for help. She talked with fond regard about those big soppy-eyed rescue dogs carrying brandy to stranded travellers in the mountains, neither of us able to come up with anything associated with my father until I gave up and the answer just flew off the end of my fingers. St Bernard's was the name of the hospital on the outskirts of London in which Bella was quarantined when she caught an infectious disease.

It was different with Dave 'Boy' Green. He came back to me effortlessly with a sudden flurry of flailing fists like it was yesterday, the sweet curatorial thrill the first time I tore his picture out of the back of a newspaper, his upper lip pulled down over his mouthguard in the time-honoured way that made him look goofy and punk. As a true fan I refused even to countenance his bathetic nickname, The Fen Tiger, always feeling too much embarrassment on his behalf in the subtly mocking juxtaposition of his pastoral origins in Cambridgeshire with the hungry roar in him of the exotic wild animal, and believed the 'Boy' in his professional name, clearly chosen for him by somebody other than himself, made him sound a bit lightweight, diminished, low-status.

He trained at a gym in Huntington, near his home, and Katie and I went to visit him there when she was still with Dad, staying at a bed and breakfast the night before our appointment because his training session started very early and there were no early trains.

Hank Williams was playing on the car stereo when our minicab arrived in the morning, the driver keeping an eye on us in the rear-view mirror the whole way to the gym like we might do a runner at a crossroads in the middle of nowhere and cheat him out of his fare. The flooded fields on either side of the road were as white as the sky.

I used up a couple of rolls of black and white film, the light from the high windows bouncing off the shiny floor where Dave Green was working out, reflections and shadows creating technical difficulties I had no skills to overcome. His manager just accepted our fandom as Dave's due and didn't judge us on our appearance, our cropped hair and funny clothes, and allowed us to wait in the yard while Dave had a shower and got changed after his training session. We hung around, not sure what we were waiting for, until our hero reappeared, his cheeks flushed from the exertion of his workout, the heat of the shower, and I saw that he was shy in our company, I tried to think what he was thinking. He was wearing a smart tailored jacket, bottle-green velvet he might have chosen because of his name, green maybe his signature colour now he was famous. His manager was easy about his fame, but Dave was not quite sure about it, probably embarrassed by us because we were girls but not like any girls he was used to. He offered us a lift to the station and we were so thrilled, although looking back I suspect he acted in response to a nudge from his manager. I sat in the front of the car because the whole worship thing was my idea, I remember the sight of his thick thighs in his smart nubbled trousers, his battered hands on the wheel. I loved him first, I discovered him, and Katie came along for the ride. She understood my enthusiasm and shared it to some extent, but not completely, her love of Dave 'Boy' Green more of a tribute to me than to him, and maybe a bit of a wind-up for Dad, a side effect that may or may not have been intentional on her part. We attended several of his fights, before she turned against me. Dad came with us once or twice, to York Hall in Bethnal Green and also to the Royal Albert Hall, one of the biggest fights of Dave 'Boy' Green's career. Dad was quite interested in him, but the real focus of his interest was Katie.

Sunday, 24 September 1989, cont.

During the early evening Dad and I had a conversation about my reaction to Susie and Ib both telling me they wanted to write. The conversation made me feel uneasy. Dad thought I was 'loopy' to mind, and I said 'Maybe I am.' He doesn't like it if I show any sign of anything less than total level-headed well-balanced good-natured sanity. I tried to explain, only making things worse.

Then the doorbell rang and it was Jane Willoughby in a denim mini skirt, bringing cold grouse, shortbread and tomatoes from Scotland. I had a tummy ache so I didn't want to eat anything. I went back into the studio and got on with the cleaning. Dad came back in and I had my last word on the subject – 'It's bad enough having so many sisters, let alone if they try and follow in your footsteps.'

Dad's big problem understanding these things stems from his reluctance to feel anything apart from his own power. In the kitchen listening to him and Jane talking about 'The Archduke', some relic of the Austrian monarchy. Once the studio was beautifully clean and smelling of damp wood I went home.

Monday, 25 September 1989

I told Pam about Dexter and she told me she would split up with Steve soon. Felt close, able to talk freely.

Tuesday, 26 September 1989

Celia came over for supper. I made spinach soufle with tomato sauce, mash and grilled bacon, and she brought a bottle of champagne. Talked for several hours. Anxious after she left because somebody kept on ringing the doorbell of the flat across the landing. The dark shape of a man on their welcome mat visible through the wired glass panel of my front door, his finger on the buzzer, his insistence disturbing me.

Wednesday, 27 September 1989

Stomach pain so I stayed in bed. Mum rang me to ask me to go with her to Ratzker's. She wanted me to collect her from Medina Road and drive down to Brick Lane and sort some bales of curtains with her. I said yes then after I put the phone down I remembered that I was ill. I rang back to explain, began to cry, and got some sympathy and understanding from her, felt like the first time in years.

Thursday, 28 September 1989

This morning received contracts from Deborah Rogers for an American deal for SEXUAL INTERCOURSE while reading ZUCKERMAN UNBOUND again, a book about being a successful writer in America.

Friday, 29 September 1989

Frances's birthday. Drove Ib to the toyshop, Inverness Street Market then Sainsbury's, and helped her get everything ready for the party. Marathon sausage roll and sandwich construction. Pat had to go to hospital for tests. Dad ate an ice-cream cornet and two of those jellies with segments of mandarin orange set in frilly waxed paper dishes. Frances a violent bully but also gorgeous. I love her so much. I gave her a Lullaby Light Show that plays Brahms' 'Lullaby' and shines the moon and stars onto the ceiling as it turns round.

I was strangely unconcerned about Pat, and can't remember exactly what was wrong with him, I think some lesions in his gut, the repercussions of a motorbike accident in which he was severely injured a few years before Frances was born. I am perturbed by my assessment of Frances's behaviour, and worry that she will be upset should she read this. She was not a violent bully, but I was unable to recognize the ordinary rough play of a two-year-old, perhaps because I did not have the confidence as a small child to express my feelings, aware from the start that my mother had too much on her shoulders. Mum used to boast smilingly how Ali and I were such wonderful good little children, at least until we were teenagers, no tantrums or fighting or fuss.

It makes me happy to think that Dad almost always showed up to celebrate the birthdays of his grandchildren, enjoying the party food and the chaos, sometimes arriving with gifts and bringing Pluto, his whippet, who was playful and always gentle with everybody. On the telephone to my children and their cousins when they were little he used to pretend to be Pluto, barking into the receiver to make them laugh, which confused them and conflated him in their imagination with the dog, as if they were one and the same person, until they began to call him Grandog and the name stuck. He signed himself Grandog in his communications with them, changing the spelling as it suited him, writing to my daughter Stella on her thirteenth birthday and ending the letter 'love from Grrr.dog', an affectionate growl.

Sunday, 1 October 1989

Dexter and Maya for lunch. Roast chicken. Gave Maya a pink Sindy bath with gold taps. She was very pleased. She asked me, 'Do you still love Daddy?'

We have split up but she can't understand because we are still eating Sunday lunch all together as if nothing has happened. I explained the two kinds of love. Maya said she knew we still loved each other in the other way.

I think there is an element of pleasure for her in the split as well as disbelief and sadness. Her wildest dreams have come true. Also loss, confusion, anger, the same as me.

Tuesday, 3 October 1989

Profuse weeping at Bridges. I am very sad. Afterwards Dexter came over briefly to collect a jersey. Cried some more. Then I remembered the idea I had in the night for a short story or novel, the fear of my father's death the source of my grief.

A man with quite a few children makes one of his daughters the sole heir and executor of his estate. How this effects their relationship. He is compelled to examine her behaviour towards others, using an informal network of gossips (friends and relations) to keep him supplied with evidence. Every now and then he hears about something unbalanced or peculiar she has said or done then rings her to question her about her motives. His own behaviour is extreme and irrational if examined in the same way but this is why he has made his daughter his sole heir. She becomes his conscience. I might have to wait until Dad is dead.

I thought I might have to wait because my idea was based on the truth of my own experience, although I went ahead anyway, which I shouldn't have done; the book took me almost five years and turned out to be the most tortuous and unsatisfactory thing I ever wrote. In real life my father had begun to lose interest in gambling by the time I was thirty, and consequently was accumulating more cash than he could easily divest himself of, the huge surplus making him think of the future, the future of his children, a whole new and surprising aspect of his personality. He had taken advice and as a result he asked me if I would assume the position of sole heir and executor of his estate. Until he mentioned his estate I had not thought that any of us would inherit anything. His embrace of a more conventional model of fatherhood must have been encouraged by his love of his children and perhaps by his legal advisors, on whom he may have wanted to make a good impression. He said it might be a bore for me, the work complicated and onerous, as if I might turn him down, but there was no chance of that.

I was not the oldest of his children but old enough to understand what I was letting myself in for. He told me he was relying on me to be fair, fairness a concept he explained was not at all the same as equality, unconcerned as he was with equality both intellectually and instinctively, but there was nothing in the will about fairness. I read through the document and was careful to point out, in case he had not taken on board the full implication of what he had written, that if I saw fit I could allocate everything to myself, say I wanted to laugh all the way to the bank and leave my siblings out of the calculations. He said he knew I wouldn't do that, and he was right, I felt way too responsible. I remember he referred to his potential beneficiaries as 'the children' when the two of us put our heads together to discuss what might happen when I was in charge, a way of talking to me about his offspring that made me feel I was no longer quite one of them.

SIX

Wednesday, 4 October 1989

Drago, a Yugoslavian poet I met through Angus, rang up and gave me a lecture on my book, then invited me over to dinner. To get out of it I said I couldn't visit strange men on my own. He thought he had offended me by making an improper suggestion. I said I would come if Angus and Cerith would come. Angus really likes him and wants me to like him. Reading SWEET DESSERTS by Lucy Ellman. Death of the father in the book made me very sad again.

Bridges more or less told me not only would it be all right but a good idea not to phone Drago about the dinner. I felt very relieved. I love it when he tells me what to do. He was very reassuring, and I felt free.

Celia came over in the evening bringing wine and a couple of mozzarella and tomato salads in plastic containers from Pizza Express.

Thursday, 5 October 1989

Phoned Paul McAdam.

I met Paul when I was part of a small team running a warehouse party in a disused railwayman's chapel in an abandoned Victorian building at the far end of Battlebridge Road in Kings Cross, overlooking the canal and railway tracks, the whole block occupied by friendly squatters who allowed us to take over the chapel every Saturday night for an agreed sum. This was 1984–5, one of the first warehouse parties. There were no pews, and the chapel held 400 or 500 people. We charged a couple of quid on the door and fifty pence or a pound for a tin of cold lager from the bar, an old bathtub full of ice behind which I stood with the strap of an Adidas bag wound round my ankle for safe keeping as it filled up with cash. By popular demand the bar also stocked brandy, the drink of choice of the local sex workers who discovered we were open until six or seven in the morning, always welcoming, cheap, and right on their doorstep. Over the course of the night up to 800 people came through and almost everybody bought drinks. My dearly beloved friend Sean Oliver played the music with drummer Bruce Smith and DJ brothers Morris and Noel Watson, amongst others.

For about three months everything ran smoothly, Sean and I taking home a couple of hundred pounds each at the end of the night, the Adidas bag full of loose change we could dip into during the week if needs be. Then one Saturday, not long before midnight, some heavies turned up and tried to extort money from us. They said they were Millwall F-Troop, and looked very menacing. I slapped one of them because he was threatening violence and I was worried about Sean, who suffered from sickle-cell anaemia – ever since we first met I had felt very protective towards him. I was surprised at myself for lashing out but not as surprised as the Millwall supporter, who had not been expecting to be assaulted and just stared at me, weighing up whether or not to hit me back. Lucky for me he decided not to retaliate, but that was not the end of it. He told us that he and his mates were taxing us 10 per cent of the door and bar and would be back next week and every week after that to collect what we owed them. I was scared and thought we should shut down – we were out of our depth – but the others were not so easily put off and found some people from South London to protect us.

When the Millwall F-Troop returned the following week, the boys from South London tumbled out of the back of a van and fought them off, and from then on we had to keep our crew on the payroll in case the Millwall F-Troop came back again. A few weeks after the skirmish I seemed to have acquired my own bodyguard, some bloke from Bermondsey who had appointed himself to stand by me all night, arms folded over his chest and his jaw set, perhaps hoping something might kick off again so he could make himself useful. We talked sometimes in the small hours if there was a lull between customers, shouting over the music. One night he said, 'I am your brother.' His manner was intense. I thought he was expressing his loyalty to me in a metaphorical way but when I said I was touched that he felt that way about me, he said 'NO, I AM YOUR BROTHER.' That was Paul McAdam.

Paul hadn't seen Dad since he was a child. I don't know why I phoned him. Kay, his mum, said he was out. I told her I was Lucian's daughter and she began to reminisce. I knew she had four children with Dad, Paul told me Dad was the love of her life, there was nobody else as far as she was concerned, so I imagined she must still have very strong feelings about him, but she spoke with a hazy smile in her voice, no trace of anger or outrage as she looked back. She told me that after the war men were scarce and could do whatever they liked, and that women let them, to make up the numbers, because so many had died. I was so struck by that sentence I wrote it down at once in case I forgot what she said. I understood she was trying to justify her unconventional behaviour – she was an unmarried mother like my own mum, her children born in the late fifties and through the sixties like us. She said she remembered Lucian, their affair was casual, he used to visit now and then on a friendly basis. It was just she kept on getting pregnant. She said she had to stop seeing him otherwise she would have ended up with ten kids. Four was enough. So they lost contact.

I found a few letters from Kay to my father after his death, one from the hospital in which she had just given birth to Jane, her first child. She asked Dad to tell the nurses he was her cousin if he wanted to come and see his daughter, and expressed her delight with the new baby, whom she loved beyond anything. I posted the letter to Jane when she was dying, and took the opportunity to apologize before it was too late for the hostility I had shown towards her in my grief after my father's death. She forgave me and said that things had been very complicated for all of us, and I much appreciated and admired her lack of resentment. We were both able to acknowledge without saying anything too emphatic that Dad had not made things easy for those he had chosen to keep close, let alone for those from whom he had distanced himself. The loneliness I assumed she must have suffered was not evident at her funeral, Golders Green Crematorium crowded with family and friends who had gathered with love to pay tribute to the life she had made for herself, the Freud Museum welcoming all of us afterwards in a significant embrace.

After my phone call with Kay I remember Mum came over to have tea before she set off for Galway to see Uncle Ron, hoping to resolve something between us before she boarded the ferry. I was beyond tact when it came to the mothers of Dad's other children and the children themselves, expecting Mum to welcome everybody as if we were one big happy family, an expectation she met handsomely, but when I told her I had spoken to Kay she wasn't very interested. It did not cross my mind that she might have seen Kay as a rival for my father's affections. I was angry and sad she was so depressed, and frightened of her hostility towards me, the fear so debilitating on occasion I would invite Debbie or one of my other friends to come round to protect me from my anxiety if Mum was on her way over.

Susie dropped in to say goodbye and I offered her some soup in an attempt to alleviate the grief we were left with once Mum had set off on her travels, a potage bonne femme I had made earlier for any such eventualities. Mum used to say she might go to Galway and never come back, a mild threat that buzzed in my ears with the same hum I used to hear when she talked about killing herself.

Susie went home with some extra soup in a covered dish, and I went round to Pam's. Her children were naked, Steve playing the jolly daddy, but Pam wasn't in. What you don't know is that I went out with Steve before Pam, and begged her not to marry him. We were making flower garlands for the bridesmaids the night before her wedding, I was overcome by fear of what Steve might do to her once they were married and told her it was not too late to back out. One of my cousins on my mum's side, booked to do the catering, backed out at the last minute. I felt very sad in the church, hoping Steve might have changed, but put a good face on my grief for Pam's sake and my own, not to show myself up or ruin her big day. Pam was wearing a dress designed and made by Clare Thom, a good friend of mine, and my aunt Bulie turned up at the reception from the West Country with buckets of coronation chicken and platters of poached salmon in the back of her Land Rover. Pam did look happy in spite of my warning; she didn't know Steve like I knew him. Then years after the divorce I asked Pam how she felt when I begged her not to marry him, if she thought I was jealous, and she said no, she knew I was right about Steve, but went ahead anyway.

Friday, 6 October 1989

Today wrote another five pages. Told Bridges I feel lonely. Without explanation he has moved six of my sessions (mid/end October) from my usual times to seven o'clock in the morning. Could be confusing, I have to be careful. Dexter is working at Pam's, redecorating the hall. I knew I would bump into him on my way home and I bumped into him. I really wanted to invite him in for comfort/sex but knew I had to resist. It's funny he's just round the corner. Trevor Laird phoned me. I suggested a drink next week. He said he would phone again.

Saturday, 7 October 1989

Looked after Frances all day. Went to Coram's Fields, looked at the ducks, rabbits, geese, chickens and the goat. Frances played on the swings. Several single dads with their children, very light rain.

Had a drink at Freds with Pam, Angus and Cerith. Angus trying to persuade me to publish this diary, not one of his best ideas.

Monday, 9 October 1989

Appointment with the clinical psychologist. I was in the room with him for nearly two hours. Very confusing. He was hostile towards psychotherapists and Freud and not even sure about the existence of the unconscious mind. He suggested I look through the self-help books at Dillons, buy a relaxation tape and make a diary of all my bad thoughts. While I was in the waiting room I felt very upset, institutionalized, like I felt at the Hackney Hospital when I came back from Italy. Made me half an hour late for Bridges. Was I glad to see him when I finally got there! Made me realize how good and trustworthy he is, how full of respect and gratitude I am.

Wednesday, 11 October 1989

Wrote the last word of the new book today. Working on it will feel very safe now. Looking forward to the sheer pleasure of editing. Although as I was writing the last sentence I began to fret about an idea for the next one.

Bridges, felt he was getting at me. I was very upset even before the session began. Couldn't really understand anything or take anything in. Miserable. Spent the evening at Pam's, talking about domestic violence. I want to do something to help her but I don't know what I can do.

Thursday, 12 October 1989

Drinks with Louise Chunn of the GUARDIAN in view of writing something for them. Home, bath. Drink at Freds with Trevor. He did phone.

Saturday, 14 October 1989

Received a letter from Barclays Bank demanding I pay back the Colville Rose guarantee money of fifty thousand pounds with interest accruing from Friday at 4% above base rate of 11%. Helpless feeling until Monday when I can speak to lawyers. Anxiety.

Sunday, 15 October 1989

Lucy came over in the evening, it was very good to see her. She brought me a bag of wonderful dried porcini from Italy, a perfect companion to the huge box of saffron she brought back from Barcelona a fortnight ago.

Monday, 16 October 1989

Woken by the postman. I was dreaming about making a film, a man hurtling towards me, I thought I was going to fall in love. And him with me. But he had more important things to attend to.

Worried my new book is too abrupt, too fragmented,

too embarrassing – all things I admire in the books of others.

Bridges after work. He interpreted my film dream as me wishing to direct everything, to be in control, the centre of everything – a desire unfulfilled in real life, particularly as he has changed six of my session times. He said this explains my anxiety over the weekend, something I put down to the responsibility of Maya, waiting for her anger to emerge, and the letter from Barclays Bank.

Tuesday, 17 October 1989

Maya's birthday. Spent yesterday evening making a cake for her, and finished it off today – it took me most of the morning to assemble and decorate it.

Call from TATLER offering me a job as guest restaurant critic. I accepted.

Bridges, then called in at Celia's. Angus was there too. I told Celia about my idea to write something about painters and family life. She was prepared to be interviewed and suggested I find Paula Rego and talk to her too. The idea is beginning to grow into something bigger than the original plan for a GUARDIAN article. I could include photos by me, some autobiographical material (the artist's daughter) and some quotes from Dad if he will cooperate – he might. Exciting idea. I am leaving the first draft of my book for a few days or even a fortnight to get some distance. Dexter came over in the afternoon to collect the cake.

Wednesday, 18 October 1989

Bridges at seven so I had to get up at half past five in the morning. It was dark and I felt very lonely. Very upsetting session about my jealousy and difficulties with other people's relationships. Managed to distort what he was saying almost out of the realms of possibility. Felt shattered by what I imagined he said. Have to wait until Friday to sort it out. Home by twenty past eight, very unsettled.

I need some new clothes because everything in my cupboard is falling to pieces. I spend too much time every week mending holes and darning. Although I have several elaborate evening outfits left over from the Café de Paris, all of which are way too fancy for a few drinks at Freds or whatever.

After the Hot Sty shut I DJ'ed with Neneh Cherry at the Wag on Tuesday nights, put on gigs for my friends' bands, worked at Battlebridge Road amongst other places, was membership secretary and music consultant at Freds for a couple of years and for eighteen months of 1987–8 worked Wednesday nights on the door of the Café de Paris, my responsibility to dispense the free tickets, not a very difficult job, and one that made me very popular and very unpopular. I had a crush on Jack, one of the other door staff, who was from Marseilles, lived in Paris and flew over once a week with Albert, a French DJ who took turns with Fat Tony on the decks, Albert's favourite tune of all time the Grace Jones version of 'La Vie En Rose', a record he played every week and that summed up the atmosphere of the club.

The door staff were divided into two categories, the bouncers and the others, meaning me, Jack and Barry. While I was dealing with the guest list (letting all my friends in for nothing and trying to recognize famous people without my glasses on) it was up to Jack and Barry to choose who was allowed to buy a ticket and the job of the bouncers to deal with the disappointed punters if they became enraged not to be let in. Jack used to get in trouble because he was not able to differentiate between a party of sex workers in shiny black vinyl and a girls' night out for supermodels, or didn't care either way, a cool attitude to the selection process, but Barry took the whole thing completely seriously, like St Peter at the pearly gates, confident in his ability to distinguish between those who were worthy and those who were not, believing that there was a fundamental distinction between the two groups and that he was in a position to adjudicate.

Brian was the head bouncer. He worked all night, took all the drugs we were palmed on the door to keep us sweet, drank steadily, got into his car after we shut and drove straight to the Tube depot to report for work – he was a train driver. Alongside him stood Francis, who was shot and killed one night when he was working in South London, and Peter Doig, who never even mentioned he was a painter.

People queued round the block to get in, and Brian had some kind of racket going, which was very lucrative. I didn't want any part in it – I was paid fifty pounds a night, double my rent for a few hours work, plus tips, which seemed like enough money for anybody – but Brian explained to me that as long as I refused to take anything extra from him I would be the weak link in the chain, the only one not involved if anything blew up in his face, and therefore not to be trusted. I tried to hold out but he cajoled me with affection and low-level menace until I capitulated.

Wednesday, 18 October 1989, cont.

Dexter came over after work to collect some dress fabric to take to Clare Thom's for me – he is still working at Pam's and Clare lives near him. I chucked the bag out of the window when he rang the doorbell because I have been seeing too much of him. Five hours on Sunday when he came to collect Maya, an hour or so on Monday when he came to drop off the cake ingredients, likewise on Tuesday to collect the cake. ENOUGH.

Went to bed very early. Debbie rang late and I had a long talk with her about her difficulties and unhappiness. I asked her if she wanted to come round to supper on Friday and she began the usual non-committal thing she does, not saying yes or no, expressing too much reluctance, unable to make up her mind. I got irritated and told her I was upset enough already after my break-up with Dexter and did not want to be messed about on top of everything.

Thursday, 19 October 1989

Bought some black silk for the petticoat to wear under the dress that Clare is making for me. I hope it will be ready in time for the LRB party. Bought TATLER to see what it is like and had a cup of tea at Patisserie Valerie. Bumped into Dexter on the way home and asked him to take the silk to Clare's. I knew I was hurting him.

Met Pam at Freds for a drink then went to see Michael Clark. Leigh was brilliant as the banana on the cover of the Velvet Underground record. Gorgeous sequinned costumes and bare-breasted women with shaved heads under the syrupy lights. Michael and his boyfriend executed a naked duet centre stage on a double bed, licking and sucking, anus and penis, for at least twenty minutes, then Michael performed in a drug-addict costume spiked with syringes to the head, groin, legs, arms and back, a terrible jerky addict dance. Honesty and exposure. I had a panic attack and nearly passed out. Too sad for Michael. Was taken to see Nureyev at Sadler's Wells when I was a teenager and fell asleep.

Friday, 20 October 1989

Bridges at the crack of dawn again. Not as unsettling as last time. Negative capability required to get through all this uncertainty about everything. Wrote to Paula Rego, shampooed the worst parts of the hall and sitting-room carpet. A storm woke me at four in the morning, wind banging on the door of the fire escape. I thought the noise was bombs going off but I turned on the radio and was reassured when I heard about the storm on the news. Nothing like as strong as the storm last October when I was still at Portobello Road.

Saturday, 21 October 1989

Met Lucy at Maison Bertaux. We talked in detail about her meeting with BN, a man so elusive he shares the same quality of unreality as HH. Both of us lost our appetite in the excitement of contemplating the forthcoming LRB party, an event at which both these fantasy figures will be walking around like ordinary mortals. The consequence of finishing the first draft of my new book seems to be the awakening in me of an insatiable desire for items of kitchen equipment. I bought myself a mandoline or universal slicer from Ferrari's and a lovely brown lidded terrine for Angus because it is his birthday tomorrow. I spent the afternoon daydreaming. It was peaceful.

I didn't connect my insatiable desire for kitchen equipment with my feelings for HH, whom I had not even met but after a couple of work calls was already thinking of with intense interest and hope for my future. I really thought it might have worked out between us, we could have fallen for each other, you never know how that sort of thing is going to turn out. At least I was aware of the absurdity of my longing, which may have meant I was in with a chance.

Sunday, 22 October 1989

Dinner with Angus and Cerith. Dad was the only other guest. His Rolls-Royce was parked outside, a surprise to see it in my street. Delicious soup with baby vegetables, steak and oyster pie with mash, steamed baby lettuce and parsnips, followed by mango with cream and Greek yogurt. Lovely food. Dad quite relaxed, talking freely. Short happy sleep.

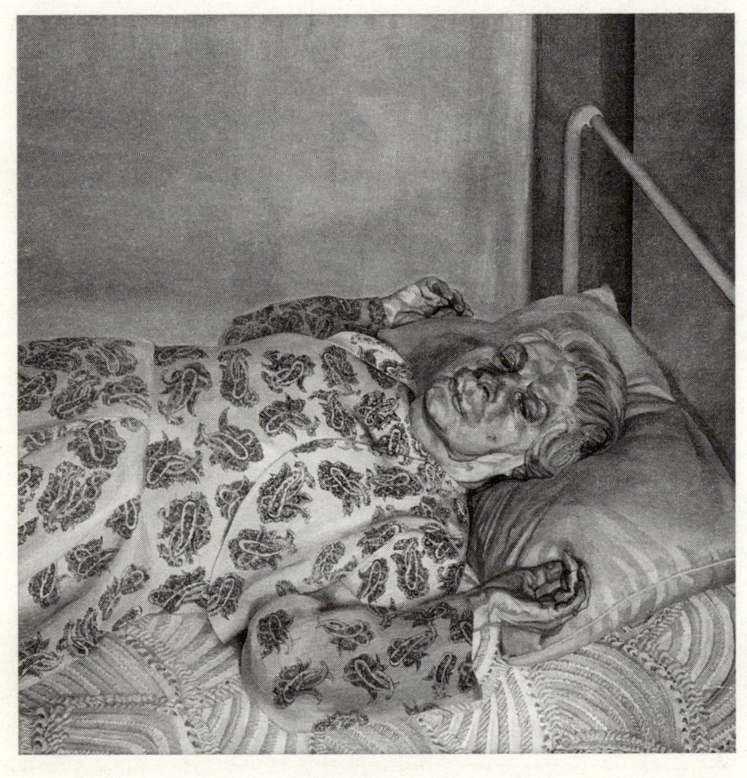

The Painter's Mother Resting I (1975–6)

LUCIAN FREUD

SEVEN

Monday, 23 October 1989

Up at a quarter to six to see Bridges.

Long telephone conversations with Paul McAdam and his brother David McAdam, who have fallen out with each other. Then making arrangements on the phone with my uncle Stephen's wife Ann to invite the McAdam family to the funeral.

Dad's mother died. I asked him if he was sad, and he said no, not really. His response made me feel sad on his behalf, also relieved he was not devastated. I was used to him working seven days a week whatever happened, and it occurs to me now, looking back, that his total commitment to work, even if it made him unavailable much of the time, was reassuring in its consistency.

I am also struck by the level of my involvement with the McAdams and my assumption of responsibility for their inclusion in the arrangements for the funeral. My negotiations on their behalf with Stephen's wife was an example of the good organizational skills for which I was known and shows some type of kindness on my part towards them. I was kind, but that was not my only motivation. Those phone conversations with Ann made me feel central to events, a way to play down or erase my own sense of unbelonging. Not that it was as simple as all that, because I found out from the McAdams that they actually knew Dad's parents and used to see them when they were little, Kay having made contact with them against my father's wishes and behind his back, not something my mum would have contemplated.

Tuesday, 24 October 1989

Fell asleep while reading and woke up two or three minutes before the doorbell rang – Mum coming to tea, and I had completely forgotten. Ran to the shops to buy milk, bread and biscuits.

Wednesday, 25 October 1989

With Lucy to highly anticipated LRB party, wearing my new Clare dress. Drank several glasses of white wine and spent most of the evening talking to HH, who agreed to read my new book. A comedy of expectations and wishful thinking. He was clever, serious, funny, understanding as I thought he would be. Home drunk about ten, ate salad, rang Lucy to discuss the evening.

Thursday, 26 October 1989

Met Pam for a drink at the Plough. Paul McAdam and Jane arrived later as arranged. Jane kept on touching my sleeve lightly to imply goodwill, intimacy. Felt tired, heard some more of Paul's side of the argument between him and David. Heard all about David's side on Monday. Jane making sensible comments in arbitration. A drunk tramp came over to our table and began to pester us. I told him to go away, I said we were having a family conference because our grandmother had just died. That got rid of him. Afterwards, once the McAdams had gone, I said to Pam 'If Jane is my half-sister then I'm a turnip,' although later on I realized I shouldn't have said that, I knew I was wrong.

Friday, 27 October 1989

Dawn raid on Bridges again, for the last time. We talked about the Colville case, HH, me having delusions about being special, about being knocked off my perch, and how I am in danger of getting back on it again on Monday when I resume my normal session times. Shaken and weak on leaving, Bridges newly confrontational, using the words MAD and DELUSIONAL to describe my thought processes. I suppose he knows what he is doing, although I begin to be affected by doubt, a feature of my therapy that I assume is all part of the problem I have therapy to try and sort out in the first place. I am looking forward to telling him how I feel on Monday. I feel he is angry. I know he will deny it and tell me that I am the angry one.

Spoke to the solicitor at Goodman Derrick about the Colville Rose and was reassured by her firm plan of action.

Met Lucy for tea in Piccadilly, ran up and down Berwick Street to get some shopping as the stalls were shutting up for the day. Missed the fishmongers so went to Chinatown and bought a grey mullet. When I got home I looked for a grey mullet recipe. Elizabeth David very derogatory about it.

I cooked and ate the fish in spite of her scorn, the flesh not as muddy as she said it would be. My adherence to the tenets of Elizabeth David was not only about the taste of the food, the preparation and combinations of ingredients, but also about taste as in good taste, the authoritative tone of her prose and snob insider knowledge, her way always the right way – the bronzed chicken on a white oval dish with a sprig of watercress, the summer pudding made only of red currants and raspberries if one were unable to obtain mulberries – no strawberries or other faux pas – and the important vegetables prepared with a view not only to the clarity of their flavour but to their appearance on the table, everything laid out like a still life in my mind's eye, the quintessence of beauty and simplicity. I had read all her books from cover to cover as if they were novels and never questioned the appealing strictures of the domestic arrangements as she described them in her enthralling prose, the wilder Mediterranean aspects of her knowledge tempered by her judgemental English sensibility, every paragraph a lesson in desirable womanhood. Her certainty about everything – even when she was wrong – and her assumption that her reader must share her unerring discernment and high level of basic skills soothed me and allowed me to feel I too could become confident and lovable like her.

Sunday, 29 October 1989

Getting ready to go to the wake for Dad's mum. I was anxious about it, tried to ring Annie and Bella, but neither of them were in. Felt I needed to tell Annie that the McAdams were coming, and to make sure that Bella had been invited.

To St John's Wood Terrace, the house where Dad's parents lived and his mother had lived on after his father's death. The house was shabby, dark brown wood and worn furniture, German books and foreign people.

It was not the first time I had been to the house. I used to visit sometimes, to read to my grandmother, but she was so detached I was not sure she understood or remembered we were related. I read Goethe in translation, *The Sorrows of Young Werther*, and have no recollection of the story, although I can still feel the mournful substance of it, my grandmother's head bowed and her hands folded in her lap in complete stillness; Goethe was her favourite writer. I wanted to get to know her but it was too late, I was too nervous to get anywhere near, not confident I was welcome in her home, the shield of her silence keeping me back with all my hopes and regrets. Dad always said she should have been allowed to die when she tried to kill herself after Ernst's death, he was angry one of her carers called an ambulance, angry she had been saved from herself, although he began to paint her round about then, over and over again, every portrait illuminated by intense loving kindness, his love for her drawn out by the quiet distance of her resignation, the distant heart of her extreme grief.

Sunday, 29 October 1989, cont.

We watched a home movie of the family at Walberswick, Ernst fishing, Annie as a child looking beautiful in a kilt. The room was blacked out with thin hangings over the windows, and was full of people, old women and children mostly, none of whom I had seen before except Annie. I sat next to her. A cousin of Dad's called Walter was the projectionist, making a commentary in heavily accented English. Restless children moaning, 'I want to go home.'

The whole McAdam family turned up with Kay, a little woman with grey hair. Then Bella and Esther. We were all given labels, our names in capital letters on rectangles of sticky white paper embellished with gold stars like those given for good work at primary school, the stars awarded on this occasion to identify us as Lucian's children. There were not enough to go round. Later on, when I told Dad about the stars, he said that they sounded like something out of the camps.

I met Ann who had lived upstairs from my grandmother, a very nice and very sad woman, who had suffered a loss similar to Susie's, the death of a fiancé, at about the same time. I was introduced to Walter, thick hair standing up 'en brosse' as Dad had once described it to me, pronouncing the French words self-consciously as if he was not sure he could get away with it. Dad said Walter was some kind of war hero.

Walter: 'You are not the one who wrote that book are you, um um SEXUAL INTERCOURSE?'

Me: 'I am.'

W: 'Oh my God, how could you have done such a thing? My friends were telephoning me to ask me if I were related to you and I had to admit it. I was blushing down the telephone.'

'I'm sorry to have caused you embarrassment. Did you read it?'

'No, too strong meat for me. Did your father approve of it?'

'Yes.'

'And your mother? Didn't you offend your mother?'

'She read it and enjoyed it.'

'Why did you have to use such a crude title?'

'I can think of cruder ways of putting it.'

'Why so crude?'

'It's best to call a spade a spade.'

'But no need to call it a shovel!'

After my conversation with Walter I met a horrible man called Dr Phillips, a famous gynaecologist, who asked me nosy questions about Dad, was obsessed with family trees and being a Freud, and mentioned twice that he was related to the Rothschilds. I fielded his questions as best I could. Walter's wife was nice, Annette, and she too asked questions. I was in the hall pointing out my siblings to her. Dad's brother Stephen did a double take and peered round every time in amazement – must have been the first he had heard of us. Annette asked me how many of us there were and I was unable to help her. I ate some cake, dark chocolate, my grandmother's favourite.

I felt close to Annie after the bad time last time. That was pleasing. Stephen's teeth like Ken Dodd, and he was wearing a purple and orange tie. After a conversation with a woman from the Freud Museum I walked round the block with Annie to get some fresh air. She talked about her neediness, Paul's neediness (today was the first time she had met him) and her non-relationship with Dad since they had fallen out, the pain of all that.

She also told me that earlier on in the evening Stephen had expounded his preposterous theory of Dad's illegitimacy. Stephen claims to believe that Dad must be illegitimate because he is thin, with hair, while Stephen and Clement are both fat and bald. Dad has told me this story before, adding his question to Stephen about infidelity – 'Can you imagine my mother, who is also your mother, doing such a thing?' Dad is utterly convinced his mother could never have had an affair – totally unthinkable. I had the same feeling about her, and anyway, Dad looks more like Sigmund than Clement or Stephen. I asked Annie more or less exactly the same question Dad had asked Stephen. 'Can you imagine her having an affair?'

'Yes,' said Annie. 'She really used to confuse me when I was young with her talk of sex and contraception.'

I don't know when exactly but quite late in the day Dad mentioned in passing he had always been his mother's favourite, news to me but no revelation as far as he was concerned, he was just stating the obvious, Clement and Stephen both duds in his opinion and his mother responding with inevitable helplessness to the incontrovertibly superior intelligence, force of personality and sheer physical allure of her middle child. He was precocious as a young boy, his early talent revealed in a sheaf of childhood drawings left behind when he died, each sheet dated and named on the back by his mother to identify the artist, a few by Clement and Stephen but the majority by my father, his pictures so much more affecting in every way that even without the names it would not have been difficult to work out which ones were his, not that a mother must love a son more than his brothers because he can draw with more vivacity and loveliness.

He told me that her favouritism had been stifling, acutely uncomfortable for him, not a source of joy or pride – I think he felt implicated by association in the shame of her intemperate feelings, although I am not sure he would have preferred to be shunted aside in favour of one of his brothers. He was sandwiched between Clement and Stephen, both of whom loathed him in boyhood, mainly but not entirely I suspect as a consequence of her adoration. He said he felt got at from all sides.

Sunday, 29 October 1989, cont.

I got into my car and drove home from St John's Wood Terrace. The phone was ringing as I put my key in the door. It was Dad, wanting a full account of the wake. I obliged, then spoke to Lucy for ages. Felt a little disorientated – the clocks have gone back.

It doesn't seem to have crossed my mind at any point that Dad might have wanted to attend the memorial gathering, I just took it for granted that was never going to happen. He was eager to hear my anecdotes about his relatives as long as he didn't have to spend any time with them, unwilling as I see it to contaminate himself by proximity to all their emotions and memories, the claustrophobia of everything they had suffered just to survive, much of the family wiped out by the Nazis. He always swerved funerals, even those of his close friends.

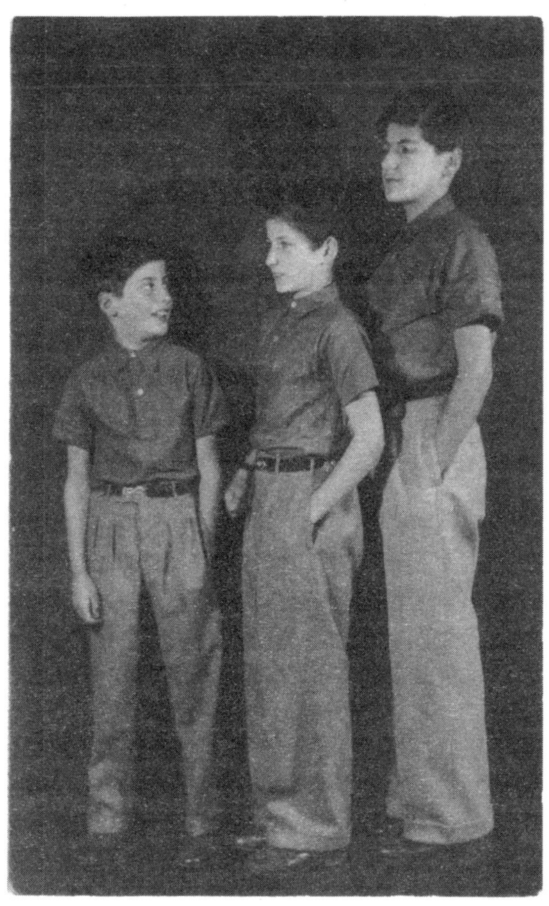

Clement, Lucian and Stephen Freud
Photographer Unknown

Monday, 30 October 1989

HH phoned and we have agreed to meet on Wednesday lunchtime, although exactly where is as yet undecided. He is going to ring again. Not sleeping at all well. Relieved to see Bridges and discuss with him how bad I felt after the session last Friday.

Tuesday, 31 October 1989

Spent the day reading my new book in view of giving it to HH on Wednesday. I might call it WOMANCHILD. Was unable to tell whether it works or not, or even what it is about. I am hoping HH will be able to tell me. Seeing him tomorrow and am getting myself worked up into a state. Also seeing Dan Jacobson about my UCL reading next week.

Supper with Lucy at Alastair Little's basement, conducting research for my TATLER article. Very good food. Alastair came out of the kitchen and talked to me about rocket and lambs' lettuce. I was enjoying myself so much, drinking wine and talking with Lucy about everything, when Sean, Hussein, Tim Burke and Chris Burkham came into the bar and disrupted my evening. Sean pressed up against me on the bench seat and we had an awkward monosyllabic conversation.

Hussein was Sean's manager and good friend. Sean was wearing a white shirt and some old suit jacket that looked unaccountably glamorous on him, his clothes borrowed and thrown together wherever he found himself when he woke up, everything effortless but with unerring intent, some shoestring fashion god or goddess always smiling on him when he was getting ready to go out. I felt moved, proud and uncomfortable in his presence as he squeezed in beside me, the physical warmth and slight softness of his bulk almost the same but something had changed. He was very close but uneasy with me, and I remembered suddenly how much I missed him. We were not estranged in the least but no longer together every day one way or another, no longer neighbours in Notting Hill – he was busy with his music, maybe had some new friends.

How much love I felt for him still. In the beginning he used to ring my doorbell at Northwold Road on the off chance when he was at a loose end, a young kid in a squat on Southgate Road busking to make ends meet, still a bit shy and a long way from home – he was from Bury St Edmunds. We would listen to records on the sofa in the sitting room, him stretched out with his feet in my lap.

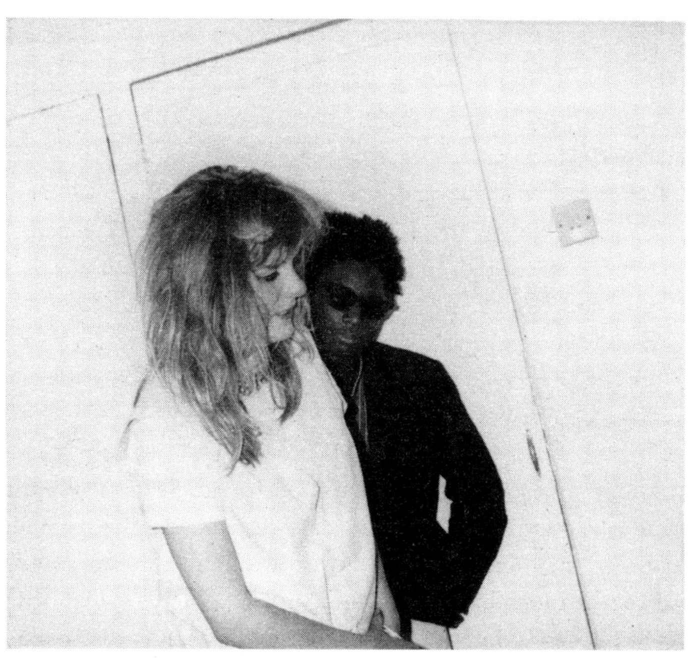

Sophie and Sean at Northwold Road, 1981

ROSE BOYT

We both loved music. He was with two other musicians when we first met, Gareth Sager from The Pop Group and the pianist Mark Springer, and I was with Sophie de Stempel, at some party in Chelsea, a big room with piles of old books and vases of flowers arranged on little end tables. Gareth, Mark and Sean had a car, but nowhere to sleep, and I had spare rooms, but no way to get home. The whole thing was Gareth's idea; he said they would drive me to Clapton if they could all stay the night, an arrangement that suited everybody. I woke up in the morning and could smell coffee and hear voices. Gareth had been to the shops and was making breakfast. We all became very close and looked out for one another from then on, and through Sean I met Andi, his sister, and Neneh, her best friend, two women I still hold with love in my heart, along with Naima, Miquita, Phoebe, Thelonious, Tyson and Mabel, all their wonderful children.

Tuesday, 31 October 1989, cont.

Hussein sat up at the bar on a high stool, insulting Tim Burke, shouting at the waiters, picking up food from the dishes the sous chef was plating up, acting swinish and gross. My mood collapsed completely when the conversation turned to the Colville Rose. The whole restaurant was listening, and Hussein was shaking his head as if to say 'I told you so' even though he didn't warn me. I started to feel very bad so we left, refusing the drinks Hussein offered us as we pulled on our coats. Then to Freds. I don't know why I didn't just go home. Lucy went to the loo and Esther asked me if we could all go to the Wag together. I said I didn't want to go in a gang. She said 'It's not a gang, it's only me and Jane McAdam.'

As soon as Lucy came back from the loo we just left without saying goodbye to anybody. The Wag was packed. Andi looked wonderful in a red and green fun-fur dress and matching coat with gold shiny lining, a big furry leopard-print hat on her head. I stood at the bar with Lucy, unable to enjoy myself, worried I had said the wrong thing to Neneh, her face tense round the mouth. She told me that now she was famous she had to talk to everybody she met whether she liked it or not, a sort of egalitarian gesture in case anybody thought fame had gone to her head. Lucy and I stuck it out until the end, then went home. Some sadness about the past, repetition, emptiness.

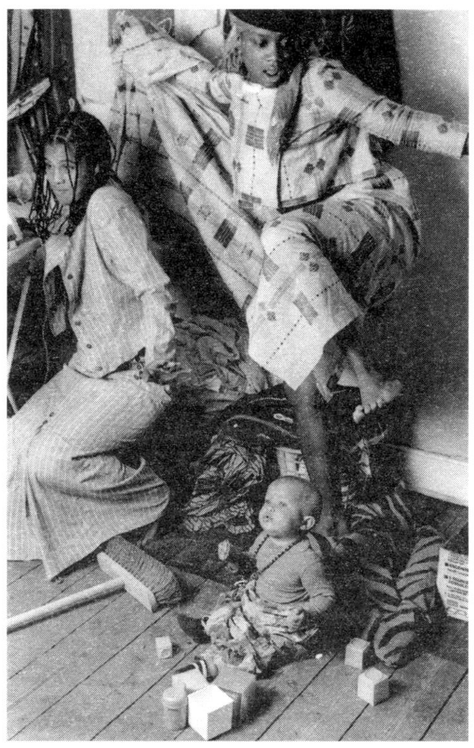

Andi and Neneh at Portobello Road with baby Naima

ROSE BOYT

Wednesday, 1 November 1989

Woke up too early, extremely agitated. Waited for HH to ring and began to give up hope. He rang at ten. Seemed to me like the last minute.

Walking up the steps of Foster Court began to laugh at myself, my self-assurance dropping away. Sat in the English Department common room waiting for Dan Jacobson. A girl came over to talk to me, her legs shaking a little bit; she was the organizer of the reading I am doing next week and was nervous of me. Once I got into Dan Jacobson's office I felt reassured – he was helpful, and said all the right things. He told me to raise my eyes to the audience during the reading, not to be embarrassed by obscenities, to avoid long passages of dialogue, not to adhere too rigidly to the text if anything sounded off, to write bridging passages if necessary, to be entertaining. He told me that Robert Lowell used to stop between lines when he was reading to the public to explain classical references, and that Dickens annotated, added and crossed out whole chunks of his novels to produce good reading texts. So I've got some work to do before next Tuesday.

The gap between noon when I got home and a quarter to one when HH was coming to pick me up seemed interminable. I read to pass the time. Brushed my hair a few hundred times, tried to cover my spots with Hide and Heal but decided they looked better naked and cleaned it off.

The doorbell rang – he was a few minutes late. I ran down the stairs with a disconnected sense of distance from myself. I felt very uncomfortable, but once I was walking and talking with him in the street I began to recover.

We went to a Japanese restaurant in Tottenham Court Road. I had two glasses of beer – that made me feel a bit more relaxed. I talked too much about my family but it was not the end of the world. I asked him if he had seen SEX, LIES, AND VIDEOTAPE and he said he hadn't, maybe we should go together one night, and I said that would be nice. I asked him about Bellow's THE BELLAROSA CONNECTION and he said he didn't think much of it, he said he thought it was about lamenting the loss of Jewishness in America, the sadness of that, a subject he didn't seem to think much of – not how I had read the book at all. I'm going to read it again and see.

After lunch he walked me home and went off carrying the red folder containing about the most revealing thing I could possibly have written, worse almost than if I had given him this diary.

A very dark afternoon, with rain. Esther rang to have a go at me about my horrible behaviour towards her on Tuesday night, when Lucy and I abandoned her to go to the Wag. She unleashed a whole lifetime's worth of anger down the telephone. I was shocked by her fury but managed to apologize.

Friday, 3 November 1989

No news from HH about the book. He has only had it for a couple of days.

Later a bad phone call from Dad. Asked him for the money for the Bridges bill as agreed and he said 'It must have gone up, are you sure that man hasn't got you in his clutches, are you sure you aren't dependant on him or addicted to psychotherapy, the man who runs the Freud copyright is completely bent, I once met an analyst who was a complete crook preying on the weak and needy.' I defended myself and Bridges in the face of this onslaught and just about managed to keep myself in one piece although I had to ring Lucy afterwards and tell her all about it.

I received the first two years of my psychotherapy on the NHS, then after I had used up my quota and managed an open-ended break I asked my father whether he could pay if Bridges would see me privately. Dad replied immediately and said he was happy to help out, no questions, which made me very happy, although the relentlessness of my monthly demand for the payment and my dependence on him was soon to become problematic for both of us, not that I am not eternally grateful for the funds. He paid the bill in cash sometimes, money that felt like a direct message from him to my therapist as I handed over the stuffed envelope, the used notes tainted by my father's hostility and rivalry, also tangible proof of his undeniable generosity towards me.

He referred to my therapist as THE VENAL SADIST and I remember I had to look up the word *venal*, very relieved to discover that it only meant capable of being bought or obtained for money, susceptible to corruption, rather than containing something sexual towards me as I had feared, as far as I knew the word seeming to share the same root as *venereal*. I had added a sexual element to my father's use of the word *venal*, confused perhaps by the uncomfortable three-cornered relationship, and in an equal and opposite misunderstanding had removed the component of sexual excitement from the cruelty implied in his accusation of sadism, leaving behind only the hurt and pain, although the exploits of the Marquis de Sade were not unknown to me. I could see no sex in sadism, my unconscious distortion of the nickname a reaction to the spite of my father's attack.

Sunday, 5 November 1989

Beginning to have the fantasy or dread that HH doesn't like my book or that he is dead.

Monday, 6 November 1989

Swam early then came home and went back to bed as unable to bear the suspense of waiting for the phone to ring. Spent the afternoon re-examining the parts of SEXUAL INTERCOURSE I intend to read on Tuesday. Unable to get on with my TATLER article because the suspense over the book is killing me.

Paula Rego came over at half past six. Promising hour with her – she seemed fairly keen to be part of my book about painting and family. While she was still here HH rang up and said he liked my book, he thought it was 'terrific'. A cause for celebration! To explain why it had taken him 'so long' to ring me he told me that his aunt had just died and he was caught up in a family crisis. It was lovely to talk to him and he seemed to want to talk to me but I had to say 'Paula Rego is here' because it seemed too rude to leave Paula on her own in the kitchen while HH and I had a long chat. He said he would phone back in the morning to arrange meeting up.

Tuesday, 7 November 1989

Still waking horribly early to face the dark dawn on my own. Reading TWO SERIOUS LADIES by Jane Bowles, not a wise book. Finished THE BELLAROSA CONNECTION again. HH was right, it is about Jewishness.

I so wanted HH to be right, I so wanted to believe in him. I can't read Bellow anymore but back then I was still under his influence, not wise to the low status he afforded women in his work because unwittingly I identified with them and failed to question his misogyny. He seduced me with the exuberance of his prose and suspended my ability to think clearly, inducing in me a state of worshipfulness with which I was only too familiar, dazzled as I was by my father's genius in the same way.

Tuesday, 7 November 1989, cont.

HH rang up to say he would come over on Thursday evening. I am looking forward to it with trepidation and excitement.

My reading of SEXUAL INTERCOURSE – some people walked out about two minutes after I began, white and trembling with anger or shock. Most of the students looked embarrassed, a little stunned. Lucy came with me for moral support. That was very good of her. Afterwards went back to my flat and I made a bit of supper and bored Lucy to death about HH. I must try to cut down on talking about him otherwise I'll drive her round the bend.

Wednesday, 8 November 1989

Mum came over and we went shopping to buy some material for her yearly skirt. Found some good fabric in Berwick Street, had lunch at Mildred's, Mum told me she is going to start having psychotherapy. The best news I have heard for a very long time.

Bridges, then went over to Neneh's. Andi and Tessa P, some boys upstairs in the back room making a demo with Cameron, Naima and Miquita watching TV in the bedroom, Neneh feeding baby Tyson in the kitchen, the nanny playing Connect4 with one of the band. I took some photographs. I felt sad when I got home, sad I wasn't married with a baby.

It was Sean's birthday, but we don't seem to be celebrating him. He must have been enjoying himself elsewhere. Tessa Pollitt, bass player of The Slits, is the mother of his daughter Phoebe, Cameron is Neneh's husband, Naima is Neneh's daughter, Miquita Andi's daughter. Phoebe was not Sean's only child – he had another baby a few months after Phoebe was born, with Carole Taylor, another girlfriend of his. They called him Thelonious, after Thelonious Monk, the jazz pianist. I learnt from Sean, not just about music, and came to believe (erroneously) he had something in common with my father, wondering whether through my friendship with him I might begin to understand the point of all the women in my father's life, what they were for.

Thursday, 9 November 1989

Ran down to Oddbins to get a bottle of wine, nearly had a heart attack and had to lie down on the sitting-room floor to calm myself. HH turned up a bit late with a bottle of wine. Had a marvellous evening. He said Sigmund said the two most important things in life are work and love. I was drunk, we ate some salami and cheese and salad, he stayed until twelve then had to go home and write a piece. He said he thought my book was very very good. After he left I felt like I loved him. Went to sleep at one and woke up at four and couldn't get back to sleep.

I am reminded by this description of our meeting that I didn't actually cook anything for him, the supper a casual assembly of good things, everything on the table deceptively effortless; I wanted to feed him but I wasn't prepared to put on my apron and knock him out with one of my signature dishes. I was afraid to reveal too soon my suggestive domestic proficiency and my readiness, in case he was one of those people who scare easily, reluctant to raise the stakes in that intimate way. Also to cook performatively is nerve-wracking and I didn't want to make myself even more tense in the kitchen, my instinctive caution holding me back in my behaviour if not in my hopes and dreams.

I don't mention this in the diary but as well as admiring my book I remember he really liked the wine I had bought, a sparkling red burgundy, chosen because the bottle and label looked substantial, although had I realized it mattered so much I might have been more circumspect in my choice. He inspected the bottle and opened it once he had had a good look, and when he raised his glass to his lips and took a small mouthful he was astonished the wine was so delicious. I was glad he enjoyed the burgundy but was surprised when he asked me how I had discovered it, he wanted me to explain how the whole thing had come about, almost as if he were hoping I might confess that the man in the shop had chosen it for me. I didn't tell him I had taken a chance in the off-licence on the corner, thinking red might go better with the cheese and that bubbles were more festive for a special occasion. I didn't say I felt we were celebrating. I shrugged, puzzled by his interest in the details of my choice, and realized he was inadvertently expressing slight amazement I knew something he didn't know. He was unsettled in himself until I told him the wine was a fluke and that I knew nothing about anything. Just one of those minor incidents when you are getting to know somebody and they inadvertently betray an aspect of themselves in relation to you, something that you might do well to heed when you feel it, important as it is not to try and hold on to hope at the expense of your true feelings.

Friday, 10 November 1989

Bridges told me I was afraid of something deadly in myself, that was what my phobia was about, a fear of the emergence of something terrible in me.

I remember only too vividly my fear that something terrible might emerge, the constant threat of insanity, and how that fear lessened as I made progress in my treatment, my relief that everything inside me was just me and could be accommodated if I learnt to accept myself, not that I am aiming to offer advice to anybody who might suffer in a similar way.

But now I wonder if Bridges took seriously enough the real danger of my childhood journeys, what happened at sea, the devastating impact of that life on my sense of security. I admit I tended to anecdotalize my experience for my own protection until my life sounded like something out of a storybook, and there were elements of joy in what happened – seeing the world was a great privilege – but I was numb to the truth of my mum's marvellous recklessness. I didn't feel the terror myself when I should have been feeling it, when it was happening, mostly shut down to the threat and able to convince myself I was a brave sailor to save myself from the shame of admitting nobody was looking after us properly. My pride occluded my feelings, but Bridges should have been able to open his eyes and my own to what went on, the reality of my experience.

I recently described to my new therapist a night on the ship in a sudden storm when we were trying to enter a harbour. Uwe was swearing and shouting for help but the bosun and mate had resigned at the end of the last trip so there was nobody but us to obey him. Ali took the helm to allow Uwe to tether the boom to the main mast, and Mum and I were on deck in the lashing rain and wild seas, trying to follow orders to the best of our ability, nobody wearing life jackets because we had got out of the habit. The ship bucked and groaned backwards at speed, but we couldn't see anything. A splintering crash at the stern and I was thrown down and doused under a wave, the lifeboat breaking on some invisible buttress or metal hull of a moored vessel.

In the morning we were all very happy only the lifeboat was smashed. I longed for a new mate, a new bosun, any extra adult to make up the deficit and spread the responsibility, but nobody wanted to join us on board, a rejection that I felt reflected badly on all of us and added to my unease. We continued on our journey with scant provisions, the loss of the lifeboat not addressed openly because it would have been impossible for Mum to admit she just accepted the risk for Uwe's sake and kept going. She was determined to stay with him, a feeling I understand but would not call love exactly, not that it is up to me to name the unnameable contents of her heart. His captainship was almost untenable, and Mum was maybe a bit uncomfortable about the facts of our life now, no longer able to pretend it was really quite sensible. I told this story to my therapist because I needed her help to work out that our life on the ship was not just an adventure as I had chosen to convince myself, but was fraught with real danger, from the sea and from Uwe, no cowardice on my part I was so secretly frightened I hardly felt anything. When I think of myself as a child at sea in my bunk I feel trapped still with the enduring fear of attack, no way to escape, a panic of nausea not dissimilar to seasickness, as if I am still back there, and I don't know how I endured it. It was terrifying for me. I still feel so much sorrow for that poor child.

Saturday, 11 November 1989

Made Mum's skirt. Wrote the TATLER article but decided to scrap it. Maya to stay, Laura stayed too. They kept me up most of the night. I didn't have the strength to stand up to them. In the end I let them sleep in my bed with me.

Sunday, 12 November 1989

Lola very naughty, Maya jealous, Dexter very late to collect Maya. I was very cross. Ib's for Mum's birthday. She was very pleased with her present.

Monday, 13 November 1989

For my birthday Lucy bought me a beautiful dark navy pleated skirt with a wide belt, and a man's jersey, the collar piped in green velvet. Perfect clothes for me, the most luxurious clothes I have ever possessed.

This is the outfit I am wearing in the painting.

Monday, 13 November 1989, cont.

Angus and Cerith came over after Bridges to help with preparations for tomorrow.

Tuesday, 14 November 1989

My birthday. Pam dropped in early from the fishmonger's with last-minute shopping, Mum came over to help, Angus and Cerith came over again. Celia turned up with presents and wine. Debbie ironing the tablecloth and hoovering. Went off to Bridges, came back and had a bath, last-minute preparations and then the guests began to arrive.

Francis Wyndham first as always then
Ib and Pat
Bella and Esther
Ali and Mum
Pam and Debbie
Lucy
Tom and Erin
Lulu and Nick
Anne Norman
Susie and Tom Browne
Dad
Clare Thom
Angus and Cerith

Lovely party.

Written by hand on the bottom of the list –

HH rang in the afternoon to say he couldn't come. I was disappointed. Some friends gathering around, some nowhere to be seen.

Friday, 17 November 1989

Bridges, talk of my hurt feelings, how easily I am hurt, and how I hide this from other people, and from myself. According to him the reluctance that comes over me as I sit outside in my car waiting for my appointment is an inversion of my fantasy that he is reluctant to see me. He described two worlds of mine, the paranoid one where nobody cares about anybody, and the world of truth and wisdom I want to be a part of.

When I got home I finished the TATLER piece and Rory Ross sent a bike for it. I now have clear space, nothing hanging over me.

Tuesday, 21 November 1989

Still nothing from HH. I find waiting very hard. He said he would ring at the end of last week. Bridges. Applied for a job at a new restaurant opening round the corner. Interview on Friday. Read AUGIE MARCH, many phone calls, nothing from HH. What is the matter with him?

Two strange dreams about old flames.

Friday, 24 November 1989

Bridges first thing, restaurant job interview cancelled until further notice.

In the afternoon mustered the courage to ring HH.

He did not apologize but asked me if I would like to meet up next Friday after work and I said I would. A bit anxious after the call but relieved – I couldn't wait any longer. He said he had had bronchitis, but was a bit better. I think my anger came out on the phone, I hope not too much, not enough to frighten him off. The anxiety began to wear off after a while but I am looking forward to talking to Bridges about it. Bridges pointed out that some of my anger at not receiving the call at the end of last week as promised was the anger unexpressed years ago when he didn't reply immediately to my letter of application for psychotherapy. Not to mention anger unexpressed long before that.

Bought some wool and a pattern to knit Frances a dress for Christmas. Stayed in and started it.

Saturday, 25 November 1989

Pat brought Frances over and Dexter and Maya came over at four. And Debbie with a child she was looking after. Maya moaning and the woman downstairs rang up twice to complain about the noise of my niece jumping on and off the furniture. I was outraged and said that my niece never jumped on and off the furniture. Debbie said such horrible things about Maya I had to ask her to leave. Once everyone was gone Maya was fine.

Thinking about a father rejected by his child. Like Dad telling me in amazement about seeing Victor Willing and his children outside the building on Shaftesbury Avenue where Katie used to have her studio, his children helping him out of a car with some paintings, Dad telling me he was amazed Victor's children should help him, seeing as he was so horrible.

The Will. Considering the idea I had before about a father leaving everything to his adult child as executor, and the adult child beginning to behave oddly under the pressure of scrutiny – or is it the father behaving oddly?

Ugliness, a man complaining about his ugliness. A woman looking for a man, a husband. Beauty, the surface, about surface, and depth. Keats.

I have always felt confused about the importance of surfaces, what they might reveal, my father's valorization of the appearance of people and objects, not wishing to believe as he believed that looks mattered above everything as I have said, and yet I would fall in love then on the same basis. Discovering beauty and truth conflated so indivisibly in Keats I understood the poet was writing about art in general and form in particular, but feel uneasy now, loving him so much, that he might have shared with my father the belief that to be lovable a person must possess a lovable surface, my father's habit of judging and feeling applied even to his own children and grandchildren. I remember him complaining about a young person he had no reason to attack. He said he supposed she was beautiful, turning up his nose as if in her case such a tribute were just another one of the faults he perceived in her, a justification of his irrational dislike.

His taste in people was unconventional; he was able to discern attractive aspects in both men and women that nobody else might have been able to see. He said that one of the things that was so lovely about Celia was her use of the phrase 'ever so', an expression that encapsulated for him a whole world of femininity and charm. He felt much affection for her but in spite of his feelings he painted her as *Naked Girl With Egg*, a portrait in which the egg, hard boiled and cut in half in an eared dish, puns with her naked breasts, a comparison that made her feel humiliated.

Talking about work he said he hoped that the paint would become flesh rather than just representing it, the paint itself felt more deeply than anything else in his life, obsessed as he was by the potential of the substance, its possibilities. The transubstantiation he tried for was not about creating personality, not that personality is fixed, although he believed that people don't change. He said he wanted to paint a person, not their likeness – he was making flesh, but for me the true beauty and truth of the portraits is experienced in the way the paint surface reveals how he saw his subjects, their specificity under his gaze, from his perspective, and how he felt, not just how much he loved or admired his sitters, but how much he loved and hated to be caught up, that ambivalence.

Monday, 27 November 1989

Went to the supermarket for Pam because she is ill and the children were hungry. Made supper for them, told them a bedtime story and went home to bed.

Wednesday, 29 November 1989

Woke up feeling dejected, rejected, miserable. Talk at Bridges of my terrible jealousy and sense of fatherlessness.

Supper with Celia, she was very complimentary about my cooking. Afterwards at Freds somebody approached me about working at a new club. Maybe. Must write to Dad and ask him for some money to get me out of the debt I am in and to get by until my ship comes in. Asking him is very difficult for me. Home to bed and sleep.

Thursday, 30 November 1989

Took back the table I had borrowed from Angus and Cerith. In their sitting room I noticed all this handsome new old furniture made of dark wood with dark red and green cushions. It felt familiar but I couldn't think why, uneasiness and then I realized it was furniture from my grandmother's house – Dad must have given it to Angus – I think it was designed by Ernst. Felt terrible, angry and sad, very hurt, Dad clearly oblivious to the fact that I might have wanted something from his parents to remember them by.

The furniture was designed by Ernst. Not that I had even met Ernst, but that made it even worse. My father had kept from his parents not only the births of his illegitimate children but also the children themselves, ourselves, his secrecy motivated by the claustrophobia of his mother's delight and possible opprobrium over the babies, the inevitability of Ernst's great shock at his son's irresponsible attitude towards fatherhood. Dad hoodwinked them by omission, too many women in his life and too many children for him to begin to explain himself, all the pregnancies unplanned as far as I know but the sheer number of them suggesting he must have wanted to father us even if he didn't want to take care of us on a daily basis, not that that would have been practical even had he not needed to work, so many of us more or less the same age. His secrecy deprived us of our grandparents and the culture they brought with them from Berlin, and they were deprived of us, all of us apart from Annie and Annabel, who were born within wedlock, and the McAdam children, whom they saw on occasion at least when they were little because Kay McAdam made sure there was some contact.

Angus was a little sheepish when he realized I had recognized the furniture, my grandparents' sofa bench and stout chairs now arranged in his home, items he had a perfect right to possess over and above any claim of my own because my father had given them to him. I said nothing to him of any consequence, tried to cover my shock and left as soon as I possibly could without flouncing out of there, too proud to show hurt or even to feel it until I got back to my own flat, nor did I say anything to my father about those covetable dark relics of Berlin and Ernst's bourgeois modernism, all that was left of those days in my father's possession diverted away from myself and my siblings. I would never have complained about something like that to my father, afraid he might think me importunate in my wish to belong to him and his family, not considering myself entitled to make a claim against his instinct for disruption, his almost deliberate refusal to imagine the ordinary human cost of his actions. I had become adept at persuading myself to accept he was free to make his own choices, and experienced my anger and hurt and sadness in silence.

I got used to seeing the furniture at Angus and Cerith's and managed to distance myself from my desire for it, having accepted my loss. Angus had the worn chairs reupholstered at great expense, assuming they were a permanent addition to his home, and I admired the hard-wearing horsehair fabric he had chosen, a perfect blend of practicality and luxury, in a deep shade of red. I accepted the furniture was his and not mine, until, no longer working from Angus, my father employed a couple of old friends from Paddington to repossess the heirlooms, and gave them to me as a wedding present.

It is possible he wanted to acknowledge my marriage with a significant gift and decided to retrieve the furniture on my account, having intuited how much I minded about it, or maybe he regretted his gift to Angus and wanted the furniture suddenly for himself, only to discover he had no spare houseroom when it arrived on his doorstep. Either way I got what I wanted, although Angus told me how horrible it was for him when the men pushed past him into the flat, walked out with the chairs and returned a few minutes later for the bench sofa. I am certain had my father asked nicely Angus would have returned everything, no need for the strong-arm tactics.

Of course I was sympathetic, and found myself apologizing on my father's behalf – Angus was so hurt and incredulous Dad had sent Mick and the boys round to do his dirty work. I remember my father compensated Angus financially for the cost of the reupholstery after the repossession, in the name of fairness or some tit-for-tat motive to come out on top in the altercation, the give and take of heirlooms and cash expressing the love and spite between them, both of them caught up in the intensity of their feelings.

Thursday, 30 November 1989, cont.

In the evening invited Angus and Cerith over for a drink to show no hard feelings or to console myself somehow for the hard feelings that had overwhelmed me earlier over the furniture. Then we went back to their flat for supper. They invited me again for tomorrow night, and to bring HH with me, a special evening – maybe they are trying to make amends too.

Friday, 1 December 1989

Bridges, talked at length about Dad and money; I am trying to steel myself to ask for some, the meaning of this, my difficulty, why I haven't got any of my own at the moment. Job interview on Saturday.

Home, cleaned the flat, knitting, ironed a shirt for the evening, couldn't believe HH would actually turn up, wrote a letter to Dad and decided against sending it.

Bath at six, ready and waiting on the sofa, listening to SUPER BAD, sipping vodka and tonic, waited two hours, realized he wasn't going to show, spoke to Lucy on the phone, cried, felt very angry, sad, baffled, rang HH at home (got the number from directory enquiries) and at the LRB, no answer, no answer, felt so bad I wanted to ring Bridges, then went over to A and C's alone.

We discussed the subject of HH's absence. All day I felt the impossibility of him turning up but dismissed my fears as a paranoid fantasy. I remember when I rang him on Friday he sounded abstracted, a bit tense.

Luckily Lucy rang in the afternoon and asked me if I wanted to go to her parents' house in the country for the weekend and so I postponed my job interview until Wednesday and accepted her invitation.

Saturday, 2 December 1989

A meandering motorway avoidance journey, we arrived about lunchtime. Felt very close to Lucy and thankful for her friendship. Her father so gently welcoming.

Sunday, 3 December 1989

Arrived back in London late Sunday night, extremely glad to be home.

Monday, 4 December 1989

Spoke to Dad on the phone, asked him for some money. He said fine, come over on Wednesday at half seven to collect it. A little bit depressed after the phone call.

Just plucked up enough courage to phone HH. Waiting and waiting to speak to him until a robot voice said 'The other party has cleared' and the line went dead. I felt absolutely terrible, imagining that he didn't want to speak to me. Rang back, he answered the phone, I said, 'Where were you on Friday?' or something like that and he told me I had got the date wrong, it was next Friday, the 8th, Dad's birthday.

I think HE got the date wrong but I didn't let on. I made out I agreed it was my mistake, although I am not completely sure either way. I told him that I had begun to think he was mad or dead or something and he apologized for being the cause of my psychopathic thoughts. So that's it, we are going to meet up next Friday as we may or may not have originally planned.

Friday, 8 December 1989

Dad's birthday. Up at half seven for Bridges, went over to Mum's afterwards to look at some old things from Pauline who used to work at Hughes' rag-yard but now works at a new yard called Derek's. I bought a beautiful nightdress for Lucy, a dress for Debbie, a blouse for Celia – my Christmas shopping – and six yards of georgette crêpe in navy with a small white sprig pattern to make something for me. Home, HH phoned and told me that he has to go up north tonight for a football game so that's our date off again until Sunday.

Sunday, 10 December 1989

I had just got out of the bath at 5.45 when the doorbell rang. It was HH, fifteen minutes early. I told him to wait a minute on the doorstep, got dressed quickly then buzzed him up. Didn't have time to put on my make-up because I was worried we would be late for the film – I didn't want to get to the cinema and find all the tickets had sold out. He bought the tickets. I wanted to offer him half the money but couldn't do it. Had a cup of tea at Benigra's on Tottenham Court Road and he told me it was the anniversary of his father's death a few days ago, he turned his head away and spoke to the wall.

We saw SEX, LIES, AND VIDEOTAPE. HH really liked it, made a joke about the age of the director – he was only twenty-six – 'Doesn't it make you sick,' meaning sick with jealousy. I said it didn't make me sick. Partly because it wasn't really a good film, partly because I want things to be good, I want to like new things. The film didn't move me. HH said it didn't move him either but that didn't matter. I don't know what does matter then.

Afterwards we had a drink at the Plough. HH told me about the agoraphobic attack he had suffered up a mountain at the weekend, the weekend that followed the Friday night I thought we were scheduled to meet. Again he told me I had got it wrong, we had agreed to meet on the eighth of December, not the first.

Then he told me that he had postponed the deadline of his Saul Bellow article, and not for the first time, so he could get away from it all. Hence the mountain at the weekend. He said he had lied to the editor of the LRB – must have been Karl Miller – pretending he thought the deadline was the eighth. Just like our date, I thought. He told a lie about confounding the first and the eighth, a sort of confession. Had he lied to me too? How shitty. Or was it all me?

I was too polite and too aware of the state he was in to say anything more about the missed date, although the confession about his lie to Karl Miller was followed by a moment or two of horrible silence while I processed what he had just told me. I didn't look at his face, I don't know whether or not he became conscious of what he had said once he had said it, if he was able to understand in the silence between us the implication at least for me of his anecdote. And later, on the street corner (he was walking me home from the pub) he asked me what my psychotherapist was like. He told me two anecdotes about analysis, one the story of a woman who discovered, after years of treatment, that her analyst was an alcoholic, and the other about a therapist who was sick in a session, actually vomited in the presence of his patient. I thought that HH was envious of my relationship with Bridges. On the doorstep – I regret this – I asked him if he wanted to come in for a cup of coffee but he said no and hurried off. I was so disappointed and miserable I went to bed and cried.

Monday, 11 December 1989

The misery of disappointment, then Bridges was very helpful. He made me see that everything was quite simple. HH didn't want to sweep me off my feet, and I wasn't all that keen on him anyway. I felt so rejected this morning, and now I am over it.

EIGHT

Tuesday, 12 December 1989

Finished editing the article for TATLER and sent it off on a bike. Bridges, then Pam's for Laura's birthday. Finished LONDON FIELDS, too many mistakes about Notting Hill. In the first few pages Martin Amis claims that in Notting Hill black men go out with white women but black women don't go out with white men. So what about Andi and John Waddington, Linda and Jimmy, Neneh and Cameron, Ngosi and John Tate, Jeni Innocent and Paul Cook? Also Amis doesn't seem to know that there is a real part of London called London Fields.

Wednesday, 13 December 1989

Museum St Café for TATLER photos, more Christmas shopping. Got a letter from Paula Rego saying she can't do the book because she is under contract to Phaidon not to collaborate on anything because they are doing a book of her work. I need to reassess what to do. Jobs, writing, everything. Uncertainty but exciting this empty space just before Christmas, without pressure. Somehow things feel all right. Made myself some supper after Bridges and relaxed.

I sound relieved not to have to write a book about painting and parenthood. I was still in thrall to my father, had not achieved enough distance to see clearly, and was much too lonely and unstable to dwell fruitfully on my own experience.

Friday, 15 December 1989

Kai invited everybody over for supper. Mum came to tea at mine first, her mood not too bad when we were alone together, just talking about this and that, but once I had driven her home, waited for a bleak hour or so while she got herself ready (she did the washing up) then driven her to Kai's, she completely lost the ability to enjoy herself. She is obviously very unhappy, anxious, black round the eyes, scrutinizing me and Ib as if she wanted to kill us.

On the way home she told me that the psychiatrist or therapist she has been seeing has gone away. At the end of the penultimate session he suggested she attend a psychiatric hospital as a day patient in his absence, as if he was going to make provision for her over the holidays, but didn't arrange anything. Very worrying. I am afraid he wouldn't have suggested the outpatients department unless he believed there was a danger of suicide. In Mum's case it looks more like she is planning a murder. She is unable/unwilling to attend to anyone else's problems. She never complains about Ali or Kai. I dropped her off at Medina Road then went home myself, feeling very anxious on her behalf.

Sunday, 17 December 1989

Did nothing all day, didn't even go to the shop for the papers. Rang Cerith, who told me that Angus was over at Dad's mum's house collecting some more of her furniture. This information toppled me. I had asked them over for tea and Cerith said he would ring me later but did not. They have borrowed my big frying pan, a beautiful old damask tablecloth, a cookery book and my lovely jersey from Westaway and Westaway, none of which they show any sign of returning. Very angry. Rang Bella and we had a little talk. Made me feel a bit better. She said she really minded about the furniture too.

Monday, 18 December 1989

Bridges, sobbed and got snotty, had to wipe it on my sleeve because I didn't have any tissues. Still crying on the stairs on the way to the loo, but managed to dry up on the way to the car.

Tuesday, 19 December 1989

Bridges, my anger because of the holidays. He said that if I want to get married there is work to be done sorting out this anger and my feeling that I am not lovable. I can't believe I will ever get married. I am demoralized by unresolved feelings of rejection, my parents lacking the wherewithal to look after me properly when I was small and needed somebody to look after me properly.

Thursday, 21 December 1989

At last completed marking the proofs of the TATLER article. Went to Hanover Square to give them in, took Lola shopping and to a gallery, helped her wrap her presents, supper with Lucy at Museum Street Café.

Friday, 22 December 1989

Last Bridges, felt much better, recognizing the destructive parts of myself. Supermarket, Dexter over with Maya, Pam's Christmas party.

```
Saturday, 23 December 1989
   Hoxton to see Eileen with Frances.
```

I met Eileen in 1976, when I was at the Queen Mary Hostel on Hoxton Street. She was married already with two small children, a boy and a girl, and a big dog called Sheba. Dad came round to her flat in Haggerston once while I was there, talked easily with her husband about racing then fell asleep almost mid-sentence because in the extreme summer heat the volatile glue she used for her outdoor work gave off fumes that were asphyxiating if you were not used to them – she was sticking shoes for a shoe factory on Hackney Road, her home full of boxes of uppers and soles. We became lifelong friends and she is the subject of some of my best photographs, a series called Lily, Eileen, Donna, Rosie and Florence, five generations of her family portrayed in colour on her sofa, her granddaughter Rosie my god-daughter.

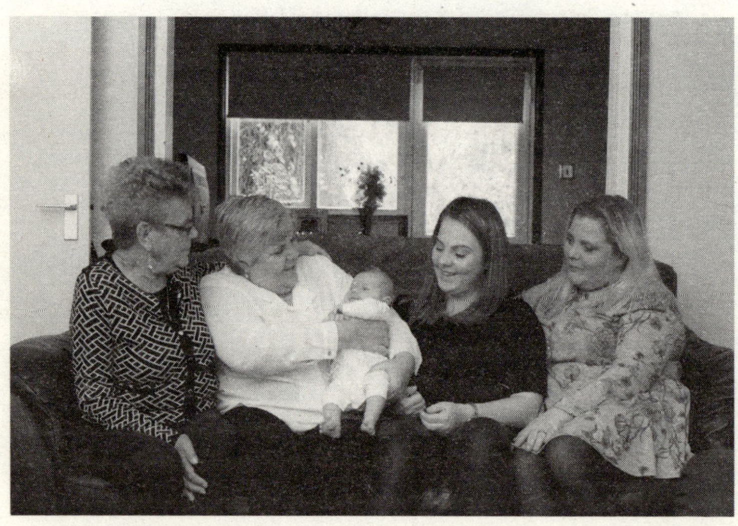

Lily, Eileen, Donna, Rosie and Florence (2017)

ROSE BOYT

Saturday, 23 December, cont.

Freds in the evening to meet Debbie, Esther, Paul McAdam and Jane and Lucy McAdam.

Sunday, 24 December 1989

Wrapped presents, hoovered, washed the kitchen and bathroom floor, went to Janey's party. Joan Collins was there, and Dominie Mauconduit, invited by Bella.

Janey was one of Dad's sitters, and Dominie was an old friend from the punk days. She had severed ties with her family in Australia and during the late seventies was moving round the London homes of various friends and acquaintances, working part-time in the sex industry like many of the young women and one or two of the young men on the punk scene.

I was awed by the subversive sexiness of the outfits she put together before she set off for work at Shepherd Market when she was staying with me and Bella at Clarendon Gardens, every detail of her appearance carefully considered, amongst her most memorable ensembles the tightly belted trench coat worn as a dress, the mustard man's suit of tropical wool paired with high heels and nothing underneath, and the silk pussy-bow blouse and knee-length skirt of muted plaid worn with bare legs and glossy pink lipstick like a fantasy librarian. Every one of her looks was a winning combination of scary and vulnerable, as if dressing up as a sex worker was not quite the same as being a sex worker, the exercise of her artistry in self-presentation making the sex work more of a game.

Before she went out she checked herself in the mirror to see how she came across, trying on the pout she would employ once she was outside Tiddy Dols where she plied her trade, her swagger defiant and wilful because she would have fun and get paid in the process, making it look easy, while I settled down for the evening smelling of chip fat after my shift at the cafe on Edgware Road where I worked four days a week, hard graft but not unenjoyable, Joe Strummer and other punk legends in and out because they lived in a squat round the corner.

Dominie flashed her eyes at me sideways from under her eyelashes and said goodbye, but when the door closed behind her, despite the sudden pain in my chest telling me she was prepared to put herself through things I was not prepared to put myself through, I kept my nose in my book, not even conscious she was unhappy. If she came home with champagne and I drank a couple of glasses was I complicit in her abasement, if she was abased, should I toast the success of her enterprise and allow myself to enjoy her immoral earnings? Who was I to judge her? One of my family members wanted to tag along but Dominie was having none of it, able to draw the line but not on her own account, like sex work was good enough for her but not for us, although we were all teenagers still, Dominie only a year or so older than me. She thought we needed protection from the world into which she was able to immerse herself for a few hours whenever she felt like it, no harm done as long as her luck held, all punters required to hand over the cash before anything happened and not subjecting her to anything off limits, although once she came back home to me with a black eye, a piratical bruise she incorporated into her look when she went back out the next day.

She must have been unhappy though, because she decided to travel to South America by ship, a working passage on a commercial vessel, perhaps wishing to see the world or just to get away from how she was living, tired of the sex work and unable to stop it. She packed a bag and set off for Heathrow, travelling easily, her ship departing from some German port. She took her pet rat on the plane in a small cage, having checked first with the authorities, but some zealous customs official at the other end suspected she was a member of the Baader–Meinhof Gang and sent her back to England. She was arrested as she disembarked, no longer under suspicion of terrorism but charged with a rabies offence and held in a cell pending trial, mourning the rat, which had been put down at the airport. The judge handed down a five-year ban from the UK and she was deported to Australia, the country she loathed – she had no friends, no life there. After a few months in Melbourne she travelled to Paris, got married and attended the École des Beaux-Arts, studying under Christian Boltanski, making watery paintings in her own blood. I visited her a few times at the Hôtel Amelot when she was still single, once with Katie, the three of us sharing a big room with several beds, two French windows overlooking the street, ten francs a night between us.

I remember Dad telling me that when Dominie was at Holland Park she asked him if she could go to the ladies, which he said proved she spent her whole life in nightclubs. I did bump into her there once or twice when we were teenagers, and wondered what was going on, but it has only just occurred to me that he might have been availing himself of her services, not that I can picture her demanding payment up front before she took off her clothes. I imagine she just went for it in the knowledge or hope he would recompense her later on, trusting him to cough up at least enough for a taxi if she missed the last Tube and him handing over two fifties as he showed her off the premises, way too much money to cover her fare wherever she was headed after their rendezvous. He would not have allowed her to stay the night had she wanted to sleep in a safe place after the sex, although he was always perfectly mannerly towards her, perfectly able to find some way to save her and himself from the real nature of the transaction, that's if anything happened between them in reality. He liked her well enough but didn't want to paint her. She liked him but I don't think she liked him any more than she liked any of the other men she spent time with in her professional capacity. He told me he never paid for sex. He told me Dominie said she was too skint sometimes even to treat herself to a newspaper. I can remember thinking she was no poorer than the rest of us, no poorer than me.

Monday, 25 December 1989

Christmas Day. Ib's, Bella's, Angus and Cerith's.

Wednesday, 27 December 1989

Shopping with Kai. Jake Auerbach's party with Susannah Clapp. Julia was so lovely. Paula Rego was quite drunk, a bit awkward, but we managed.

Thursday, 28 December 1989

Freds with Cerith in the evening then to Gaz's.

Friday, 29 December 1989

I feel more or less ready to finish my book in the New Year. Then to start work on my next one. I have to find a regular source of income. I must keep training my memory, keep trying to see out of the blur caused by anxiety and my cut-off feelings, not to throw the baby out with the bathwater. Also to think about the meaning of FORM, and about photographs as part of this diary, as illustrations, and to value DAYDREAMING, incidentally a good title for a novel. And not to be always worrying about the future at the expense of the present. Ha!

Saturday, 30 December 1989

Berwick Street then spent the day cooking and making preparations for New Year's Eve – Lucy and I are having a party. In the evening she came over and we got on with preparations together quietly and talked as we worked – so enjoyable. Made a veal breast stuffed with veal, pork, sweetbreads, artichokes and peas, which has to be wrapped in muslin and weighted down overnight – used the LAROUSSE GASTRONOMIQUE amongst other books for the purpose. This dish created a lot of calf's-foot broth.

My labour-intensive menu was very influenced by Angus, who was always encouraging me with slight pressure to extend my repertoire, and I was always trying to impress him. As well as the stuffed veal breast I made a salad of octopus, squid, prawns and mussels. Lucy's brother Tom came over with bunches of roses and a magnum of champagne.

> Monday, 1 January 1990
>
> Clearing up after the party. Ib, Frances and Pat came over for supper.

After they went, Susie rang and told me the very bad news that Mum had left home and gone to live with her ex-boyfriend Tom in his short-life house in Mornington Crescent. We talked for a long time, and Susie was very upset, more upset even than me. It was not as though Mum didn't know that life with Tom was untenable, why she had split up with him in the first place. But now she wanted to give it another go, this time in his house, maybe hoping she would find his behaviour easier to manage in a new location. Her decision felt deadly, not suicide exactly but a version of it.

I phoned Ali, looking for comfort, and he said that Mum's behaviour was typical of that of the adult child of alcoholic or drug-addict parents. He said that people like that invariably seek out drama, can't bear a quiet life, and find ordinary emotion too boring.

How sad I felt then, listening to his unemotional response, the twang in his voice in abeyance but not altogether gone since he had given up drugs himself, like he had been using for so long that it had become part of him. His analysis of Mum was drawn from the Twelve Steps, the recovery programme he had embraced and that seemed to have saved him from himself, although I was not entirely convinced then that he was drug free. It seemed reductive and disrespectful to talk about Mum like that, and besides, I hadn't thought of her parents in that way, Major Boyt and Mrs Boyt mentioned so seldom and with such obfuscatory details it was hard to learn anything real about them – Mum had plenty to hide when it came to her own upbringing. She didn't say much but now I come to think of it I do recall her telling me that Linda took a lot of pills prescribed by the doctor to make her feel better. That must have been what Ali was talking about.

I was not sure about his reading of Mum – he was detached, seemingly unmoved by her calamitous behaviour, the wisdom of his analysis protecting him from the corrosive force of her unhappiness, but he was the expert and knew what he was talking about. What really hurt was that Mum had told him she was afraid to tell me she had got back with Tom. She was afraid of me and had confided in him. And I picked up or imagined an element of relish in his voice when he told me. He had not thought I might have minded how she regarded me.

Mum was afraid of me because she didn't know me, which made me feel even worse, but maybe she was right to be scared. I *was* angry and upset, although not nearly as angry as she was. And it was not just Ali and Susie she had already told. I realize now that Ib must have known too, but kept the news to herself when she came over for supper on New Year's Day, keeping me in the dark for her own reasons. I can see myself laughing with her and Frances at the table like one of the characters in a play who inevitably looks a bit stupid or pitiful because everybody else knows something they don't know.

I am not sure if Mum loved Tom but at some point during her time with him she told me that he had endured mental anguish through no fault of his own his whole life, and had tried everything, even psychoanalysis, but it didn't work on him, and I thought about the slightly funny shape of his skull, the bones pushed out of whack as if by the torment. She described him as irreparably damaged so I wouldn't judge him or her by association, hoping to engender in me some sympathy for his suffering. She said when he was at Medina Road with her and off drugs for a while the Turks who lived next door would leave little taster bags for him on the garden wall to tempt him back, free samples that caused him to dust off the boiled metal syringe he had put away in a safe place since the last time he had injected himself, his delight maybe cut with sorrow and shame he was off again down that same old path. Or maybe he just accepted himself without judgement and welcomed any relief he could find from his anguish. She told me he couldn't help himself, nobody could help getting back into it under those circumstances.

Tuesday, 2 January 1990

New ideas freewheeling effortlessly in the pool this morning. Decided to insert some new work in my book on the mother's mother, relating to what Ali said about Mum yesterday, how she had suffered.

Wednesday, 3 January 1990

A thank-you letter from Francis Wyndham for the party. Also a letter from Sophie de Stempel. I recognized her handwriting at once on the envelope. I have seen her twice in the last week, once at Janey's, once at Gaz's, but I swerved her because I haven't recovered from the last time she wrote to me. That letter was ages ago, when I was still at Portobello Road, and I know she was having a very bad time back then. Still, I was devastated by her unfounded accusations, and they still hurt.

The devastating letter was not about Dad, but I believe that in some inevitable yet indirect way he was behind the sudden violence of her animosity towards me, my love for her and her love of him bound to turn out badly for both of us at some point, the real miracle that we both recovered and became close again. Time passed, I bumped into her at some party and knew I was over it, we were able to start again where we left off.

Thursday, 4 January 1990

Received a letter from Mum about moving in with Tom.

The letter might be in my boxes of papers but I can't even begin to look, reluctant to experience the grief I know I would feel if I found it, reluctant to experience the grief I would feel if it is lost. Mum loved me and didn't want me to be upset with her, the only phrase I can recall word for word is 'circumstances beyond my control and not of my own making', meaning that she had been swept away by some ineluctable force.

Thursday, 4 January 1990, cont.

Worked all day on my book, wrote to Susannah Clapp asking her if she would read it, then went for a job interview as a receptionist at a hostess club. The club was low ceilinged, a red cave, half-naked women of all sizes moving about in the half-dark, a row of pert little bottoms at the bar mooning in fringes and G strings. Glad to say the receptionist is allowed to wear normal clothes, although I don't think I got the job, the man didn't ask me enough questions. I had a quick drink at Freds on the way home. If I do get the job I will only stick it for a short while, just so I can get some money together – it's five nights a week, which in the long run would be too much on top of my writing.

Friday, 5 January 1990

Sainsbury's and Chapel Market first thing. Misery focused on Maya – I am looking after her tonight. Anger about feeding her – she tries to control everything by accepting and rejecting food, just the way her distress manifests itself. It is partly my fault because I try so hard and then get disappointed. Muttering under my breath in the supermarket, and by the time I have slogged all the way up the stairs with my shopping and my empty purse I feel inordinately outraged. It would be much easier for both of us if I gave in and let her eat nothing but Rice Krispies and chocolate biscuits. She complains about everything. And the anger makes me feel miserable. GUILTY. And conscious of the little girl in me who wants to be looked after.

I have just written a letter to Mum – Happy New Year and all that, nothing much, a few loving words to show I am not angry (ha ha) and now I feel like crying.

I could have been more forgiving, I wish I had been more forgiving.

And I feel like crying now it is all too late to make any difference. I don't mind shedding a few tears, it's not like I won't be able to stop, but surely I can find some other way to deal with the guilt of my disloyalty after everything I have said about her, some other way to console myself for my loss now she is dead and I would do anything to bring her back. I love her and miss her painfully every day, and want to counter or offset my portrayal of her destructive side or whatever reductive shorthand I might choose in my haste and shame to sum up her struggle to cope with five illegitimate children on her own, me just retyping from my diary how I felt inadequately mothered into adulthood when I suspect her childhood was much worse than my own. The struggle is all over for her, but it's not too late for me to celebrate some of the marvellous things she made in her life as a mother and grandmother, as an artist, now I am no longer angry, to commemorate and honour her creativity.

I remember the joy of the decorations she made for me and Ib when we lived on the ship, long white candles nestled in wreaths of paper daffodils, the flowers so lively by candlelight and her face haloed against the darkness as she entered our cabin the night before Easter, the heaving sigh of the water just the other side of the heavy timbers and the mainsail boom creaking to remind us in case we forgot for a moment that we were at sea. I know she must have been smiling, her smile imbued with love and the solemnity of the ceremony she presided over for a few moments, my small heart and presumably that of my sister hurting and melting under the spell of her loveliness, the wonder and loving magic of her gifts.

The candles burned brightly, my pillow still cool under my cheek because I had only just finished putting Kai to bed in his bunk in the cabin next door, the sweet smell of his baby milk still in my hair. Kai slept with his eyes open, perhaps because he didn't want to miss anything. I was supposed to put my hair in a plait before bed – 'Like the sailors of yore' was how my mum sold it to me – but had not managed to make myself, a slip that made me feel I was losing the struggle not only to tame the tangles but also to live up to my own expectations, my mum cutting out the lumps at the back when it got too bad and throwing them overboard. She didn't mention my hair, a maternal kindness because it was Easter or an oversight on her part that made me uneasy she too was letting go of the things I knew were important for both of us, not just my hair but how to look after ourselves properly. She kissed me and my sister goodnight and went off to get on with the things she had to get on with because she had to get on, and Ib and I were tempted to peel off the drips of melted wax from the dwindling candles and hold them in the flames, big sister reminding little sister to keep her hair out of the way in case it caught fire. At seven years old I was already an expert in responsible behaviour, a miracle child and not a miracle child, loved but also desired.

The candles flickered in their papery nests, and I was enchanted by the daffodils, the delicacy of the way Mum had painted them. The smoke rose in thin spirals before it dispersed and the sea rocked us to sleep, the incessant swell soothing my sister but making me queasy as soon as I closed my eyes, a heaving sensation inside me that had to be quelled. I thought of the daffodils, Mum staying up late to make them in secret, paintbrush in hand, the intensity of her concentration as she remembered the forms and felt them, the only flowers on board the everlasting bouquet in the jug in the main cabin, the straw petals all dusty. I knew that feeling of lightness in my own hand as I wrote and drew in my diary before I gave it up, my pencils flying across the unlined paper as I conjured the wonderment of what I had seen, not just ships and harbours but my dream-life of fairies and angels. I wish nothing got lost. It comforted me to think of her remembering daffodils and making them, even Uwe with his charts spread out on the table to plot our course, his quietness when he was quiet, their bed on a platform at the back of the main cabin behind the big table, their sponge mattress and the built-in seating upholstered in blue cloth. I was alone but not alone. Mum must have come back in to snuff out the candles while we were sleeping.

We had real candles on the tree at Christmas, the metal candle-holders clipped onto the ends of the branches, and Mum made dolls out of the engine rags, their dream outfits a bit Danish because of the design of the printed fabrics, a blonde doll for Ib and a redhead for me. We never called them rag dolls because we considered that name an insulting allusion to the vulnerable actuality of their origins on the oily floor of the engine room, and loved them with extra intensity because of their low start in life. Ib christened her doll Lulubelle, a girl-child of about the same age as herself, although she had not been made in my sister's image, bore no resemblance to either of us. Lulubelle's hair was unravelled from the sleeve of a holey jersey that must once have belonged to some small Scandinavian, neat yellow kinks permanently set in the wool as long as it kept dry. Her pink mouth and blue eyes looked appealingly pretty against her pale cheeks, although Ib kissed her so often a patina of dirt spread over and between the warp and weft of the old sheet of her face, the fabric wearing thin long before my sister had had enough of her.

My doll was not a child but a woman, her womanhood perhaps a tribute to my maturity. Her hair, made of fluffy mohair, was a bright fiery rust colour, and I can still recall perfectly her facial expression, haughty and startled as if by her own beauty, green eyes like mine, the black lines of her lids and lashes drawn in fine stitches, the bright red of her lips like roses. I called her Butterfly but loved her a little less well than Ib and I loved Lulubelle, with some ambivalence, because she was not so easy to love. I held her but disappointed myself not to feel anything, the miraculous side of me deciding I was too old and too tough for the relationship anyway, always the first one on deck with a knife when Mum caught something by torchlight with the men in the lifeboat when we still had a lifeboat – I was a child able to grasp a live eel in a cloth, hold it down, hack it up and cook it on the stove in the galley, no mercy, long chunks of fish still wriggling in the hot pan.

I can no longer picture the detail of Butterfly's clothing, whether or not she wore underwear under her outer garments, but I do remember Mum made a black bikini for my Sindy doll out of an old pair of tights, and tulle curtains for her bed, a wooden four-poster with brass curtain rails, built by Uwe or the mate, in which Sindy could lie with her pointy bosoms encased in black nylon.

And she showed us the world. I remember the first time we arrived in Denmark, by ferry from Folkestone or somewhere, Uwe sent a sleigh drawn by reindeer to fetch us from the snowy harbour where we disembarked, an unforgettably wonderful experience, and to greet us when we arrived at our own ship he had covered every inch of the walls of the empty hold with pine branches, the needles fresh green and smelling of Christmas. We descended backwards down the ladder and came into a magical forest, the fragrant boughs decorated with straw hearts and stars tied with red ribbons, and he was there in the trees wearing a hat of red felt and a white beard, offering us sweets from his sack.

Mum painted a series of illustrations for a children's book once we were back in London, images of such loveliness I am amazed nobody wanted to publish them; I think she showed them to somebody but became discouraged very easily when they were not snapped up. The pictures were all lost, until a year after her death I chanced to open an old childhood scrapbook of mine, another of her lovely creations, and found five of the beautiful watercolours safely stowed at the back between two pages of sugar paper. I was so delighted to see the illustrations again in all their freshness and originality it was like Mum had come back for a moment to bless me, not that I believe in the afterlife, but I felt blessed.

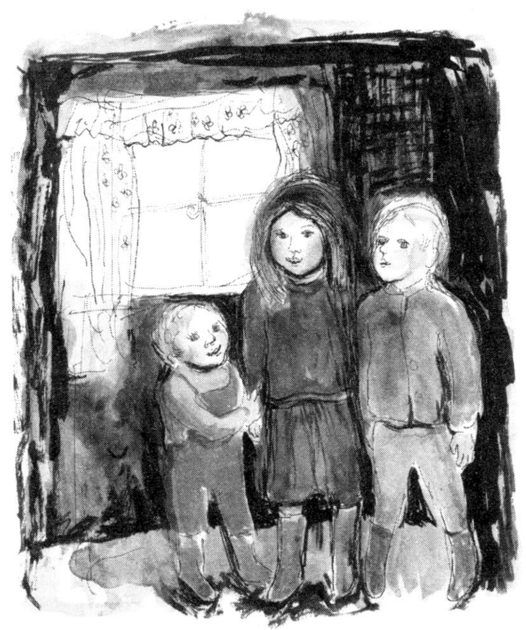

Three Children
SUZY BOYT

The children in the pictures are touchingly particularized, plainly modelled on us, which is complicated, as I never felt Mum was very pleased with how we looked in reality, the dissatisfaction with which she regarded us an aspect of the disparagement to which she subjected herself, although I might be wrong about this.

The scrapbook must have been one of the things I didn't take with me when I left home. Mum seems to have chosen the best of the pictures and put them away for safe keeping between the empty pages at the back, with or without the intention of giving them to me, knowing in spite of the critical gaze she turned on herself and her work I would treasure them if I received them. I wrapped up the scrapbook when she gave it back and put it away on top of the wardrobe without even looking in it. She didn't say anything about the illustrations otherwise I would have found them and embraced her with gratitude and joy, so happy to see myself and my siblings again through her eyes as our childhood selves, the newly discovered images proving she knew in her heart of hearts we were lovely children in spite of her uncertainties, her misgivings about us. It occurs to me now she put five pictures away because she had five children, and maybe hoped I would share them out between my brothers and sisters. And I will, when I am ready to let them go.

Tiny forget-me-nots adorn the pink cover, a tattered white paper doily forming a central decorative motif, the pages hand-stitched along the spine in red thread. My reluctance to look inside when she returned the scrapbook was not about her, I just couldn't face going back. I didn't want to see the postcards Uwe sent us when he went to sea and we stayed behind in the house outside Port of Spain, colourful pictures of tropical islands I stuck down like they were important to me, encouraged by my mum, Uwe thinking of us only when he was so drunk he could hardly write his own name. She knew how to boil flour and water on the stove to make glue, and as I applied the lumpy paste I obliterated for all time the scribble of his sentimental outpourings.

Unless. Unless I decide to steam off the postcards one day in a mad bid to discover the address of the house near Port of Spain, the forgotten street name and door number, or just to read once more the four words of the message we received after he lost the ship, just to check – *SHIP SUNK, GO HOME.* The postmark might reveal the name of the place he was washed up after the shipwreck, not that I even care, my entire self still wishing he was eaten by sharks. I don't even know if I glued that final card in my album alongside the others before we packed up and set off for London without him, if Mum didn't tear it to shreds or set it on fire.

When my daughter Stella was born Mum made three plain Viyella nightdresses for her, one pink, one cream and one pale brown, the colours of Neapolitan ice cream, and I made the effort almost every night after Stella's bath to thread her arms into the sleeves before she got too big, not to waste a moment of their usefulness.

These adorable garments fastened at the back with thin ties and were unadorned apart from a single row of feather stitch at the neck, the pattern so old-fashioned my mum might have remembered it from her own childhood after the war, her baby brother who was ten or eleven years younger than her dressed for bed in a similar way by the nursery nurse, not that I imagine she and her siblings wore clothes made by their own mother, although Mum must have inherited her creativity from somewhere. She was an excellent pattern-cutter and made us beautiful summer dresses from her own patterns when we were young, having learnt dressmaking at art school.

She brought up Ali's son Louis from babyhood until she was too ill to look after him, by which time Louis was at secondary school and Ali was ready to take over. When he was still at Mum's Louis loved *Thunderbirds* and desperately wanted a Tracy Island for Christmas. The toy was sold out everywhere, unavailable however much one was prepared to pay for it, so Mum made him one out of papier mâché, a full-size model to replicate the original in the picture in the Argos catalogue, a feat of design and construction so spectacular Louis didn't complain it wasn't the real thing and spent hours every day playing with it. Louis has just graduated from Bristol. Mum would be so proud.

Then when she was ill I drove her to Rosemary Gardens, a small park on the borders of Islington and Hackney, to get some fresh air, and she asked me to take a few photos. I offered to take some proper pictures with my camera but she was happy with the ones I had taken on my phone and asked me to have them printed for her. I thought she just wanted to look at the trees and grass when she was resting at home – it was not so easy for her to get out – but she painted a beautiful painting of the park and gave it to me. Both this painting and an oil of anemones hang in my house and I love them and look at them every day, with love for her and some sadness because I am not sure she knew how highly I value them.

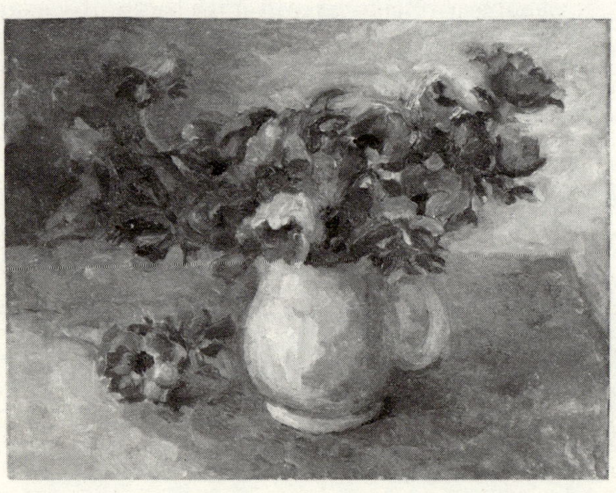

Anemones

SUZY BOYT

NINE

Friday, 5 January 1990, cont.

I am having difficulties. Hard finishing my book, hard beginning my next book, hard keeping steady with Maya, worried about money and on Sunday I am supposed to be going to St John's Wood Terrace to choose a few old things from Dad's mum's house for myself and for the others to remember her by. Stephen's wife Ann invited me. I haven't told Dad. It all feels horrible.

Sunday, 7 January 1990

Dexter and Maya at my flat. I really didn't want to go to my grandmother's. I got very upset about it, drove over there, sat in the car, phoned Ib from a telephone box, cried in the car afterwards, waited for Ali to turn up, and then at the last minute, after I had more or less decided I should go home because it was all too squalid, I was not entitled to be there, Dad would be angry with me, I knocked at the door. Ann was so nice. I filled a couple of cardboard boxes with some old things, photos of Dad when he was little, old china mostly cracked, a few old cookery books, some napkins.

Ali chose a mirror and a carpet from the garage or

shed at the end of the garden. I chose some shelves but have to wait for them to be valued before I can take them.

Angus was there, having a poke around – he must have received encouragement from Dad or at least been given permission. He had a migraine – I am not surprised.

I feel sad now, trying to remember what happened to those shelves; I must have let them go because they were too cumbersome. But I do know that Angus ended up with Ernst's library, the brown wooden bookcases designed by my grandfather and dismantled from his study, the whole dark array reassembled in Angus's spare bedroom. It seems likely he was at my grandmother's the same time as me to scope out what was available, not that he said anything to me about what he was up to. His acquisition was not a secret exactly but fudged not to rub my nose in it, although I was granted a quick look once everything had been installed, my head round the door for a moment, the bed unmade in the half-light and a few boxes of books as yet unpacked, the shelves only part full but ready and waiting for more. Angus was very happy with his gains, but I think when he saw me in my grandmother's kitchen with my small haul of mementoes to share with my actual siblings he knew it was all a bit skewed, his longed-for proximity to my father not as comfortable as he might have hoped. I don't know why Dad wanted to give him the library, maybe because he had set a precedent, having already given him Ernst's other furniture. I will never know if Angus asked for it or Dad just liked him so much he wanted him to have everything, excited by Angus as a model and keen to tie him in to himself in as many ways as possible, reliant as he was on his models once he had started to work from them, his work depending on their fidelity and constancy, his life depending on their total commitment until he was ready to let them go.

Sunday, 7 January 1990, cont.

On the way back Bridges' car was in front of me in the queue to turn right out of Avenue Road onto Elsworthy Road. I felt extremely self-conscious, but then I realized that Bridges was not in his car – a woman was driving. When I got home I felt quite exhausted. Dexter made me some tea and toast and I tried to calm down. I washed all the old china, looked through all the other stuff, the photos, and tried to decide how to divide it up. Dexter and Maya left about five. Put the napkins to boil on the stove. Some of them are ancient, monograms embroidered in the corners, the letter B for BRASCHE, Dad's mother's maiden name, and some LF for LUCIE FREUD.

Being fair is so difficult. I am Lady Bountiful, nothing is worth anything, everything is loaded with sentimental value, the relics I have to dole out not even mine. Dad rang just as I was trying to write him a letter about it and he made me feel all right about everything. I made five piles of stuff, one for Bella, one for Ib, one for Susie, one for Esther and one for myself. I am keeping the napkins.

The conscientious distribution of the dregs of our grandmother's household goods was a foreshadowing of the fair execution of my father's estate, aware as I was already of the enormity of that responsibility. When I arrived at the house Stephen's wife Ann showed me the napkins, damask yellowed along the folds and limp from disuse, heaped in a glass-fronted cupboard, and encouraged me to help myself to what was left in the kitchen, the modest domestic items set out in two rows on the table like exhibits in a small provincial museum. What I didn't say at the time, or even seem to register, was that the house had already been ransacked by the time I got there, childhood photos of Dad and his family scattered across the dusty carpets as if they were worthless. Everything had been gone through, not only by Angus but also by legitimate cousins less eager than me, not as hungry for evidence of connection.

I knelt down and gathered up the photographs, although I had no sense of claim, and felt deeply enriched just to possess them, even if only temporarily, knowing that I ought to share them out amongst my siblings and not just keep them all for myself. Under the napkins I found a folder of bevel-edged card that contained several studio photos of our grandmother, the likeness to Esther so uncannily strong round the chin in particular I decided she should have the whole collection.

Sunday, 7 January 1990, cont.

Spoke to Ali on the phone, getting to know him.

I had avoided Ali as much as possible for so long it was quite novel communicating with him post-rehab, although I still lived every day in terror of his death as I had done since we were in our early twenties. Mum just took him at his word, and even I gave him the benefit of the doubt most of the time, hoping against hope he was not going to return to his old ways. My avoidance of him was not tough love or anything tactical but just an instinct on my part not to see him if I could avoid seeing him, his presence too horribly upsetting for me because I loved him and didn't want him to die. It was his choice to take drugs and mine not to witness the state he was in, his desperation and his wounds. I wasn't judging him, but I just couldn't stand it.

Monday, 8 January 1990

Spent the evening starching the napkins and making a bag for Lucy for her birthday out of some blue and white striped horsehair fabric lined with cream linen. Very nice, and serviceable.

Tuesday, 9 January 1990

Intensive editing all day. Bridges, then Pam and Laura came over for some lentil soup because Pat has started work on Pam's kitchen and she can't make any hot food. She took a plateful back for Steve with a napkin on top.

An ambivalent phone call in the evening from Susannah Clapp in response to the letter I wrote her asking her to read my book. I was surprised she was so reluctant. She said she had made a decision when she left Cape not to read people's manuscripts, but acquiesced in the end. I went over to her flat and delivered it. Elated feeling on leaving.

Wednesday, 10 January 1990

Bella came over to collect her stuff from our grandmother and to have lunch. Very upset at Bridges as I was yesterday, anger and jealousy about him cancelling my session this Friday. Learnt how I cut things off, choose to forget things, forget him in response to feeling forgotten myself, feeling nothing but SAD instead of my real feelings of anger, jealousy, being responsible for my life and how I live it.

Supper with Lucy at the Museum Street Café then back to mine and I gave her the bag. She was very pleased with it, as Bella was earlier with her things from Dad's mum. A call from Drago the Yugoslavian poet who is also a hepatic doctor or AIDS specialist but I was right in the middle of working and he rang off fairly quickly, made me feel bad for being so short but I managed to say Happy New Year just as he was putting the phone down.

Rang Deborah Rogers and found out my American money is on its way. Hurrah.

Brief discussion with Pam about Angus, he told her he was worried in case I was pissed off with him.

Thursday, 11 January 1990

Phone call from Jeremy Norman about a new club in Chelsea. He is suggesting a period of concentrated work to get everything set up, followed by working one or two nights a week. He wants me to think of a name. Didn't get the job at the hostess club (no great loss) but the place in Chelsea sounds like a real possibility. Must try and think of a name. Suddenly the prospect of earning some money is cheering me up. Although I don't really want to go back to club work.

In the evening went to a party for Roger Pomphrey. Met up with Sean there, went on to the Zanzibar with him, then Gaz's on my own.

Friday, 12 January 1990

It suddenly hit me that Bridges has cancelled the session today, a fact I had more or less managed to push out of my mind. Began to feel very low. Went to John Lewis to buy paper patterns for a jacket and a blouse, then bought some green tartan from Westaway and Westaway. Dexter came over in the early evening ostensibly to go to a film but I was too miserable, weeping like a child, then overcome with lust and had sex on the floor in the sitting room. Afterwards couldn't stop crying, he stayed the night. Utter misery.

Monday, 15 January 1990

Up early, went to Holborn Viaduct to photograph the statues in view of describing them at the beginning of my next book. Dexter came over to put up a shelf in the kitchen. More notes on the book then Bridges. Susannah Clapp rang and invited me over to go through her notes. Very pleased with her suggestions, left feeling grateful and confident.

Tuesday, 16 January 1990

Still suffering from the shock of Friday, the sex shame and my regression to babyhood. My reaction to the let-down of Bridges going away, what being left means for me, not dealing with it, the shock of realizing how much it hurt me, not helped by my upset over the Mum and Tom situation.

Mum went away with a man (maybe Dad) and a suitcase when I was three and I didn't understand why she would leave me. The door slammed and I found myself in the echoing hall with an unfamiliar Nordic au pair who objected to my tangled hair and decided to cut it. I can't remember her name but she hurt me with her comb and snapped with the scissors too close to my ears because I was dirty and she wanted to change me. My hair fell to the floor in a scattered heap and I was changed, unrecognizable. Mum had gone and I was no longer my real self. Her sudden departure and the au pair's disdainful attack has stayed with me and has left me with a fear of losing myself, a mild to moderate terror amongst other terrors that get played out over and over again, not so much in the daytime but when I wake in the night in the dark and there is nobody there.

Tuesday, 16 January 1990, cont.

Bridges says I still have hopes for a different relationship with Mum, hopes that are always disappointed. Give up and be realistic, she is never going to be consistently supportive towards me, it is impossible.

Sean and Bruce at Freds. It was good to see them. Home on my own, feeling a little bit better.

Wednesday, 17 January 1990

Told Bridges I thought he/psychotherapy was cruel and inhumane because I am still so angry about him cancelling my session last Friday.

Thursday, 18 January 1990

More work on my book, agonizing about the morality of revealing so much. Made Rip Rig + Panic tape for Lucy. Dexter dropped in (again) and Ib and Frances came over but Frances was so wild it was all a bit tense and uncomfortable. Peace and quiet after they left, talked to Lucy on the phone.

Friday, 19 January 1990

Bridges early, another terrible time, so angry when I left I felt like slamming the door and shouting at him. He says this is about my anger and hostility towards my father. This feels dangerous, although now I have expressed how angry I feel I am a bit better. I fear he will not be able to take it if I am my true self.

Was Bridges right about my anger and hostility towards my father? Two things about Bridges. When I was first married and outraged by the inequality of married life I complained to him about the lack of effort put in by my husband domestically and with the care of his son, whose real mother was dead, and Bridges told me I should just let my husband get on with his work as that would be better for all of us in the long run, meaning I ought not to hold him back in his career, my own work not even mentioned in the equation. Then when I went back to see him for support and advice after the death of my father, to help me manage my grief and the estate (fortuitously for me by that time he had become a psychoanalytical business consultant or something like that) I happened to mention that I hadn't gone to the police when I was raped as a teenager. I told him I still remembered the name of the perpetrator and was thinking I might try and get justice before it was too late, but he just shut me down before I had a chance to work out how I felt, saying it would be too hard on my children if it went to court and I should just let it go for everybody's sake. I am not saying he didn't help me enormously but he should have stood by me rather than taking the side of the men in my life, my father, my husband, my rapist, not that they all deserve to be lumped together like that, but I am sure you can understand what I mean. I wanted him to acknowledge that my anger was justified. His attitude did not feel straightforward enough. Although once at the very end of a session when I was bemoaning my father's absence from my childhood home Bridges told me that all things considered the lack of domestic consistency on his part might have been a good thing for me, less dangerous, meaning if Dad had somehow forced himself into a conventional role and moved in with us the outcome for me may well have been worse, I may well have been more damaged. I was laughing and crying in response but had to get up off the couch because my session was over.

Sunday, 21 January 1990

Lovely weekend in the country with Lucy. Walked round the plantation many times, a safe walk in the enclosed wood, impossible to get lost. Read LIBRA by Don DeLillo and couldn't work out whether it is meant to be very confusing or if I am very confused. Some anxiety in the dark on the way home but I managed it.

Monday, 22 January 1990

Told Bridges how angry I had been on Friday, how I had wanted to kick his door in, felt better, then went to the gym with Pam. She was wearing a sexy leotard and glam tights, I wore a pair of lumpy tracksuit trousers and a baggy T-shirt with long sleeves. Intimidating and embarrassing, but I know I should try and become less inhibited.

Tuesday, 23 January 1990

More work, my book is now ready to give to my agent. Bridges, angry silence, home, peace and quiet.

Thursday, 25 January 1990

John Lewis for bias binding and thread for lampshade also bathmat. Book to Rachel Calder. Catrina lunch. Mum tea, made Chelsea buns, Pam and children for supper. Cleared up after they left and re-covered a lampshade with the remains of the yellow silk left over from lining my new jacket. The lamp is silver, a birthday present from Mum a few years ago, very beautiful.

Friday, 26 January 1990

Bridges, big upset again, about looking after the baby in me, my anger that nobody will look after it for me. Cut out blouse from pattern then went over to Susie's at five for tea. Not easy. Home on the bus then worked on the blouse until midnight.

Saturday, 27 January 1990

Frans Hals show at the Royal Academy with Lucy and Frances then Fortnum's for breakfast. Frances was jumping all over the banquette when the head waitress came over to tell us off and I recognized her – it was Anna, one of the Verde sisters, my downstairs neighbours, with whom I had rowed recently on the telephone. I could remember every word of the row. I had been outraged she dared to suggest that I allowed my niece to jump on the furniture. Caught in the act.

Tuesday, 30 January 1990

Talked to Dad about Angus, he is planning not to work from him for a while. I told him that Angus would feel terribly dropped. Dad said working from him was not easy, Angus was angry and agitated.

Wednesday, 31 January 1990

Bridges, he went to sleep in the session. First time ever.

Thursday, 1 February 1990

Phone call from Dad or it could have been yesterday, asking me to sit for a picture. Had a long talk with him about it. Great significance for me, how I long for a father, how I dread him rejecting me. I told him I was afraid of the claustrophobia of it, the commitment, afraid of letting him down, but agreed to have a trial run on the understanding that if I couldn't stand it I could back out. He referred to the naked picture of me when I was a teenager, he said when he had put his hand on me I lifted it up and gave it back to him. He mentioned incest, trying to reassure me about any fears I might have on that front. I will commit myself to this picture because I can no longer avoid dealing with him, my feelings about him.

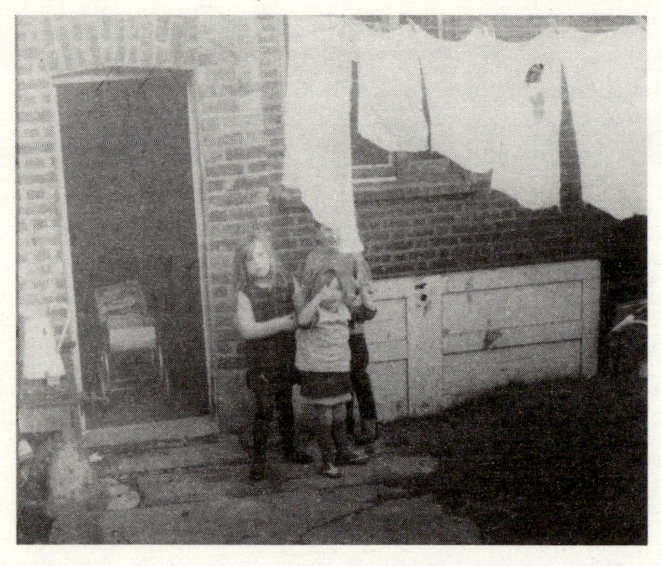

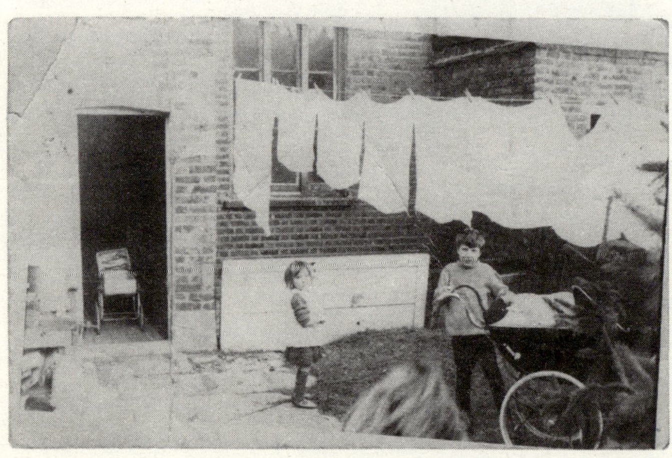

Back garden, 31 Lonsdale Square
Photographer Unknown

TEN

I would not have known he put his hand on me had I not read about the phone call in which he reminded me, but now I remember the weight of his hand in mine as I removed it from my hip or thigh, his palm cupped round some tensed part of myself I did not want him to think he could reach out and touch. His touch was unwelcome but the incident was no big deal for me when it happened, he only wanted to adjust me, not to feel me. And I can't even remember the talk about incest, a subject he may not have brought up had we met face to face to discuss sitting – it was easier for him on the telephone, and maybe for me too, if he was going to talk about us not having sex, not that I wanted to have sex with him, nor him with me, just in case you were wondering.

I remember him appearing at 31 Lonsdale Square when Uwe was with Mum before we lived on the ship, two men in the same room who could not have been more different in appearance and demeanour, my father diminished in comparison by Uwe's great height and Aryan colour, his usual jumpiness exacerbated by the rival masculine presence. Mum was probably pregnant with Kai by then – she loved being pregnant, the only time she ever felt really happy – and Dad would have had to deal with how he felt about that, a triangulated dynamic he may or may not have minded very much, although the discomfort we both felt on his arrival pinned me to the blue velvet armchair in which I had enthroned myself, the print on my dress of watery flowers in yellow and pink making me feel like a princess with two knights.

Uwe was vying for my surrender with extreme loving warmth and easy charm, plying me with sweets, an approach I preferred to my father's uneasy choreography – he stopped in passing to flick my knee or touch my nose as if to stake some claim on his way from the window to the mantelpiece and back again, energy sparking almost visibly from his eyes and his fingertips. Mum was stirring the pot at the stove with her back to us not to join in.

It occurs to me now Dad must have stayed on my account because he wanted to see me even if he was feeling the awkwardness, he wasn't going to give up on me, or perhaps he was compelled to remain because Mum was unavailable, his desire more urgent if he thought she had moved on. I don't know if he was hurt, he must have been hurt, and I felt his discomfort as my own, my unease so intense that a part of me wished he would just go home and get on with his painting. I favoured Uwe over him at that point; Uwe made me feel safe and I wished he were my real parent very briefly, before I got to know him. I loved Uwe but came to regret every moment of affection I had ever squandered on him, every time he had made me feel loved for his own ends. That was the first time I was conscious I had made a mistake in my feelings. I came back to Dad in my heart and was thankful he and not Uwe was my real father.

We had no bathroom on the ship, a detail of which for some reason I have only just become conscious, never before having felt the lack. Uwe made us line up naked on the deck every morning and doused us in seawater, letting down his bucket over the side even if he had to break the ice first, the punishing Germanic ablutions not very effective at removing dirt but supposed to improve us in other ways.

In port if Mum had enough cash she took us to the public

bathhouse, everybody jumping naked into the icy water of the plunge pools, nothing on offer and nobody looking to see what they could get if they stared hard enough. We tried to keep our eyes to ourselves in that temple of meaningless nudity, not to take any interest, but on the way back to the harbour Ali and I sniggered and gawped at the buttocks and bosoms displayed openly in the shop windows, Mum attempting to herd us past the double-page spreads as quickly as possible. The rosy-hued body parts looked so heavy and were manhandled with such unexpected leverage in the photographs I failed to connect them with my own physiognomy, the bodies in the bathhouse or the modest womanhood of our own mother, a person who swam in her jeans not to have to undress on the rocky strand and who walked naked between the sauna and steam room like the Little Mermaid treading on knives, although I was already beginning to recognize the common pressure of greed for love misery that women seemed to share and that might leak out or spill over. We referred to those magazines as BUM BOOKS when we talked about them on the way home to Marstal, naming the exposed anatomy of the protagonists in English or one of the other languages we picked up from Uwe and the rest of the crew, and as we passed by the woodyard we shouted out the name of the disgusting flowers that bobbed on the scrappy bushes and trees growing wild amongst the pallets and planks, calling them WILLY BLOMSTERS because of their phallic appearance, the long blossoms in bodily shades of purple and mauve.

I was surprised to find that the same obscene plants flourished all over Islington when we got home, and that my father was enamoured of them as he was enamoured of all emanations of life springing up in parts of the city still undeveloped after the war. He told me they were called buddleia, and I tried to admire them because he admired them, making the effort but still failing to see what he saw in them, failing to understand his enthusiasm. Eventually I did learn to enjoy the sight of those arching shrubs seeding themselves in neglected neighbouring gardens and in his own garden, along with the bay and the fig tree I gave him, but even now the flowers disgust me up close, the bracts of tiny petals crawling with insects and arousing in me if not the actual childish loathing that made me turn away and giggle in horror at the sight of those blooms bobbing over the stacks of planked wood in the woodyard behind the shipyard, exposed in the Danish sunshine, the flowering spires neither entirely flaccid nor fully erect, then the adult version of that feeling, transmuted and understood.

Until I read the diary I had completely forgotten the conversation about incest, although about a year or so after our repatriation from the Caribbean, following an outing to Soho, just the two of us, I did have a word with him about his behaviour.

Had I been two or three years older we might have spent a couple of hours at Muriel's with Francis, an elegant jazzman playing the upright piano in the dark bar and singing along if we struck lucky, Pernod my favourite tipple, my father choosing to believe if he drowned the pastis he would render it harmless on my behalf like lemon barley water, always congratulating me on my good head as I floated down the stairs in his wake on our way out, his admirable daughter determined not to fall over. But on the day in question I was still too young for afternoon drinking even in that topsy-turvy world, so he took me to Patisserie Valerie, a treat that should have been enjoyable.

He ordered a pot of tea and flicked through the evening papers, not seeming to mind we had to share the communal table with three or four elderly ladies in fur coats talking amongst themselves in Italian, and I tried not to gaze too covetously at the gateaux displayed behind the curved glass of the counter, assuming without even thinking about it that the glazed berries, rosettes of whipped cream and palisades of white chocolate were out of my reach. He addressed the waitress by name – she was called Maria, a curly-haired woman in a waist apron, not difficult to annoy when she got old if you lingered over your empty cup or spent too long in the lavatory. She cleared a space for our tea cups and put down a large plate of cakes, right in front of us – the Italian ladies had their own selection. The cakes were not as fancy as the ones behind glass but even so I was slightly bewildered by Maria's munificence, and unsure of the financial implication of it. My father hadn't ordered anything apart from the Darjeeling, which was brown and strong, not like the weak milky tea Mum gave us when we got home from school, even though she loathed tea, because of her mother, who lived on it.

I realized Maria was tempting us with the cakes, knowing we would be unable to resist. I looked round at the other customers and learnt from their example we were supposed to help ourselves from the big plate, one or two each, perhaps three in extreme circumstances, the Italian ladies consuming the evidence with dinky forks and apparently trusted to confess afterwards. I wanted the baked cheesecake and took it – Dad encouraged me – but as I ate he stuck his fingers in every single cake that remained, breaking off and scooping up small lumps of millefeuille or almond macaroon, unable to find anything to his liking but continuing in hope until every cake was spoiled, even the most unpromising, his cake fork still wrapped in his napkin. He had not intended to eat anything, that was obvious, otherwise he would have ordered something from behind the counter, a slice of the syrupy green pistachio sponge with raspberries or a tower of glistening chocolate profiteroles in a metal cup. He didn't seem to notice or care that the elderly ladies looked horrified.

I ploughed through my cake of choice, ashamed to enjoy the sodden sultanas and claggy crumb, that delicious balance of lightness and richness. I guessed that my treat deserved disdain like the broken macaroon and the millefeuille, but loved it all the same and was determined to finish it, unable to stop myself from finishing it, never once in my life having failed to finish a slice of cake. I asked him if he wanted a bite but he shook his head and smiled at me in spite of his own disappointment, raising his hand to make a scribbling sign in the air. Maria came over with her small carbon pad and assessed the damage without remarking on it or reprimanding him, not that anybody ever reprimanded him, at least not on my watch. I was worried he would kick off when she gave him the bill but he paid with a ten-pound note, one of several crumpled notes he took out of his pocket, and left a big tip, the coins in the saucer drawing my eye as I dismissed from my mind as untenable the idea of pocketing them to give to my mum. Maria scooped up the coins and shrouded the despoiled cakes with a napkin before removing them.

We drove home through empty streets in the orange Mini he had borrowed from Jane Willoughby while he was between cars, the silence between us broken occasionally by snatches of tuneless singing, one of his favourite songs by Fats Waller, 'I really hate you because your feet's too big', comedy lyrics I couldn't help but take personally because I was already a size six and a half and no reason to suppose my feet had stopped growing.

He parked outside 17 Lonsdale Square, jumped out and opened the car door for me before I could open it myself, ready to assist me, although I was only nine years old and perfectly capable of climbing out of a car on my own. I pulled down my skirt to prepare myself, full of cheesecake and conscious of the challenge ahead – in those days people went on about the rules of conduct as disseminated at Lucie Clayton College, and although I was quite certain all that undermining car etiquette was not aimed at me I lacked the confidence just to disregard it and tumble out in my own way. So I smiled, slid sideways as gracefully as possible, my knees pressed together, and shuffled from the passenger seat onto the pavement, my main concern not to flash my knickers.

In my highly sensitized state my father's fingers felt way too sharp and insistent at my folded waist, but once I was out of the car he backed off and lit a cigarette, preparing himself to approach the neo-Gothic front door of my home and give me back to my mum, who may or may not have been pregnant already with Susie. I am pretty sure she was pregnant, although I have only recently realized that Susie must have been conceived very soon after our return from our travels, as though my father was waiting for us to come back and we could all take up again where we left off.

I shielded myself behind the car door as I spoke to him, my torso framed in the car window, visible through the glass but out of his reach. I didn't say anything about his cake binge at Patisserie Valerie but as gently as I knew how I asked him never to touch me again. He must have understood something about my distress because he obeyed my edict without asking any questions, he heard me and was able to respect the blanket ban that deprived us both of the ordinary physical closeness between father and daughter, all the fatherly affection I might have received from him had I not said anything to discourage him. He might have remembered how to hold me in a gentle way, and I might have been able to let him. It makes me weep now to think of that deprivation.

My awkward exit from the orange Mini reminds me of a party where a male friend of my mother's called Ginger, a petty criminal from our neighbourhood, tickled me until I almost wet myself, which was painful and humiliating. The party was at 47 Lonsdale Square, the home of Dan and Christine Oestreicher, Dan's daughter Lucinda my best friend at the time. I was squirming on the floor, Ginger kneeling to poke me with his stiff fingers, and above me on the wall hung a large red and green picture, big geraniums and brickwork in an urban garden, painted by Tim Behrens, the man whose proposal of marriage Mum had turned down at some point in the distant past, not that either of my parents had ever mentioned Tim in that conection. Tim's twin daughters were in the same class as me and Lucinda at primary school, along with the daughter of another of my parents' friends, who used to play skipping and two-balls in the playground with us. At play-time on the first day back after the summer, our last year together before she went to boarding school, I asked this friend what she had done in the holidays. She told me that she had gone for a joyride on Paul's penis. I asked who Paul was, and she told me he was her father's best friend.

My dad locked the car and flicked his cigarette butt into the gutter. The front door of the house was always unlocked, at least during the day, the hall floor gritty and littered with brown leaves and newspaper. He bounded over the doorstep and through the litter, fuelled by all the sugar he had consumed, seemingly careless of the signs of domestic dereliction. I didn't mind him seeing how we lived, but all the rubbish blown in on the breeze made me angry with my mum. She should have been able to keep it back with a broom.

Her style was more Lady Madonna than finishing school, although her sister Bulie was sent abroad to one of those places to get her out of the way when scandal broke following their parents' divorce. Mum was photographed on the staircase of our house as Lady Madonna for a book about the Beatles, not that she was recognizable in the image, the camera lingering in a suggestive and unparticularized way on her long hair, the draped shawl of knitted lace in which baby Susie was hidden, layers of peeling paper and paint on the wall behind her. The romantic image was a wasted opportunity for all of us to be properly proud, her face blurred like she was not good enough to be seen as herself – she could have been anybody. Although we were proud anyway.

Dad and I went upstairs to the kitchen. He ate all the cheese out of the fridge and pushed his hand between her thighs from behind while we were waiting for our supper, the dry skin of his palm grating inaudibly against the fine wale of her corduroy trousers. He was sitting down and she was standing up, spoon in hand, leaning over the table to dole out the noodles, sauce of fried onion and tinned tomatoes. There was no cheese left to grate over the pasta, but she didn't admonish him, she didn't say anything, and

I am reminded of an anecdote he used to tell me about the time he went to visit Bella and Esther at the Old Laundry, the house in Sussex where they lived with their mother and stepfather Christopher, their little brother Noah and Christopher's other children. Christopher invited Dad to break bread with the family and they all sat down to eat at the long table, Christopher at the head with Bernadine beside him and Dad at the bottom end with Bella and Esther, the conversation a bit stilted inevitably but everybody managing to keep it civilized. Towards the end of the lunch, some of the children still picking at the remains of the food, Christopher put down his knife and fork and scolded Esther for thoughtlessly eating cheese, a reprimand that was the punchline of Dad's anecdote; he believed it established beyond doubt Christopher's fatuous pomposity.

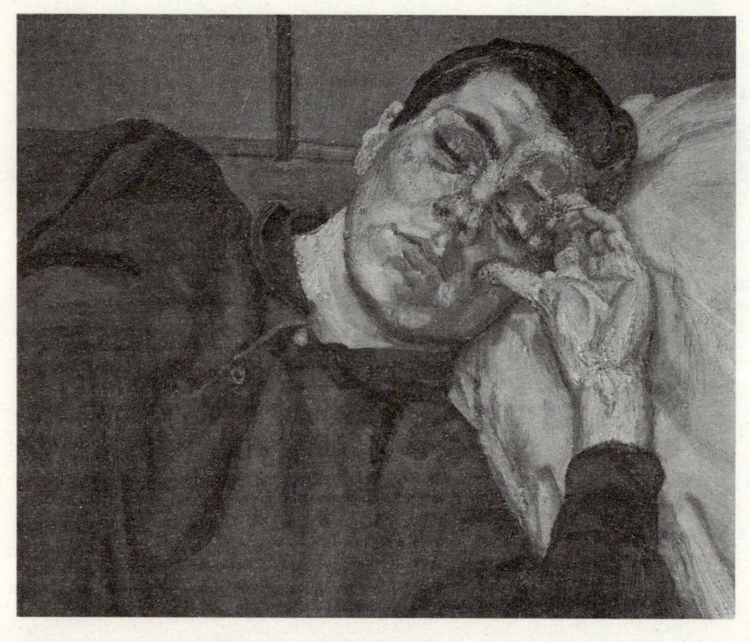

Rose (1990)

LUCIAN FREUD

ELEVEN

At my interview for university I was asked if I had a favourite poem and I said yes, 'My Mistress' Eyes are Nothing like the Sun', no contest, because it was the only poem I knew off by heart, thanks due to my father for that – I may well not have got in otherwise. The professor prompted me to talk about the way the sonnet repudiates overblown simile and ridicules a certain type of verse, but I didn't pick up on the hints because to me the poem was about love, not that I knew much about love, but I knew more about love than I knew about poetry. I thought the poem was only about sexual preference, the poet loving his mistress not because she was archetypically feminine and attractive but because she was real, maybe like me, with all my imperfections, lovable not because of or in spite of failings in relation to the ideal but just in herself. I understood the 'false compare' was about women, not about poetry. That gave me hope.

As my father's daughter I compared myself not only to the lovely half-starved women he desired and painted as I was growing up, their ribs and hip bones and cheekbones, but also to all my girl siblings, bigger or smaller than me, fatter or thinner, plainer or prettier, more or less conscientious and able to take care of themselves, more or less beloved of my father, and it took me a long time to grow out of the habit of comparison and live comfortably with them and myself, ridding myself of the shame of jealousy if not the jealousy itself in its entirety and loving them all, my sisters.

And Mum used to compare me not only to her sister Bulie, who bullied her when they were little and had a strong face, but also to the Wild Woman of Borneo, an indigenous person captured and displayed in a Victorian circus, neither comparison intended as a compliment, although I didn't mind the second one and imagined my mother had been subject to the same evaluation, perhaps when she forgot to brush her hair or bared her teeth and hissed at her mother and father or stepfather when they tried to bring her down. I hope she was able to rage.

One of the nursery rhymes she used to recite has stayed in my head because they were both in it, my parents, one way or another, not on the surface but represented just the same, as I was in Clementine, believing it was part of me in the foaming brine when my mum sang

ROSIE lips upon the water
blowing bubbles mighty fine.

The rhyme that contained both my parents was short but expressed vividly the unpredictability of the adult world, the language of which I never stopped trying to decipher, the fallout turning up the dial of my mind beyond caution, beyond recklessness.

Queen Queen Caroline
Washed her hair in turpentine
Brushed her hair with a leg of a chair
Turpentine to make it shine
Queen Queen Caroline.

The turpentine was my father, the sharp oily smell of the studio, the rags, his chef's trousers smeared with Naples yellow, burnt umber, lead white, and the invocation of the improvised hairbrush was my mother, the turned leg of the old blue velvet armchair she had inherited from her mother, not that mine would have bashed herself over the head with the chair leg should it have broken off at a party or during a rough game. She didn't use turpentine cosmetically but washed her hair in washing-up liquid at the kitchen sink, insisting it was all soap, a frugality in which she persisted until her hair was so dry and tangled she was no longer able to get it to lie flat, the avoidance of flat hair perhaps the unspoken motive behind her choice of detergent. The leg of a chair, interpolated into the poem where it does not belong, was lifted from 'Dan, Dan, The Dirty Old Man', who washed his face in a frying pan. In the amended version the Queen is unable to take care of herself properly. I wonder what happened to that heirloom armchair with its winded back like a big spoon. My mum must have shed it somewhere along the way like pretty much everything we ever owned, the damage and loss of domestic objects a memorable aspect of her housekeeping, each deliberate or careless act inculcating in me the belief that nothing was permanent, nothing was safe, nothing too precious to be broken or mislaid.

I am tentative here, not sure about what I am saying, but sometimes I wonder if I hated my father as well as loving him, the hatred almost impossible to own or admit to because we all worship him in our own way, his children – we won't have a word said against him. It was hard for me to bring my ambivalence to consciousness because I was not sure enough of him or myself to accept ambivalence as an ordinary aspect of any familial relationship, and I am sure that this unconscious emotional inconsistency contributed to my anxiety. Of course I wanted to believe in him, he was my father – I had no wish to cast him off, no wish to be cast off. We all need guidance, and he seemed to know everything. He comforted me with his certainties, but when he was in full flow at the easel, working up a scornful analysis of a mutual acquaintance or family member for example, slagging off a former friend or even a small child in all her clamorous needs, her fight for her own survival, I began to suspect his hatred of his victim might not be justified. I wanted to put him straight, but it pains me to confess he was able to make me question my own feelings towards the object of his loathing, infecting me with his warped perceptions if I was not careful to block out the caustic noise of his attack. On occasion I did find the courage to interpose myself, but when my courage failed me I felt sick of myself, complicit by default, my nausea in his presence teaching me if nothing else to ask myself why he was so spiteful. My shame was as intense as the shame I felt every time I failed to challenge casual expressions of anti-Semitism when I was young but not too young to know any better, enraged over the hate speech but keeping my mouth shut for fear of getting my head kicked in. My father was horrible sometimes, but I persisted in my love and admiration in the face of his unadmirable behaviour, and I think it was this persistence and the unexpressed anger I harboured towards him, conscious and unconscious, that flattens the tone of the diary sometimes, how my voice is not really my own, not even deadpan, like I had no point of view, as though I had been hypnotized.

In my mind's eye the portrait of 1990 was benign and peaceful, a boyish young woman thinking her own thoughts, the work similar in intent to other paintings he made at that time of some of my sisters, the new paintings all quite lovely in their own way but nothing to write home about – I can remember thinking he made us all look pretty because he was feeling kinder towards us, more tender. And likewise the sittings were more restful, his demands less extreme. I didn't offer to get undressed and he didn't ask me.

It is unclear to me now how I was able so effectively to distort reality. That painting was not easy, not for me, nor for him. I found him much less thrilling than when I was a teenager, not as marvellous, perhaps because I was no longer a teenager, unless I have misremembered how I coped with the teenage painting as well as distorting the reality of the later one. One thing of which I am now sure, holding the naked pose for hours on end under his scrutiny must have been taxing not just physically but mentally and emotionally. It was my therapist who pointed this out to me recently.

Perhaps he was even less careful this time round because I was no longer a young girl. He just said what he liked, he thought I could take it or just couldn't help himself, no holding back for my sake. He pushed further and further against his own inhibitions, a little shamefaced occasionally when subjecting me to the worst of his material, grinning when he went too far like Les Dawson performing in front of his mother-in-law. Until I read the diary I had completely forgotten all that sex talk, how often I just smiled and even laughed a little when I should have put my hands over my ears and screamed SHUT UP YOU SICK FUCK.

I had completely forgotten how often I had to dissimulate for fear of the vengeance he might mete out if I crossed him, how frequently I cut off from my true self. Not that I dwell on my fear in the diary because my false self gets into that too. I am not surprised to rediscover scenes from my life I had erased from my memory – nobody wants to recall everything – but am unsettled to find I chose to omit intensely remembered thoughts and feelings, whole scenes, as if I were hiding something even then, if only from myself. My father was much less fatherly than I remember him, the stories that don't seem to have alarmed me enough at the time causing acute disturbance in hindsight, now I am able to look back and really hear the implication of what he was saying. I have changed, and not just with the times. He became so much milder as he grew old, more loving, and it was this version of him that had stayed with me.

Friday, 2 February 1990

George Clinton with Kai. He came back with me after the gig and I made him some supper.

Saturday, 3 February 1990

Not looking after Frances today so a bit of leisure for me. Government of South Africa announced their intention of releasing Nelson Mandela. Had a little lie-in, sorted out some records, did some washing for Pam because her machine has broken down, put my hair up in pipe-cleaner curlers for Catrina's party tonight, enjoying myself. Dad rang up and I agreed to be at Holland Park tomorrow at ten for the trial-run sitting. Got ready, make-up, hairdo, new John Galliano dress that I bought in the sale. Debbie came over, then Angus and Cerith, got a cab to Leathermarket Street. I spent most of the evening behind the decks. Kirsten was with her new boyfriend. He was young, a bit bitter and chippy, not the psychotic scar-faced headcase she had led me to expect. Debbie got so pissed and angry she shouted at Catrina, passed out, woke up and was sick all up the street. Poor Debbie, it was too much for her, all the happy married couples, all the babies, me behind the decks in my new dress. Most popular records all the old ones apart from Lisa Stansfield and 'Pump Up the Jam'. I got quite drunk but managed to keep most people happy. I KEPT PEOPLE HAPPY, WHICH WAS THE WHOLE POINT.

TWELVE

Sunday, 4 February 1990

Up early, drank some coffee then drove over to Dad's, feeling a bit fragile after last night.

Dad talked to me about Marie-Laure and Charles de Noailles, a man I have read about in Buñuel's LAST BREATH and also in Proust. Dad said he had visited de Noailles' wife often in Paris, it was an arranged marriage, they lived in a great mansion but separately, in very different styles. She was a big drinker and took lovers, while her husband was conventional, discreet, although like everyone at that time had a mistress or two, but not in the public eye. Dad said that the other day he was having a chat with Balthus on the phone and Balthus told him a story about Marie-Laure. She had got herself involved with a fantastically handsome composer from Russia or Poland who lived off women and was treating her so badly that Balthus had rescued her and taken her back to her husband. Dad said she used to have big lunch parties every day, inviting Poulenc, Cocteau etc. and sometimes even her husband, from his part of the house. Charles commissioned UN CHIEN ANDALOU and was sacked from the Jockey Club for doing so because it created such a scandal. He had put up the money for the film on one condition, that Buñuel would let his friend Igor Stravinsky compose the music, but dropped the condition as soon as Buñuel protested.

I have only just realized that when Dad said Marie-Laure de Noailles took lovers, he was one of them.

Sunday, 4 February 1990, cont.

Discussed how much he loved Gorbachev. Dad said he realized that there was no alternative but for Gorby to agree to the reunification of Germany, but that he really fears the Nazi/expansionist German personality. Already there is talk of the Fatherland. Dad thinks this puts us in real danger of another Hitler figure leading the German people into war. I hope he is wrong.

He told me a story about James Pope-Hennessy, a friend of his who was murdered in a very nasty incident, the consequence of picking up rough men and taking them home with him. Dad said Pope-Hennessy liked to be knocked about and boasted in the pub about receiving a huge advance for a book, trying to impress the workmen and other local people. He had managed to get a lot of money out of a woman by pretending to be in love with her and when he died his brother gave her some back, as much as he could get hold of.

He showed me a drawing he had bought of Frank's at auction that had cost him sixty thousand pounds. Of Stella, really beautiful. He told me that Frank started seeing her when he was about seventeen, then married Julia, left her for Stella, and now Stella is in her seventies is back with Julia.

Of drinks with Robert Lowell, Lowell said, 'John

(Berryman) would have loved to be with us now.' Also of a night out with Lowell and Caroline Blackwood at the Neal Street Restaurant. Dad was with Katie, they drank thirteen bottles of German wine (Dad and Katie not drinking much) then all went on to a party. Not long after they arrived Lowell sat down next to Katie on the sofa and began to chat her up. 'What have you been doing this evening?'

Lowell told Dad something about Eliot – he absolutely loathed Henry James, hated even to hear his name mentioned. Dad says he thinks Henry James is a psychological novelist, using more or less his own invented system of psychology. He said he could see why Eliot hated him, didn't explain but told a story of Maupassant coming to London and dining with James in the West End. In the restaurant Maupassant asks Henry James to go and pick up a woman who is sitting at a nearby table. Henry James refuses. Maupassant points to another woman, and makes the same request. This continues, Henry James always refusing. 'You don't know anyone in London, do you?' says Maupassant. This according to Dad showed that Henry James was puritanical, how different from Eliot. I said refusing to accost a strange woman in a restaurant was hardly my idea of puritanism.

Dad told me how much he loves Berryman's work. I must read it.

Brief discussion of addiction. Dad told me that my views did not take passion into consideration. He talked about Mum's courage in going to live with Tom, how she followed her feelings. Didn't slag off Tom and showed sympathy for Mum. He called her heroic.

I ate a woodcock, the last of the season. It was delicious. Then over to Lucy's and hung about, went home, Celia came over in the evening but I began to feel very strange, too tired.

Monday, 5 February 1990

Talked to Bridges about sitting, my tender feelings, how I long to be loved and cared about. Lucy's again, left at half ten, home to bed.

Tuesday, 6 February 1990

Sat again from eight in the morning until half ten as agreed, a manageable amount of time, not too overwhelming for me and enough time left over to get on with my own work afterwards. Bruce Bernard was just leaving as I arrived, Dad having made them both a meaty breakfast.

During the break Dad was eating Emmenthal cheese in slabs off a huge block, and raw bacon. He recited some Hilaire Belloc poems, not for the first time, and spoke of Belloc's anti-Semitism, also about Gillian Bott, whom he loathes. In passing he said he was a sadist. A few times he stuck himself in the thigh with the end of the paintbrush. I was hoping he might have stopped doing that. Beginning round the eyes. Showed me the bunched tendons in his hand that cause him pain and will have to be operated on. Talked about getting old, the stairs to the studio. No danger as yet of him not being able to get up and down. He said his mother could still mount them at ninety. He said he had a strong heart.

Talked to Rachel Calder on the phone when I got home. She is very pleased with my book. Hurrah. Lay down on my bed and dozed. Totally out of energy.

I am pleased I have begun to sit for this picture, but it is hard and very tiring to keep myself in one piece. Bridges misunderstands my exhaustion. I can hear anger in his voice but maybe the anger is mine. He says I am exhausted from the effort of trying to get inside his head.

Wednesday, 7 February 1990

Working on my book about inheritance, might call it DAYDREAMING. Sawed up planks for some bookshelves in my office. When Dexter came over to show me how to use the drill he said there was something wrong with the wall and he would have to do it for me next week. I felt furious, and by the time I got to Bridges I was ready to explode. He took it on the chin and all was well.

Supper at Angus and Cerith's. A yeast pastry tart of blue ewe's-milk cheese, delicious Dover sole, oranges with blood-orange sauce. Cerith announced his intention to go abroad for a year or two, to work as an artist in residence in Amsterdam, and when I asked Angus if he would go too he got very angry with me. He told me he wanted to buy their flat from the council and sell it as soon as possible, and that the Amsterdam plan was only one of many, as if he were dying to get away, perhaps connected to him not sitting for Dad anymore.

Friday, 9 February 1990

Bridges cancelled. Dad's 7.45 a.m. to sit. I agreed to arrive at the new time as it is getting light a bit earlier. He made phone calls in the breaks and so it was less concentrated. I tried not to talk too much, the Bridges cancellation not such a disaster this time, although getting up early and setting off I had to make a little bit of an effort to remember the reason for my journey.

Today heard news that Babs, the woman who has been pestering Pam on the telephone and sending her nasty letters, has given birth to a child, and Steve is the father. Pam seemed amazed, although she herself had shown me a letter from the woman in which the pregnancy was mentioned.

Sunday, 11 February 1990

Maya howled for a long time and told me she is having a horrible time at home with her mum's boyfriend. I think she is depressed. Her voice sounds depressed. I tried to talk to Dexter about her but he said not now, too depressing.

Nelson Mandela has been released.

Monday, 12 February 1990

The married couple in DAYDREAMING are called Pam and Steve, and although they are not entirely based on the real Pam and Steve it is very alarming when the real Pam and Steve begin to act out in real life the horrible things that go on in the book.

Bridges, got very upset. Trepidation about sitting tomorrow.

Tuesday, 13 February 1990

Up at six fifteen. Felt very depressed in the bath, but managed not to wallow in it. I like driving through the empty streets at dawn. The sitting went well. Nothing to be afraid of.

Dad said old friends are always trying to get him to do the very things he does not want to do. For example, Jacob Rothschild and David Beaufort are trying to persuade him to go to Madrid with them in Jacob's aeroplane to see the Velázquez show. He said 'If you don't do something for ages and ages you become afraid of it.'

This talk of his fear made me feel less ashamed of my own; it was consoling and a little disconcerting for me to think that he seemed to suffer from the same difficulty – I was in good company, not that I would have wished the misery of anxiety on anybody. My father loved London, and was almost always reluctant to leave; to turn down an invitation he just said he was working, which was always true, although he travelled back and forth to New York on Concorde a few times when Susanna wanted to go there, perhaps to visit her daughter, his longing for the luxury of her company stronger even than his disinclination. Likewise when my husband invited me to Rome for my birthday two months after we first met I accepted the invitation and was able to fly with him because I really wanted to be with him.

Tuesday, 13 February 1990, cont.

Dad told me about a pantomime of Cinderella put on privately for charity during the war, a show he went to three or four times starring Cecil Beaton as one of the ugly sisters, the other played by a well-known lesbian.

I told Dad about a case of mistaken authorship. Mum's Tom found an obscene poem by Beth Damerel at Northwold Road and assumed it was by me. On the strength of this discovery he gave me a hardback first edition of EROTICA by Anaïs Nin.

The book was a Christmas present. Tom's choice of gift puzzled me, but I didn't spend too long wondering about it at the time, my first reaction surprise he had the wherewithal and desire to give me anything at all – the book was in mint condition, he had children of his own (I used to babysit for him and his wife when I was a kid) and since his divorce he lived hand to mouth, buying and selling books and spending the proceeds on drugs or alcohol.

Had he told me about Beth's poem when he gave me the book I would have been able to correct the false attribution, but he didn't say anything. Mum must have given him my address and I yielded to his quiet insistence for her sake when he turned up on my doorstep, although I really didn't want to allow him in my home. I didn't know at that point he had found the poem and taken me for the demotic bard of masochism, disempowered by desire and up for anything, but even so I could see he was holding his own thoughts about me in his head, and there was nothing I could do about it. I didn't want to be in his head in any guise.

Beth was a family friend from Lonsdale Square and had been my flatmate for three months at Northwold Road when Bella was studying fashion in Italy. Once I had moved out, to Lucy's in Notting Hill, Tom must have gone through the empty rooms, bored and looking for something to read while Mum was serving her customers. He showed her the poem and she was relieved to point out his mistake; the poem was not by me – apart from anything else she didn't recognize the handwriting.

I am sure Mum would have blushed when Tom showed her the manuscript, her boyfriend thinking her daughter was gagging for sex at any cost to herself and not afraid to shout about it, all the body parts in upper case, red Biro on a big sheet of lined paper, and I can't think why Mum showed me the poem and told me about the mistaken attribution, her motivation both girlish and unaccountable. I don't know if she was aware of his gift to me of the Anaïs Nin book. I doubt it.

The following year he gave me a brand-new Mason Pearson hairbrush, just what I wanted, and I remember I was quite pleased at the time to receive it from him, glad he was kind and wondering if the hairbrush was a sign he was not as bad as I thought he was, although it was obvious Mum must have told him what to buy me and may well have paid for it, thinking of me and perhaps hoping I might warm to Tom in his generosity, hoping I might be able to see what she saw in him.

Also, he wanted me to like him. He continued to ring my doorbell when he was looking for second-hand books on the Golborne Road and under the Westway, maybe assuming because of my mum he had certain rights over me too, buy one get one free, a makeshift stepfather trying to establish some type of relationship. He admired Shane McGowan and perhaps hoped to bump into him – he knew we were friends, and wanted Shane to work with him on a musical film about the canal. The sight of him at my door with his shoulder bag and elegant scarf made me recoil in revulsion and dread but I was too polite for Mum's sake to tell him to go away, even when he was really out of it, his greeting laboriously chewed in his spitty mouth, one shoulder propped against the door jamb to steady himself, his long head lolling against the rendered brick. The sex message of the first gift was lost on me at the time, at least consciously, but now, reading this diary and thinking of him, I feel compelled to lump him together in hindsight with other men in my mum's life who were drawn to something polite and defenceless in me, a longing for love and lack of confidence in myself they thought they might be able to exploit. All those men made me hate myself. The hatred dirge in my head comes out sometimes even now, out loud, not directed at myself but at various male targets, the men in my mum's life and all the men I have ever allowed to humiliate me and make me feel like a piece of shit. I hate you, I hate you, I hate you.

Tuesday, 13 February 1990, cont.

The mistaken authorship of the obscene poem reminded Dad of another case of the same. A man called Paddy Swift didn't speak to him for thirty years and when Dad finally asked him 'Why the silent treatment?' Paddy

> Swift said it was because of the letter. 'What letter?' Dad asked. Paddy Swift said he had received a letter accusing him, amongst other things, of copying Dad's work, and had assumed it was from Dad. Dad thought the silent treatment had been meted out because he had had an affair with Oonagh Ryan, one of the Ryan Maidens, daughters of a large well-off Dublin family, Oonagh being one of Paddy Swift's girlfriends, although at the time Paddy himself was living with an American 'poetess' who according to Dad was horrible to him.
>
> Oonagh was known as Princess Oonagh because she had been married to a Belgian prince who had ended up in a straitjacket. Dad said she reminded him of Nora Joyce. This was Dublin in the forties. Paddy Swift ended up having children with Oonagh. Dad said that before she was a mother Oonagh used to go on in public about rape, she used to say that if anyone raped her daughter she would forgive him, a man must do what he must do, according to Dad a sort of erotic dirty talk that got everyone going. Paddy used to tell her off, he was shocked, but Dad said he really fancied her.

I am reluctant to say anything about Oonagh's erotic dirty talk and the beguiling effect it had on my father but feel obliged not to pass over the subject without comment, particularly as I failed to rebuke him even mildly when he told me about her rape talk and their affair.

I felt nothing much as he reminisced about her, and even had I been able to register the adverse effect on me of his anecdote I would not have chosen to take my father to task about his sexuality or his openness about it. He remarked that Oonagh was not yet a mother when she talked about rape, perhaps suspecting that if she had been she would have felt differently, hoping she would have felt differently, her lack of maternal care explained away by her childlessness, although maybe I am clutching at straws here. Her understanding and acceptance of a man's needs, however extreme, must have sounded promising to my father, but I am not sure he would have fancied Oonagh had the daughter been real, Oonagh's rape talk an invitation in all but name, his regard for motherhood complicating his more abject feelings about women. I understand now that Oonagh was winding him round her little finger with her fantasies of sexual violence, not that I am trying to exonerate him, and he was unaware as he reminisced that anything he said might have disgusted me. He talked, I was captive in the studio of my own volition, and what strikes me as I look back is how unaware we both were of my feelings as a daughter, even if he didn't yet know I myself had been raped as a teenager. He was perfectly open about the sexual excitement he felt when Oonagh spoke of her sacrifice of her fantasy child to some blameless rapist, and I was just scribbling it all down in the bathroom, not even passing comment on his shamelessness when I typed up my notes in the morning.

Tuesday, 13 February 1990, cont.

Also talk about Wings Day, Mum's stepfather, after the recent article about him in THE SUNDAY TIMES; he was a war hero and escaped several times from captivity in prisoner-of-war camps. Then Major Boyt, Grandpa, Mum's father. Dad said he was horrible. In the break we talked about Mandela. Dad said he was princelike, Dad said in fact he was an African Prince.

Home, Lucy came over after sitting for Celia. Everything much better suddenly at Bridges, acknowledging the guilt of thinking people are thinking bad things, the blurring of boundaries, failing to distinguish what is me, what is others, feeling you know what other people are thinking.

Home, nice phone call from Dad, made a tape for the car, early night.

Wednesday, 14 February 1990

Received the proofs of SEXUAL INTERCOURSE from America. Wondered and wondered whether to reinstate missing passage of Norman with chocolate round his mouth telling Mr Green about hanging the dog, went swimming, rang Francis Wyndham and decided to take his advice – he said I should reinstate the passage.

After work rang Angus to pick his brains about something and he was extremely rude and more or less put the phone down on me. He really hurt Pam's feelings on Monday saying he could no longer attend her birthday dinner on Saturday nor go to the run-through of Steve's new show on Friday although previously he had accepted both invitations.

Today saw my restaurant article in TATLER, chopped to pieces, they missed out all the best bits. Also a letter from Mum, sounding very cheerful and sending me 'millions of love'.

Bridges, about the baby in me.

Thursday, 15 February 1990

Ate rack of lamb for breakfast at Dad's not to hurt his feelings because he had made it specially, then sitting.

He sang,

'When you call round for a visit
My parents ask what is it?'

He said that's what Caroline Blackwood used to sing to him (after Hutch) to the tune of 'These Foolish Things'. He said that's the way he wants to be, always has – on the wrong side. He told me he had married

Caroline for her sake (because of her parents) and said he has never been chased by a woman because he is always too busy chasing, always chasing so doesn't know what it might be like to be sought after, to be picked up, never gives the woman the chance.

Caroline's family loathed him because he was 'not even nice' which I remember him saying meant because he was Jewish. My sister Susie said to me that he fled the Nazis then managed to gain the love and respect of the most anti-Semitic social group in existence outside Germany, London society being notoriously difficult to infiltrate, and I replied that he certainly managed to get some of his own back.

Thursday, 15 February 1990, cont.

Talk also of Torquil Norman, the monster. Dad said Tim Behrens' mother, who wasn't the least bit spiteful or social, said that Torquil was a fake, no Norman and no Torquil, meaning not from an old family, which explains his friendlessness, doesn't know anybody, in fact a Jew.

Also Dad talking about Steve, which amuses me. Dad said he thinks Steve is a bit brilliant. He loves to side with him against Pam. Steve's bad behaviour appeals, while Torquil's perfection appals him, makes him feel disapproved of. I am sure he is right about that, Torquil does disapprove of him.

Torquil was the husband of Anne Norman, my mum's best friend from the Slade. Anne was a painter and had five children, the same as Mum, although Anne lived in comfort and financial security and was able to continue to paint. Torquil was not only wealthy and handsome but loved Anne in a way that allowed her to be happy. Both of them stuck by Mum and all of us, whatever happened, and

Dad loved to pick them to pieces, maybe because Torquil's conventional benevolence and sense of responsibility made him feel guilty and ashamed of himself, although he actively denied those aspects of his personality. I think that's why he found Torquil so monstrous.

Any possible amusement to be found in his admiration of Steve should have been due to the irony in his inability to recognize his identification with Steve's cruelty, but I don't think I understood that. His admiration wasn't amusing, and now I can see only too clearly how I was spoilt by my desire to please and accept my father, not to judge him. If I had judged him I would have lost him, and I didn't want to lose him. I lost myself not just in my silence when I might have countered his voice with my own but in my inability under his influence to experience my true feelings of compassion and loyalty.

Thursday, 15 February 1990, cont.

Back home and finished writing a letter to the American editor Jean-Isabel McNutt explaining that I don't want to translate SEXUAL INTERCOURSE into American and that every single one of the three thousand commas she had added to it are unnecessary. Hope I can persuade them to leave it alone.

Long argument on the phone with Dexter. I was able to say what I wanted to say about Maya. He is leaving too much up to me, he doesn't consider my feelings, he asks too much of me, takes me for granted, he is leaning on me.

Then the phone rang again. Six o'clock, Laura is still at school because nobody has come to collect her. I rushed round to St Joseph's to pick her up. Nobody at home at Pam's and so I took her over to Ib's. Muddle and lack of comfort. Ate, Ib obviously very tired, took Laura home.

Pam phoned the police as soon as I showed up with Laura because it transpired that Babs, the mother of Steve's new baby, had taken to talking to Laura on the phone in a threatening way. The police kept on referring to 'Hubby' like Steve was a normal person, but Steve is the problem and there is not much the police can do about that. Left about midnight and went home to bed.

Friday, 16 February 1990

Bridges early, looking into my internalized father figure, the connection between the one who turns away from pain and the cruel inhumane one.

At home rang Angus and got the cold shoulder again. Then he rang back, came over and explained himself, something about me knowing about the end of his sitting for Dad before he did and then telling everyone. I told him I didn't tell everyone, he believed me, and we hugged and made up. I said I thought it was sadistic of Dad the way he had ended it – he gave Angus no warning then asked Cerith to sit instead. Felt much better having sorted things out.

Wrote to Jeremy Norman to tell him I would not be able to work for him. I told him about sitting and he understood about me dropping him in it. He is calling the club Embargo, one of the awful names I suggested.

Went over to Rachel Calder's to give in the SEXUAL INTERCOURSE manuscript, Lucy came over for supper.

Saturday, 17 February 1990

Dad's even earlier because of the light coming in earlier. This means I have to get up at a quarter to six.

He told me an anecdote about Martin Summers, of

the Lefevre Gallery, taking a woman he thought was Barbra Streisand to Annabel's. When he discovered that this woman was in fact a Streisand lookalike he lost interest. Some time later he met the real Barbra Streisand at a party and told her the story, hoping to endear himself to her. She stared at him and said, 'What are you, creep, some kind of starfucker?'

Also a story about Paul Hamlyn (Hamburger) in Berlin, the three Freud children and the two Hamburger children, Paul and Michael, Dad's oldest friend, walking in the park with their nurses. The form was to ask the nurses for money to give to the beggars, so when they saw a terrifying white-faced red-haired blind man sitting on the edge of the path they all applied for change and gingerly approached him, dropping coins in his hat and running away to catch up with their nurses. All the boys walked on, except for Paul, who doubled back along the path and emptied the contents of the beggar's hat into his own pockets. He was a millionaire by the time he was twenty-six.

Monday, 19 February 1990

Dreamt of a car chase with two murderers in the back of my car, me daredevil driving, trying to shake my passengers off my back by increasing my speed.

Bridges said I was depressed and I began to feel depressed. Spent the evening being depressed.

Tuesday, 20 February 1990

Up early, went to Dad's, arrived at half past seven as requested but it was too dark to sit until half past nine. Ib came to sit at half past ten but Dad said he had got on very well anyway.

Told Dad about Leigh Bowery at The Fridge on

> Thursday evening as told to me by Nicola, Leigh's girlfriend. Leigh stuck a hosepipe up his bum, Nicola turned on the tap, and Leigh's bowels filled up with water. He plugged his anus with a tampon and went on stage, hoping to contain the water until a point in the act when he would lie on his back, point his bum at the ceiling and become a human fountain, but the act went wrong and the water burst out unexpectedly and sprayed the audience with shit-coloured liquid. Dad doubted the physical possibility of this story, then went on to say that he himself could drink water up his behind. Talk about homosexuality. Dad said it was very rare to find a man who had no homosexual experience or inclination, apart from himself of course, but went on to say that he could possibly fancy a boy if it looked like a girl. He explained to me that without some kind of a spark sex wasn't possible for a man. I thought that went without saying.

I have only just realized he meant that a woman could have sex even if she was not in the least bit interested, out of obligation or if a man raped her, for example, taking it for granted that women have sex when they don't want to have sex and failing to take into consideration the fact that a man could be victim of the same crime. He referred to the boy as 'it' in his sexual musings, dehumanizing the young person and releasing himself from responsibility for his own feelings in the process. I remember at school one of the girls telling me that Lucian Freud was a homosexual and I thought she had confused him with Francis, who was known at that time as the horror painter, a term sometimes applied to my father. It was only after his death that I heard of my father's supposed sexual activity with Auden and Spender, Dad never having mentioned it, maybe with some shame or in the belief that I could accept anything sexual he wished to express as long the object was female. William

Feaver came round to my house to tell me about it with gleeful intention to shock before completion of his own book, motivated perhaps by envy of my father, who did not like him enough to paint him and paid him one million pounds not to publish. I assume Feaver gives full details of what was supposed to have happened but I can't bring myself to read what he has written. It's not that I mind about my father having sexual contact with the two poets if that is what went on, as long as the sex was consensual and did him no harm. Both poets were considerably older than him, regardless of their gender, and he was a vulnerable adolescent, a dynamic he was to repeat with the boot on the other foot not just with Mum and Bernadine but Celia and Katie and Sophie amongst others. I don't want to read Bill's version because I would rather not hear my father's distinctive voice parroted by the author in some muddled and mean-spirited imitative act.

THIRTEEN

A family member was living at Kent Terrace and my father told me he used to call it Cunt Terrace because a gynaecologist arranged abortions from his dreary consulting room in one of the houses, the procedures performed at a clinic in St John's Wood, everything perfectly legal, the doctor always very sympathetic and easy-going, snippets of information that made me think of those siblings of mine that never happened, not that I am anti-abortion, the cost of those terminations to the women involved an inevitable side effect of my father's selfish behaviour. In a recent telephone conversation with one of my family members I had assumed he was the same way with her, going on about sex and the repercussions of sex when she was sitting, but she said no, not at all, he never told her anything. She asked me why he was like that with me and not her and I said maybe because I was older and he felt I was more available for sex talk because he had sex with my friends when we were young, a similar violation of my daughterhood. She said it couldn't be that, because he had sex with her friends too, and I remembered one of them in particular he used to talk about with some interest. We were both quiet for a few moments, two sisters breathing together down the line, then I said maybe because of the bad things that had happened to me I was more of a victim, more open.

Tuesday, 20 February 1990, cont.

After the sexual spark conversation Dad told me an anecdote about a boarding house, told to him by the second-best safe cracksman in the country, who used to live underneath him at Delamere Terrace.

A bunch of Irish labourers were behaving so badly in the boarding house – farting, swearing, horsing around – that the landlady came upstairs and shouted at them – 'Get out of here, pack up your things and get out!' One of the labourers got his penis out of his trousers, put it on the table and said 'With a weapon like this I should have no trouble finding new lodgings.' The landlady said 'I wasn't talking to you, your dinner is in the oven.'

Then he told me that at Delamere young men used to shit over the railings onto old people coming out of their flats in the basement. Also that Tony Lambton said that nostrils were the most disgusting part of the body, they smelt so horrible.

When Ib arrived I asked her about the tummy ache she had been complaining of recently and she said she had discovered she was pregnant again.

Main topic of discussion today at therapy how much I adore Bridges. That seemed to get things straight. Everything felt much better.

Wednesday, 21 February 1990

Long phone call with Susie. She is very unhappy. Didn't realize how deeply this upset me and tried to go on with work. Pam came round in a state after the dentist, shaken and bloodied, with only one less wisdom tooth, so she will have go through the whole thing again next week.

Bridges, drowning, couldn't really work out what

> was going on. He said that I want to be perfect, number one, in relation to him and Dad, but I am not sure if that was the cause of my misery.
>
> Felt quite shaky and upset afterwards, then Jane McAdam came over. I found myself going round in circles, talking about sitting, the subject I had been discussing at Bridges. I am trying to keep up my resolve to tell Dad that I can only handle sitting twice a week as a rule rather than three times because it is too knackering and does my head in. Jane stayed the night.

It didn't occur to me how difficult it must have been for me, let alone Jane, my long-suffering new sister, me trying to welcome her into my home but lacking the good grace not to moan on about sitting when she might have loved to spend time with our mutual parent. My lack of empathy for her and myself makes me flinch now with sorrow over the pain of the predicament of her and her sister and two brothers, my phenomenal tactlessness expressing the unconscious hostility I must have felt towards her as well as my conviction in my confusion that I was the lucky one or at least wanted to come across like that. I don't know how she was feeling because I just took it for granted her estrangement from Dad was agony for her as it would have been for me, not that this assumption did anything to stop me from exacerbating any sense of loss to which she might have been subject.

Jane was keen to get to know me and my father through me if that was even her plan, and when she did make contact with him I was amazed to discover that he had allowed her to set up a modelling stand in his studio so she could teach him how to make sculpture. The modesty of his belief he might apprentice himself to her for his benefit was endearing in the respect he showed for her talent, but when I thought of their hands in the clay I felt tortured temporarily by the threat of their intimacy. I feared she would find favour with him and usurp me, which was a real possibility, and kept quiet on the whole topic of Jane while I waited it out, the little figure they constructed swaddled in cling film between her visits to stop it from drying out. I wanted him to be kind but wasn't surprised when he told me it hadn't worked out with Jane in the studio, he preferred to work on his own. I was sad for her but pleased she had gone, hardly even able to feel my own pleasure or admit to myself I felt threatened.

Thursday, 22 February 1990

Up at 6.45, set off for Dad's about half past seven, managed to get there only three minutes late because I drove very fast. Anxious. Much talk of Kay McAdam, mother of Paul and Jane, Lucy and David. How Dad felt no sense of responsibility for her, even when she was living in a basement flat near him in Paddington and the Irish tenants in the flat above jammed filthy mattresses infected with bedbugs into the gaps of the door that connected the cellar stairs with their hallway, as Dad put it, 'Filthy rubbish for the slag downstairs, the one with the children.' Dad said he advised her to call in the sanitation department. 'I have no sense of duty,' he said.

He tried to convince me and himself that Kay had many other boyfriends, although Jane and Paul think he was the only one. He said he can't understand how come all the children are his, what an amazing chance that would be, seeing as she had so many men on the go. Perhaps there were no other men.

Dad says he met a man at the Colony who told him to go and see his children. When he asked about them he was told that Kay was living with a man, a friend of the man in the bar. Paul and Jane have no recollection of any other man.

Then he says she was with a man with a beard, who slashed the tyres of his Alvis, invisibly, which Dad called an attempt at murder because the tyres could have burst at speed and killed him.

And there was another man, for whose sake Kay asked Dad to sign a paper saying the children were not his so she could get married to him, a marriage that never happened.

Also Ted, a man with scars, called Kay A GOOD SORT, which Dad said proved that he had had her.

AND Charlie Lumley – Dad arranged for him to hide out at Kay's mum's when he was on the run.

Dad said Kay had a persecution mania, that she was very easy-going but all her troubles came out in the mania. He wants to believe she wasn't too choosy about her sexual partners in order to absolve himself somehow from the blame of the family's poverty and his lack of interest in the children, although he is a million miles from admitting any guilt. As far as he remembers it, he told her that if she went to his mother to ask for money that would be the end of it and as she did go to his mother he took that as farewell. Who could blame her for going to his mother? The children were probably hungry.

He was very romantic about Paddington, the people who lived in his old neighbourhood, many of whom he worked from. I remember him marvelling at the impossible elegance of the women who emerged onto the street from the slum dwellings, a door opening and the sight of a high-heeled sandal and pale skirt on the broken doorstep, my father unable to understand how those women presented themselves with such charming smartness, their appearance entirely untainted by the extreme squalor of their surroundings. I asked him if he thought they were sex workers and he said no, he thought not. He said girls on the game use small signals to let you know, dangling their keys unnecessarily from the ends of their fingers for example, jangling their keys to draw attention to themselves in a particular way.

Thursday, 22 February 1990, cont.

A plan to paint Leigh and Cerith together, finally finishing Angus off, also talking about Orton and Halliwell, Dad said maybe there is an Orton and Halliwell situation in all queer couples.

Another anecdote – Charles Forte, while being interviewed by Dan Farson, was asked why he sold a small patty of cheap mince between two slices of stale bun for seven shillings and sixpence. When Forte tried to deny it and asked Farson where he got his information from Farson produced a hamburger out of his pocket. Forte asked him where he had found the evidence, not believing that he himself could have been responsible, and Farson said from the Forte milk bar right next to the TV studio.

Also a story of the profligate Duchess of Devonshire as painted in yellow by Reynolds. The Duchess, having gambled away all the money settled on her by her husband and afraid to ask him for more, went to Mr Coutts of Coutts Bank and asked him for two hundred and fifty thousand pounds, offering in return to introduce his daughters at court. He gave her the money but she never got round to making the introductions.

And his favourite subject, justice applauded, equality derided. Plainly something he read in Nietzsche as an adolescent and has never grown out of. He likes the grandeur of it. Painful to see him battling with guilt and using these formulas to keep the truth at bay. I managed to say 'I do not want to sit again until Tuesday,' so left with a sense of freedom.

Friday, 23 February 1990

Bridges first thing, feeling a bit more stable after the difficulties of the last few days, Dad's power, his cruelty, what is him, what is me.

Saturday, 24 February 1990

Lucy's for lunch with Frances. Lucinda and David Jane arrived from Cambridge with their two children. The atmosphere a bit strained – they know Celia's son Frank, my little brother, because their children go to the same school, and they told me how he had pushed their youngest child down the stairs at a children's party. Their youngest, Matthew, wouldn't let Frances play with any of his toys, so I can see Frank's objection to him.

Monday, 26 February 1990

Told Bridges the dream I had about him telling me that I couldn't have psychotherapy anymore and then turning himself into a little crisp-haired frizzy brown man. He told me his holiday dates. The Easter break is very long. Four weeks.

Tuesday, 27 February 1990

Dad's first thing. Woke up feeling very depressed but it cleared off a bit as the sitting progressed. He played me 'Makin' Whoopee' by Eddie Cantor on his record player and said how much he loves it. We talked about drowning, death by drowning coming to mind because on his balcony the shanty town of sheet polythene protecting the leaky roof was flapping and billowing like sails in a storm. He told me that if he had a choice of ways to die he would choose death by drowning, the least unpleasant way to go. He said the humiliation of being ground on the seabed was so bad it made you laugh. I got caught in the aftermath of a tidal wave when we lived in the Caribbean. The sea knocked me over, took me down to the bottom, held me down and ripped off my knickers. I came up naked, fighting for life, my thighs and stomach grazed on the sand.

Talk of drowning led to THE MILL ON THE FLOSS, everybody drowned at the end to get George Eliot out of an impossible plot situation. I said moral positivism was a good philosophy for a novelist – everything will be all right in the end if you try to understand yourself and others and get at the truth and do what is right. A good idea with which to shape a novel, because it gives tension to the plot, is not just subject matter but form too, a journey of discovery. He said Nietzsche's ideas would be better to work with, then the phone rang and he went off to answer it, so I was saved. I noticed a copy of the portable Nietzsche on the bed in the studio so he's obviously been reading it, looking for catchphrases with which to shore himself up.

What next? Mean talk about Janey, her monthly miseries. Dad said he shouted at her once, 'WHAT ARE WE IN MOURNING FOR?' He said that even if somebody loved every inch of her from her fingers to her toes she would still suffer. He said he tries to be considerate on a day-to-day basis although he knows he is basically inconsiderate. He told me a story about Gillian Bott. She made a skirt for Janey and when she delivered it she told Janey she was sick of all her own friends. 'I am sick of all my friends, the life I lead, could you introduce me to some of yours?'

I told Dad that David Rosenthal phoned me from Random House in America with good news – they are going to print ten thousand copies of SEXUAL INTERCOURSE. I added that David Rosenthal says 'fuck' all the time and Dad said maybe he was trying to put me at my ease.

Also of John McEwen, Katie's younger brother, who is going to marry Vivienne Haig this autumn. I said he had a habit of putting his hand up to his mouth and giggling. Dad said that gesture was just like Robin, John's father – he used to do the same thing.

We talked about weakness, but not in relation to ourselves or each other. He said WEAKNESS COULD BE A FORM OF STRENGTH.

Then he mentioned an article he had read in THE INDEPENDENT. The journalist, a woman, described spending the night for the first time with a man who woke up at four in the morning and sat on the edge of the bed with his head in his hands and said he was not ready, he needed more space. Dad ridiculed the woman who wrote the article for seeing this event as an example of fear of commitment. He said, 'Doesn't it even occur to her that it might not have been the best night of his life?' He read the problem as sexual distaste on the man's part. Although he did say that everyone was familiar with that feeling, of needing more space.

Some painting time wasted because Dad was on the phone to Charles Saatchi, trying to make arrangements about the wall and floor colour of the gallery for the forthcoming show of some of his and Frank's pictures in the Saatchi collection. Dad and Frank both mad keen for charcoal grey walls and a darker shade of the same colour on the floor.

Ib turned up at ten thirty so my sitting was terminated painlessly – that was a help.

My agent rang to say Frances Coady likes my new book and is going to buy it. Bridges. Talked about my depression, the holidays, then went to the supermarket.

Wednesday, 28 February 1990

Bridges in the evening. Three mysteries, why I keep on losing him, why can't I stay with him, why doesn't he want me? I continue to be oblique rather than direct. Home, supper, BROOKSIDE made me weep. Storms overnight.

Thursday, 1 March 1990

Dad's first thing. He seemed in a very good mood, work on the picture going very well. I have an enormous nose in it but I don't mind. He was having difficulty with a letter he was trying to write to Chris Bramham, said he just found it so hard to write, to spell. Ended up copying a quote out of TWILIGHT OF THE IDOLS, about Art and Frenzy. He said that Eliot had said that Nietzsche was good for cheering yourself up. That is about the long and the short of it. Part of the quote, not the bit in the letter, is about the Swollen Will and I suggested it should be called the Swollen Willy. The page that struck Dad as so marvellous seemed psychotic to me. I remember cheering myself up with similar when I was a teenage spiky-head in bondage trousers. Cheering yourself up with Nietzsche to spur yourself on for life/art is a bit like using pornography to get yourself in the mood for sex.

Also talk of the poll tax, Dad didn't know what it was, he thought it was something to do with pole cats. He couldn't understand why they should get lots of money.

He gave me a beautiful regency lyre chair because I said I was looking for an armchair to sit in and read. I am extremely pleased. No more reading on the floor in front of the fire.

And talk of Anne and Torquil again. Dad said he thinks Anne is so arrogant, has such a terrible cruel side, turning away from other people's suffering, a narrow scope, no compassion.

I said to Dad that people who are out of touch with their real selves are often out of touch with the reality outside themselves and he agreed with me. This is subtly in THE DEAN'S DECEMBER, a glimmer of this idea, and I want to use it also in my next book, the distortion of the image of the self that leads to distortion of the perception of the outside world. Then about Angus, I told Dad about the Yugoslavian doctor poet and said that Angus had given him my number. Dad said maybe that was why we were not getting on. I said 'No, that is not it, ANGUS IS UPSET ABOUT THE WAY IN WHICH YOU TERMINATED THE SITTING ARRANGEMENT.'

He said that Angus must be wretched. I said yes. Then he told me a few things about the end of the sitting. According to Dad, Angus had shouted at him, said that Dad was putting the thumbscrews on him, and Dad said he couldn't help minding about Angus being late. And Angus had borrowed eight thousand pounds. Dad said that that was a good thing, Angus would not be able to repay him to get his own back. I said I thought that was not good, because Angus is so fond of him. I

> said Angus must have felt dropped, and the termination of the arrangement coming so soon after the angry outburst probably made it worse, made him feel he had been sacked because of it. Dad said yes, there was a bit of that in it.
>
> Then Dad said he had been invited to a Saatchi dinner and could invite a friend or two. He mentioned Angus in connection with the event and I encouraged him. I said that I wouldn't mind going too and Dad said he would put my name down on the list. I don't know whether he will, he is unsure whether or not he will go himself, but I said it would interest me.

Angus was wretched, and my nudging intercession on his behalf lifted me above my unconscious identification with him and brought me closer to my father, who seemed to want to make amends with him if only in a mild way. I was harbouring resentment towards my dear friend, my unfelt wishes revealed in my retaliatory deployment of the word *termination* – nobody wants to be terminated. Angus had been suffering but unlike me he was able to shout about it, true to his feelings even if his expectations were unrealistic, the consequence of his angry outburst the end of a long working relationship.

The outcome had a horribly predictable inevitability to it, looking back, my father tending to shut down suddenly if anybody expressed too much loving wretchedness over him in the studio, too much pain or disrespect in response to his demands; he had a long history of falling out with people. Had I been planning to express any anger about my father's behaviour towards me, the stealthy way he increased the length of my sittings for example, adding on extra time at both ends outside our agreement as the painting progressed with no discussion or recognition of the impact on me, I would have been warned off by his treatment of Angus. I did and still do feel genuine compassion for my old friend, although in the end he was so angry and upset he asked me to choose between him and my father, as if I might have chosen him. And even as I was speaking out on his behalf I managed to invite myself to the Saatchi dinner, not wishing to be passed ovcr.

Friday, 2 March 1990

Brainstorm at Bridges, about my loathing of the feeling of dependence, my indirectness, turning away from closeness, why I lose him. Mum's after the session.

Monday, 5 March 1990

I am so looking forward to reading in front of the fire in my new armchair in preparation for DAYDREAMING. Hard to remain in a state of flux. I'm going to read EMMA, JANE EYRE and WUTHERING HEIGHTS. I am thinking about the sado-masochism of romance, hence my choice of reading.

Tuesday, 6 March 1990

Failed to set the alarm clock properly but luckily I woke up at seven anyway so with a bit of a rush managed to get to Dad's on time. The sitting was fairly painless today, and Dad was keeping me entertained with his stories.

Talk of speeding up a picture when it is nearly finished, a trick he applied yesterday to the one of Susie – pretending there is only one day left, that urgency, but without panic. He said she seemed well, he had bought her some Ella Fitzgerald tickets. Then said she was still hunched with sadness.

Of D. H. Lawrence, 'The Rocking-Horse Winner', about gambling, he said what a brilliant story. Talk of his own gambling, he used Victor Chandler with whom he is very friendly, and I said that their friendship, the money between them, would make a good short story. Dad talked about giving it up, which he appears more or less to have done now, although he said he would probably have one on the National. He said that even with a small bet of three grand a day that was three quarters of a million a year down the pan.

He told me that just before he stopped he had had a brilliant win with Victor, six hundred and seventy thousand in one day, but his previous losses were so great he was still twenty-five thousand down at the end of it. So he went on and on. He said imagine the voices in his head – THE WANKER, HE WAS ON A WINNING STREAK AND HE STOPPED – that was why he continued. Until he lost the lot and then some. The voices in his head do not sound very helpful.

He used to say you can't lose, whether you win or lose you still get the hit, but I don't know about that.

I am trying to imagine such loss. His claim that you still get the hit either way might have been disingenuous, to protect himself from pity, unless he was just talking about the adrenalin rush, equal in both outcomes, the buzz of destitution as loud as the buzz of success. Still, divesting himself of everything must have been liberating at least from the possibility of placing another bet, the relief of having to stop when you can't stop, and also from the possibility of taking responsibility for anything or anybody, empty pockets the perfect defence against the expectations of others. He painted the bookmakers who skinned him alive, their rapaciousness just one aspect of those friendships, and felt great respect and affection for them, although they triumphed over him, their homes full of his paintings. He took me with him to the Playboy

Club for the company and always gave me a chip to keep safe until he lost everything, knowing he would lose everything, the last chip still in my pocket so we could cash it in to get home. We didn't travel by bus but in one of the slick limos that were parked up round the corner, my father smiling calmly on the back seat as we sped down Park Lane as if he were relieved to be divested of everything apart from the fare, and me trying not to feel sorry for him. His forethought in the face of his compulsion reminds me of a story my brother told me after he gave up drugs but continued to reminisce fondly about some details of his former life. He bought a large bag of heroin, split it in two and posted one half to himself in the expectation the envelope would arrive the next day when he needed it, a combination of harm reduction and forward planning that seemed like a good idea at the time. He went home but had nothing left by midnight and was back out on the street again, fishing for his package in the postbox with a bent coat-hanger.

Tuesday, 6 March 1990, cont.

Anyway, Dad said that the brilliant win and huge loss with Victor made him stop. He said that when he went to see Dr Gormley about Ali after Ali had left some expensive drug clinic without completing the treatment Dad had complained about the money going down the drain and Gormley had said 'It's not money down the drain, the visit to the clinic will have spoilt his drug-taking for him for ever.' Dad said it was the same really for him, so much money was not money down the drain because such huge bets had spoiled his gambling for him – three or four thousand on a horse meant nothing now, a win of twelve thousand or so was somehow irrelevant after such vast amounts.

Well that is a massive relief. He said it was no coincidence buying all the flats, meaning he had been able to afford to buy flats for his children since he had given up gambling. I was glad he connected gambling to drug addiction. Both habits make the addict heartless.

Dad said he had remarked how robust Ali was, and Ali had pointed out to him that he is in fact fragile in some ways. Dad said that Ali was sentimental also, about women – he had met a girl whose nickname was Abdul the Turk and Ali had liked it because it went well with his nickname, invented by Dad, Albert the Dutchman.

He told me he had met Virginia Woolf when he was about sixteen, and she seemed really horrible. I said I had been unable to read any of her books. Then Dad said Kai referred to his girlfriends as 'the missus' even when they were quite new.

Then we talked about Mum. I told him that Ali had said that she was a typical adult child of an alcoholic or drug addict, and therefore would always look for abuse in a relationship, preferably with another addict. Dad said that Ali told him he thought Mum going to live with Tom was a self-destructive act, and I said Ali viewed Mum's relationship as an addiction, a sort of slow suicide, and one that she no longer has the strength to conquer. I said I agreed with Ali about Mum's behaviour – I could not see the heroism in her following her feelings.

Also about Pamela. Dad said there was something vulnerable, nestish, incestuous, open about her that made her attractive, that's what he liked about her. Insinuated or implied that he was seeing her in the Lonsdale Square days, I had no idea, she was Mum's friend. I used to like her. She betrayed Mum.

Then he said he thought it was wrong for a battered woman to leave her man – pointless, when there was nothing she could do about her sexual tastes. I said yes there was, she could try and get out, get over it, get help, find an escape from the habit of being abused, rather than submit to it. Obviously Dad would sec it his way, but he did listen to what I was saying. He talked about Delamere Terrace in Paddington, the Saturday night fights between men and women ending in crutches and plastered arms, how everyone would laugh it off in the pub the next day. He said that the men would say, 'I gave her a good seeing to last night.' He said that it was no coincidence people used the same phrase for both fucking and wife-beating.

But I also remember him telling me that making love was not called making love for nothing, because it could make you love somebody. He told me that when he was in love or very excited about somebody and happened to go out on his own to a party he found that his feelings made him very amorous towards other girls or women, much more amorous than usual, and I thought that meant he tried to dissipate his love to protect himself from it, from the consequences of it, inadvertently, maybe to avoid the pain of getting hurt. He was alarmingly vulnerable in love and never fully committed himself to anybody who was fully committed to him, and as far as I know never made anybody very happy, even himself, not that he aimed for happiness, or even regarded it as a worthwhile goal.

Thursday, 8 March 1990

Dad's first thing. So much talk. Described Scargill as a gun-toting psychopath. Then told me about his teenage visit to Dr Hoffer, a psychoanalyst. According to Dad Hoffer pronounced that Dad was homosexual because of the shape of his father's hat, 'a porkpie hat (not very Jewish) shaped like the end of a circumcised penis.' Dad said he 'had' a girl a week later. Hoffer was very nice, Dad went three or four times, at seventeen, because of his kleptomania, and afterwards Dr Hoffer sent him a bottle of whisky and bought one of his pictures. Dad said he was always stealing, and had done something really very bad. And added that Dr Hoffer left his bride-to-be at the altar when she confessed she was pregnant by somebody else. Dad found his behaviour very disappointing. He said 'It was enough to make you feel like an Old Testament Jew.' And then 'David Astor saw my aunt Anna for thirty years, bought a house at Walberswick (not true) to be near her in the holidays, I always wanted to ask him whether they had an affair.'

Of MY therapist, Dad's opinion formed on the basis of second-hand information received from Angus, about Bridges and his holidays. Dad sees Bridges as manipulative and again referred to him as the Venal Sadist, which I don't find very funny. I got a bit heated, trying to put Dad right – Angus had told him that Bridges presented the holidays as part of the treatment, which Dad thought was monstrous. I told him that it was not like that at all, that the holidays were recognized as not good for me, but however much I explained I couldn't really convince him of how much Bridges has helped me. Dad wants to see him as sadistic. He asked me whether I thought Bridges was more intelligent than me and I said yes and that shut him up. Dad said he was more or less only joking, obviously feeling guilty about the things he had said.

So Angus has been telling Dad things I told him in confidence about my therapy. Dad tried to convince me that Angus had spoken out of concern for me, because he was worried.

Writing the cheque for Bridges he asked me why my psychotherapist was called Jon. I said it was probably because his full name was Jonathan. So he began to write JONATHAN on the cheque, didn't know how to spell the end part so settled for JONATH followed by a beautifully drawn question mark. I told Dad that Bridges would send round the men in the white coats to take him away and he asked me not to give Bridges his address.

Annabel's anorexia, the drip, near death. Dad said her childhood was 'classic' as a case history of anorexia, meaning his split with Kitty when Annabel was tiny. He said the not eating part of anorexia was only one of the symptoms, and death a complication or occupational hazard. He has Freudian ideas of his own and yet so piss-taking about psychoanalysis. I keep on reminding him of its seriousness and how it helps people who are really disturbed. Of deriding it he said 'I only mean how they have it in America, like a parlour game, they even have it for dogs.'

Next he told me about the time he was giving a talk at a mental hospital on how art therapy is not art, about the intentionality of art, how art is wrought. He said he asked a patient at the back why he painted and the man said 'To chastise females, they should be chastised, whipped, stripped, because they are evil.' Another sadist. Dad said that the psychiatric nurse, 'a queer minder like the queers on Old Compton Street,' was egging him on. 'Mad people's pictures are so boring,' he said, 'because of the repetitive nature of madness, they make patterns, too mad to organize a composition.'

Of Pamela's son, according to Dad the child's drawings a classic case of the child's condition on the father leaving home, excitement about becoming head of the family, confusion, hatred.

Dad on the weekend, an American invention according to him, connected with popular wealth and leisure, a modern thing, reminded him of an old German song called 'Weekend and Sunshine', about happiness in the wood with a girl, a little car, the sun shining.

He said Lucy should read Nietzsche. 'She hasn't realized that duty stinks.' He asked me if he had read me the bit about frenzy. YES YOU HAVE! I defend her when he goes on about her, but not angrily. I should protest with more force.

I talked to him about loathing dependence. Dad said 'What about when you are in love?' I lied, and said that was different. We spoke about being out of touch with one's feelings. Dad hit the nail on the head – 'That would really make you panic.'

I find myself finishing his sentences for him but on this occasion I couldn't have done. While I was thinking about panic he went on talking but I lost it all. I felt lost.

About painting, few painters get better towards the end of their life, Matisse, Titian, I asked about Rembrandt and Dad said he peaked young and then stayed there. He knows he is getting better and better, although earlier he said he didn't completely believe in himself as an artist. He said he had friends who did, presumably meaning Frank, maybe Mike Andrews. He said 'If you are really perceptive and look at your work and know it is as good as anything then you really believe in yourself as an artist.' I said it was all wrapped up in the way you viewed yourself generally but Dad said he thought it was different, art being separate from the rest of life. 'I think of it as a sediment there is not much of, and hope to add to it.' I knew that he had his doubts. He said ART IS WROUGHT was the sentence if you were only allowed one sentence about it.

Got back, wrote this and began to feel very angry.

FOURTEEN

Monday, 12 March 1990

Finished EMMA, now reading JANE EYRE. Bridges, feel fragile but not too fragile.

Reading *Emma* for the first time when I was a teenager I was profoundly shocked by the relationship between Emma and Mr Knightley, not having seen it coming because she was a young girl and he was a patronizing old man, why would she want to have sex with him? I had believed I was safe with Jane Austen, nothing obscene was going to happen, then Emma capitulated and I felt disgusted not only by her suitor but also by Emma's father and the author, both of whom allowed Knightley to take what he wanted and failed to condemn his behaviour. Austen seemed to think he was doing Emma a favour. And Emma was supposed to be grateful because he owned a big house.

Monday, 12 March 1990, cont.

Just after I got home Kate Tilley (the elderly woman who lived at my grandmother's house and used to look after her) rang me sounding desperate then turned up, suicidal, and I spent the evening with her at UCH in the casualty department, trying to get her some help.

I had forgotten about Kate Tilley. Dad told me that her brother was Kenneth More, the famous English film actor, and I knew from the haughty resignation of her demeanour in my grandmother's kitchen Kate resented him in spite of her pride, not wholeheartedly but with the part of herself that couldn't understand why he had prospered and she hadn't. She hardly mentioned him but claimed some of his glamour by proxy and not only by proxy – she was leggy and tall, wore high-waisted trousers and soft knitted shirts in olive or dusty pink, and knotted a square of stiff yellow nylon to one side of her long throat, the pointed corners flying away over her shoulder.

At the Guinness home for the elderly, where she ended up after the death of my grandmother, she made spiteful enquiries about my appearance, having outlived the usual social niceties, and insisted with a sly smile I ate two chocolate digestives with my tea in the lounge when I visited her, supervising their consumption as if her life depended on it, her mood elevated by my capitulation as if she would become even thinner by comparison.

I don't know why she thought of me when she felt like killing herself. I didn't want to look after her, but I had been encouraged by Stephen's wife to visit the home and had been drawn in, not wishing to allow Ann to shoulder all the responsibility. Maybe Kate phoned Ann and Ann suggested she phone me.

The casualty department was very busy, and I was frightened I would be there all night, in sole charge of Kate until the arrival of the duty psychiatrist, who showed up not long before dawn. A bed became available at Friern Barnet and I was immensely relieved to realize there was no expectation from anybody that I might travel with the patient in the back of the ambulance. Kate shrugged her shoulders and waved quite generously all things considered before they closed the doors, reassuring me she would be all right and giving me permission to go home, her eyes full of tears because I had abandoned her. I almost jumped up and perched beside her on the shiny black trolley to which she had been strapped in a seated position for her own good, but I was too anxious and managed to stop myself.

I was shaken, frightened and very upset when I got home, and it was almost time to go to work. I rang Dexter for comfort, but he was a bit offish with me and suddenly I knew he had a new girlfriend. I had to phone Ib to confide in her, hoping she might be able to help, and she did her best, but afterwards I was still so upset I began to feel trapped by my father, phobic about seeing him, my resilience depleted by Kate's spite and her longing for death, not to mention Dexter's dishonesty, although I did understand he was entitled to get over me and meet someone new since I no longer wanted to be with him.

I didn't think to cancel my sitting because that would have felt even worse, to let Dad down on top of everything, and I didn't have his telephone number. I could have called his agent and asked him to ask Dad to phone me, but even then I wouldn't have talked about Dexter; I felt too stupid about him, although I might have talked about Kate, I could have blamed my upset on her suicidality; she had tried to make her death wish my responsibility, an extra sensitive subject for me because of Mum's threats. He might have let me off work had I spoken up, I could have asked him to go easy on me under the circumstances, but I had to hide everything. I arrived on time with a brave face pulled over my distress like a mask, my anxiety exacerbated by my belief in the necessity of pretending that nothing was wrong with me, not just my hands trembling but my knees knocking together under my navy-blue skirt.

He must have guessed I was upset but was not gentle in response, quite the opposite, although he might have been kind had he been in a different mood. His unkindness was a reaction to my vulnerability. I told him briefly about Kate, trying to be matter-of-fact, and he said he had never liked her. Then I sat perfectly still and silent in the grey light of the studio and he felt compelled to tell me in too much disgusting detail about a recent visit he had made to the VD clinic. He said he preferred sex with strangers, preferred just to have the exciting bit of the relationship without the courtship, the intimacy without the closeness, the marriage. His eyes were alight and I felt bruised by the cruelty of his enthusiasm.

Tuesday, 13 March 1990

Rang Dexter when I got home after sitting, he said he couldn't talk because he was doing the washing, said he would ring back, I knew he was lying, there was somebody there, felt betrayed, rang back, questioned him outright, he said yes, he was seeing someone.

This was a calamity for me right then, the Bridges holiday coming up, my part in Kate's hospitalization, the shock of Dexter seeing somebody or whatever is going on with him, lying to me, still lying even after he had admitted he was seeing somebody, my struggles with sitting, Dad turning into a sex monster in my head.

Cried and cried, broken down. Bridges was quite brutal. He pointed out to me I was being self-destructive because of the holidays, making myself ill. Lucy came over and stayed the night.

Thursday, 15 March 1990

Sitting, I was quiet again, and thankfully Dad was a little less voluble than on Tuesday. He talked about his eating habits, how he eats nervously, sometimes he thinks suddenly WHAT AM I DOING? and has to spit the contents of his mouth into the bin.

After sitting I went over to Bella's to look at her new collection. She was lovely, very understanding, and I really loved the clothes.

Rushed back to see Dexter but he was very late, even later than me. Had a bit of a talk. The pain comes and goes. He has met somebody else and I am left out. I really don't want to get back with him. There is hope here. The woman he is seeing is a classical dancer, and he has a sudden passion for opera. He walked me up to UCL for the Stanley Fish lecture.

The lecture was on Marvell. Met Lucy outside Dillons as arranged. Walking the corridors of UCL feeling confident and sensible, rather than out of my head on Ativan. The lecture was very exciting. I asked a challenging question at the end. I was shaking with the shock of my hand shooting up and my mouth opening. Afterwards Stephen Fender invited us to have a drink in the Housman room, sitting round a table with Danny Karlin, Stephen Fender, Phil Horne, Lucy and Angus and Cerith, drinking enormous vodkas and talking. Dreary Stanley Spencer paintings on the walls. Phil Horne congratulated me on my question, my courage. I felt proud and happy.

Friday, 16 March 1990

The last Bridges session. Shook hands at the end, he was really lovely saying goodbye, made me smile. I felt a bit shaky as I tottered off to the supermarket to get shopping for the weekend, but managed to take with me the feeling of his support, that fondness.

Back home Rachel Calder phoned to tell me that David Godwin at Cape was less than enthusiastic about my new book so it is being sent on to Chatto. A bit of a blow. I just hope Chatto are keen.

Monday, 19 March 1990

Prepared quotes for the back cover of the paperback edition of SEXUAL INTERCOURSE. I am emerging out of the shock of last week, although still feeling fragile.

Sat up with Lucy in her bedroom while she packed to go off to Bhutan for two weeks, talking until two in the morning. Talked myself in and out of anxiety, said goodbye, went home to bed.

Tuesday, 20 March 1990

First day with no Bridges and no Lucy. Dad's first thing. He talked about getting old, infirm. Also about the ugliness of tourists, their bewilderment making them ugly. Defined beauty as understanding, the visible manifestation of understanding. He said tourists are so ugly because they are lost, they don't know where they are going.

Thursday, 22 March 1990

Felt rested. Sitting for Dad again. Some amusing talk about Charles Clore and the Stork Club. He gave me a leg of lamb, very handy because Susannah Clapp is coming to supper on Saturday.

JANE EYRE. Lola came over to make some little cakes and play with coloured paper. Had a bath, got dressed up and went to the Saatchi Gallery to see the show I have been hearing so much about from Dad. Ib and Pat were in a Greek restaurant near the gallery with Frances, who wanted to come with me to the show and so I took her with me. She was wearing the stripy dress I had knitted for her. The gallery was so crowded I couldn't really see much. Harry Diamond, Julia and Jake, Paula Rego and Sophie de Stempel. I almost spoke to Sophie. A glamorous light, like London daylight. I must go back and see the show in real daylight. Afterwards went to the Globe, Gaz's, Freds.

Monday, 26 March 1990

Some good work but began to feel very anxious about the Saatchi dinner tonight. At five went to the post office to post the box of carnation soaps I bought for Kate, who is still in the mental hospital.

The Saatchi dinner was at the River Café. I wore my best dress, took a bus to Knightsbridge and got a taxi from there. The driver went the wrong way up the Cromwell Road and down the Talgarth Road and I felt very tense. At the bar a crowd of people milling around, and various people from the gallery came over and introduced themselves. I was surprised and felt important momentarily to be recognized. Frank and Julia arrived with Jake and his girlfriend, then Dad and Bella. Bella wanted me to go to the loo with her to discuss the suit she was wearing, one of the things from her new collection. I was touched and said I thought she looked great, very stylish and original. The Freud and Auerbach table was in the middle of the room and I was at the James Kirkman table, next to Gordon Watson, a friend of the collector Janet Green, who was sitting next to Dad. Bella was on his other side and I had to be brave because I felt pushed out not to have been chosen, although I decided I was better off in the company of strangers, in front of whom I had nothing to lose. Gordon Watson was extremely friendly. He kept on topping up my glass and asking me questions. I realized he wanted to get me drunk so I would tell him Dad's secrets. I don't mention seeing Angus and Cerith so I suspect they refused the invitation or that Dad decided against inviting them.

Tuesday, 27 March 1990

Sitting early. Felt a bit strange after all the red wine last night. Dad was very chatty. He told me about his assault on Jay Landesman. Jay put his arm round Dad at a party and Dad kicked him. 'My foot went right up his behind. I had to give it a good tug to get it out.' Jay said 'You are lucky I am in a good mood.'

Dad talked about Janet Green and monogamy. He told me that she goes out with a super-rich financier called Gilbert de Botton, about whom she went on and on to Dad on a previous occasion, how much she adored him, but last night seemed to have changed tack. She asked Dad about monogamy at the dinner, he told her he tried for it, then went on to talk about it to me, saying how good it was to have one person who was important to him for everything, in every way! Janet apparently was of the opinion that no one was monogamous; it sounds like she was making a pass at him, and seemed to have lost much of her allure in his eyes. I was heartened, Dad talking to me about his good intentions. He also told me he had been to look at a country house with Susanna, apparently without any very settled agenda, but anyway the trip was without consequence because the house was horrible. I wish he would get himself a country house, then I could stay in it. Also he might get a horse, and I would love that.

Dad's financial state must be looking up. He is going to pay for Frances to go to a little private school near Ib's, then suggested having a dinner for Ali's birthday on Sunday. I am going to make it at my flat and he is going to fund it. Oysters and everything. I'll have to hire an oyster opener from the Jubilee Catering Company.

He asked me whether I thought Frank Paul was all right. I said I thought he was young for his age emotionally and was a bit eccentric, a loner at school, but there wasn't too much to worry about. Although Celia has been worried about him in the past. Didn't tell Dad anything that Celia had said, because I assume that anything she tells me is said in confidence.

Talk of a dinner at Gilbert de Botton's with Martin Amis. Dad said one of the things he disliked about going out was waking up in the morning and running through his head all the things he had said the night before, stupid or otherwise. He said he thought there had been a misunderstanding at the Saatchi dinner last night, that Janet Green now thought he was puritanical. Of Kay, Saatchi's girlfriend, and the lyrics of 'Diamonds are a Girl's Best Friend'.

He talked about Ib's shyness as a child, then his brother Stephen's pathological meanness and his theory of Dad's illegitimacy. I interpreted his spite. Stephen was born first and then Dad, a year and a half later, when Stephen was one and a half, the new baby the cause of his emnity. Our conversation led to the story of the illegitimacy of Kitty's grandmother, whose mother was governess to the children of Lord Grey of Falloden; Lord Grey got the governess pregnant and she was given a cottage in the grounds to live with her daughter. That child was Kitty's grandmother, Annie and Annabel's great-grandmother.

After sitting went to Primrose Hill on my own and lay down on a bench at the top. Home, Lola and Johnnie came over for tea. Wild phone call with Debbie, I turned her terrible anger and brought about some kind of a resolution.

Wednesday, 28 March 1990

Ordered the meat and the oysters for Sunday.

Thursday, 29 March 1990

Sitting first thing. Dad suddenly announced he was going to give me five thousand pounds on the 6th April, my wages for sitting. Best bit of news for a long time. Afterwards went to Bella's to say goodbye before she goes to New York. Booked the oyster opener from the catering agency.

I was delighted to receive news of the cheque but I don't know why Dad didn't just pay me each time I sat like it was a job of work, so I could stop worrying about paying the bills and get on with my book. He was very generous with handouts when he felt like it but that was not the same thing as wages, regular sums that would have released me from the sense of dependence on him and his mood in relation to me. It did not cross my mind that I might negotiate with him for my time, although without me he would not have been able to paint me. I did not feel that power because he was always more powerful. He controlled the terms and conditions. That was the arrangement between us.

He never used debit or credit cards, preferring wads of new notes in his pockets, and once explained to me that he regarded money as ammunition, as if it were possible to spend it to kill people. He was quite interested in Damien Hirst but whenever we bumped into him or he came up in conversation Dad deprecated his cold love of cash, his avariciousness something to smile about, in his view the young artist more excited by his earnings than by making his work. Money was important to my father but not more important than painting.

I told him I heard on the news some footballers earned ten grand a week and he snorted in disbelief, insisting that was the sum they received annually. I refused to back down and he took it personally, asking in disbelief why footballers might need all that money. He was openly affronted, as if their earnings cast shade on him, his own earnings.

FIFTEEN

Saturday, 31 March 1990

Woken first thing by Lola on the phone, asking me for Sellotape. Then Pam came on the line and told me that Sean had died last night at about midnight, two heart attacks following a severe bout of sickle-cell anaemia.

In fact the time of death was ten past one this morning. At first I was just shocked, went out to buy some bleach and some typing paper, then called for Celia. It began to hit me when I told her. We had a cup of coffee at Uncle Sam's Deli then I went home and washed the kitchen floor, defrosted the fridge, began to make bread. Dad rang and I cried on the phone to him. He was lovely. Pam rang and she came over from work. Dexter rang and I told him. He was unable to offer me comfort, said stupid things about Sean and said he would ring later. I rang Hussein and he said 'You made me friends with Sean' and began to cry. I rang Roger, who like Hussein had been at the hospital. Roger was very kind. Pam sent a message to a neighbour of Andi's to see if she needed any help or support but she said Neneh was coming up from the country to collect Miquita and Phoebe.

The last time I saw Sean was after Roger's party, when we talked together about his life, his plans, his desire to marry Sam, his lovely girlfriend. I loved him so much. I'm finding it so hard to understand he is dead, so hard to remember. I am anxious and numb, the sun is shining. Over to Carole's with Pam and her children and Frances in her pram to give Thelonious a present for his birthday.

I was too shocked to say anything much in the diary about Thelonious, Sean's son, but I loved him (I still love him) and looked after him every Thursday night for a few months while Carole was working a late shift at a Mexican restaurant, Theo beside me under the duvet in clean pyjamas that smelt of unfamiliar washing powder, spare pillows in a heap on the floor on his side in case he fell out of my single bed. The rise and fall of his breath lulled me to sleep as he slept, and in the morning I paid extra attention not to crash when I drove him home to his mum's, my precious charge swaddled with utmost care in a blanket and wedged in the well in the back of my car because I had no car seat. The grief when we arrived on his birthday was gritty and raw, too many of us crowding into Carole's flat all at once with the pram, party food laid out on the table and everybody behaving with formality not to feel the heartbreak of a child losing his dad on his birthday. The flat was full of children and Carole carried on with spectacular courage as if nothing had happened, determined nothing would ruin her son's big day.

Saturday, 31 March 1990, cont.

Lola and John stayed for the party and Pam and Frances and I went to Coram's Fields. Occasional feelings of panic, the sun is so hot. Then back at Pam's we made some food for the children and at half past seven Pat came to collect Frances. I wanted to go home to make Ali's cake but Pam felt unable to be on her own suddenly because Steve phoned to say he would not be able to get home and she is pregnant again. I went home, gathered up my ingredients and utensils and went back to Pam's. She was Johnny to my Fanny. Drinking Jameson's to keep going. Home about half one, there was a message from Sam, saying she needs to speak to me. Slept.

Sunday, 1 April 1990

Ali's birthday. The man from the Jubilee Catering Agency phoned to say his girlfriend had just had a haemorrhage so he would not be able to come over and open the oysters. Got the lunch ready and had a few big phone calls, with Dexter, and others, my memory all shot to pieces with the shock of Sean's death. Spoke to Sam on the phone and arranged to meet her tonight at Hussein's. Forgot to put the meat in the oven, there it was sitting on the table when I returned to the kitchen after a call.

Mum more or less ignored me when she arrived – she came into the sitting room and hurried away from me towards Kai and had some kind of little scene with him, like they were making up after an argument, and continued to ignore me for rest of the lunch party. Later I talked to Ib, I told her how hard it was for me holding it all in not to spoil Ali's birthday, there was no room for my sadness, and she told me that she had in fact told Mum about Sean's death on Saturday.

I can hardly believe Mum knew. I can hardly believe she would be so cold, so unable to give me even a word of support or condolence. I told Ib I was amazed by Mum's behaviour, and she said in Mum's defence 'Maybe Mum thought that if she mentioned it you would burst into tears.' So what if I did? Ib is possessive of Mum and desperate to remain at the centre of things, perhaps because she is pregnant, just like when Susie's Robert died, nobody seeming to possess any spare room for any grief but their own. She tried to console me by saying, 'Well at least it's not as bad as when Allan died,' Allan some friend of hers who killed himself, but that did not make me feel any better. I am dealing quite well with the realization that neither Ib nor Mum are much use at the moment, neither of them having the emotional capacity right now to think about me. Kai, Pat and Lily did all the washing up and cleaned the kitchen so that was very helpful and kind.

In the evening went over to Hussein's as planned. Hussein hugged me and we cried on each other's shoulders. Then a big hug with Tessa, then Sam, the woman Sean told me he wanted to marry. Much comfort from sharing grief and from cuddling Phoebe, her sweet twitchy smile just like Sean's. Hussein's girlfriend is having a baby so some hope. Talk of recriminations, the druggy friends and their part in Sean's death. Plans for Thelonious and Phoebe, Hussein's intention to support them and start a trust, discussions and decisions. Listened to a tape of Sean's new tunes and cried in the bedroom. Gave Sam and Tessa and Phoebe a lift home. Dropped Sam off first. I said to Tessa it must be a nightmare for her, hearing Sam go on about Sean. I don't know why I said that. I shouldn't have said that. I wish I hadn't said that.

I asked Tessa about the circumstances of Sean's death – on Wednesday the coroner is going to give the result of his report. There is a question of criminal responsibility, in which case the cremation on Friday will not be going ahead. Tessa told me that Sean regularly used heroin as a painkiller for sickle-cell attacks, because he couldn't bear to go to hospital, and that 'heroin makes the cells of your blood multiply so can be good for sickle-cell sufferers, because they do not have enough blood cells.'

Monday, 2 April 1990

Nothing.

Tuesday, 3 April 1990

Up as usual at half past six. Sitting. Dad said how much he liked Sean.

Home, phone calls from various people to express their sympathy. Dexter has been ringing every day. Since his stupid quip when I told him about Sean's death I have gone cold on him. He is confused, like my mother.

Wednesday, 4 April 1990

Very sunny, then began to snow. Waiting for the coroner's report. Phone call from Lucy first thing. I am going to see her later. Drowning in tears.

Rachel Calder phoned to tell me that Chatto want to buy my book. Am dying to get back to work but my head isn't working properly, I can't remember anything.

Thursday, 5 April 1990

Sitting. Dad spoke of his desire to paint family portraits, meaning his children, which moved me. He showed me Frank's school report at age five. Frank's reading aloud fluent and expressive, mathematics very good, writing vivid. Also mentioned his keenness to be alone, which Dad said reminded him of himself at that age.

Dad said when he was growing up he found his own parents terribly boring. His desire to be a waif, a changeling or a foundling, the stifling feeling of family, his desire to escape. He asked me if I understood that stifling feeling. I said 'Yes, although I don't have any personal experience of it.'

I complained to him about Mum, her total failure to address me on the subject of Sean's death, even just to acknowledge it. He said Mum not saying anything about Sean was part of her murderous side, and also related to her self-destructiveness. I said maybe it was about her own fear of death, all these things connect. I said I didn't think Dad was so self-destructive and then he told me an anecdote about the first week he was allowed to travel to school alone, without his governess, each day counting to ten on the kerb and running across the road with his eyes closed. On the last day a car hit him, he spun into the air, the car hit him again as he came down. He didn't tell his parents, this was in Berlin, the crowd wanted to lynch the driver, Dad got up and limped home. In the bath the governess was shocked by the bruises, and Dad made up a story to hide the truth of what had happened.

Then he talked about gambling again, the feeling that even if you lose you can't lose, you still get the hit. He talked about Mum and Susie as a child, their closeness. Also about the proposed painting of Leigh, naked in an armchair, and wondering whether to use Cerith or Angus and Cerith, a bit of action in the back. He is going to use the red armchair in the bathroom. Talked again of his fondness for Sean.

Anecdotes about driving accidents, his first ever

drive, after a party at Lord Rothermere's when Ann Fleming lent him a car and he ended up having a big accident. Also another case involving Jane Willoughby, but he got off. Used a woman from Delamere as a false witness. He got somebody else to sit his driving test for him.

After sitting went to Hussein's again and he asked me to phone people to tell them about the funeral. The coroner has finally given the go-ahead. Spoke to people I have not spoken to in years. Numb feeling, also sick with sadness, and anxiety. Home, and in the afternoon Pam came over after her termination and I looked after her. Not exactly what the doctor ordered for me but managed to keep it together. Had a few drinks, met Andi at a Japanese restaurant, held her hand, drank a lot of sake and ate some raw fish. Then to Freds, drank more, shed some tears, Dexter appeared just at that moment and made it worse with a hug followed by an abrupt exit because his friends were waiting for him. Went to Gaz's on my own and talked to Shanne who used to go out with Shane, drank a pint of water, walked home in tears and passed out.

Friday, 6 April 1990

Woke up with a hangover after a short sleep and phoned Shane to tell him about the funeral. He'll be the next one to go. Walked to Camden, bought some flowers and got a bus to Hampstead to meet Lucy. I was early and felt so weak and desperate I had a large vodka and tonic in a pub. Lucy drove us to the crematorium.

The grass was bright green, black-clad figures moving across it to the little chapel. A strange muffled silence like deafness. Embraced other mourners, and took a seat at the back with Lucy and others. There was no music, a green smell of grass clippings – the doors of the chapel were open. I heard Andi howling outside and broke down then, hearing her pain. Over the PA the familiar beat and lyrics of 'Blessed Are Those Who Struggle' by The Last Poets. The coffin was brought in, Hussein at one corner, Gerry Prince at another, grim faces. I had to look away.

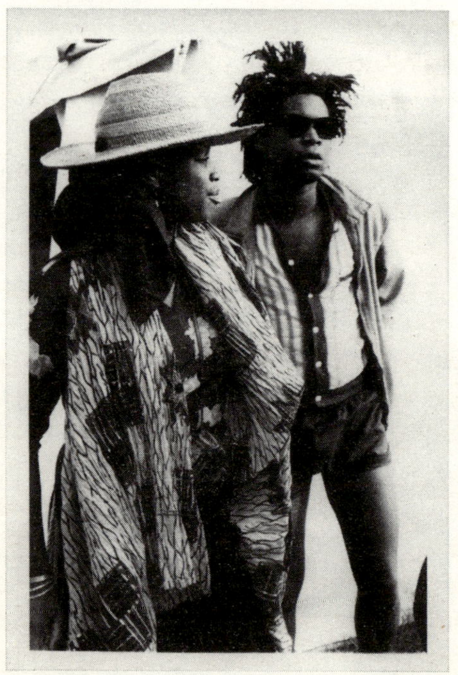

Andi and Sean at Bracknell (1983)
ROSE BOYT

The pastor from Sean's father's church conducted the service. He said that death was a monster, and not even a mother's tears could lure it from its inexorable course. He used a cricket analogy – when the umpire tells you to go, you go, and there is no argument. Sean's uncle, Gerry's father, told us stories of Sean as a child, and made the congregation laugh. The next tune was 'I Can't Get Next To You' by The Temptations. Andi read a poem, and Neneh some of the first elegy of Rilke, inexpressively – she was too sad. They played 'Sunken Love', such a beautiful record, and then that was more or less it. I was glad we were spared the short orange curtains opening at the back of the chapel, the wooden box gliding away, but I felt abject terror as we filed past, afraid to see Sean's face in death, but the coffin was closed.

Saturday, 7 April 1990

Dexter rang. I wanted him to apologize for his reaction to Sean's death – when I told him that Sean was dead he asked me if he had died of a drug overdose – but he didn't want to apologize. I got so miserable talking to him I had to call Ib and get her to come over. Spent the afternoon wandering about in the sunshine, another horribly sunny day. Went to bed at ten. The phone woke me at twelve. It was Susie, from New York, asking about tomorrow, the plans for Lola and Johnnie's christening. Susie and I are the godmothers. I slept at last and had five nightmares. One was about being admitted to a mental hospital.

Sunday, 8 April 1990

The christening. I found myself in a church swearing I am of the Catholic faith and will renounce Satan, my fingers crossed behind my back. The priest was giggling because John called him the princess. Afterwards a big tea with champagne at Pam's, then Angus rang up to invite me to supper. Lucy rang and arranged to come over so that was very nice, the four of us together at Angus and Cerith's. Angus said not to hide my grief and I was so touched he held out his hand to me like that. Afterwards Lucy came back to mine and we drank herbal tea and stayed up until four. I was miserably sad about Sean and obsessing about Dexter. I have got to give it up. I must not ask him any more questions. I may have to decide not to see him for a while. The only way out.

Tuesday, 10 April 1990

Sitting for Dad in the morning. He was worried about an etching of Sophie that was going wrong – he had worked and worked on the head until he bodged it up and was agitated about it, whether or not he would be able to save it with stopping-out varnish. So we had an early break and to distract me from my grief he told me all about the antics of his friend Gully Mason.

While at Eton Gully Mason decided to dress up as his grandfather, some Lord, and make an appointment to see the headmaster, in order to discuss his own progress. Gully paid a visit to Nathan's in Jermyn Street and had himself made up as an elderly man with a white beard and set off for Eton on the train. He had lunch with the headmaster as arranged, and made enquiries about himself, asking whether he would make a worthy heir to the family fortune. The headmaster was completely taken in. Gully was so thrilled with his success he decided to remain in disguise and discuss his sex life with his housemaster – a white mackintosh had been found in his locker, and it was well known in the school he had a predilection for putting it on and bathing small boys. Gully wanted to find out from his housemaster whether this would be held against him and impede the progress of his school career in any way. The housemaster reported that he was perfectly pleased with him. Gully was so elated he did a little leap in the air in the corridor, but was spotted by a maths master, who set a detective on him. He was followed back to Nathan's, the game was up, and he was sacked.

Gully's father found something incriminating in Gully's bathroom, some eyeshadow or something, and to prove to his father he was a real man Gully took a job in the mines. Soon a batch of poems arrived at the offices of HORIZON magazine, rugged mining verses that showed real talent – 'the bitchy earth clung to me' – and they were published. Somebody at HORIZON wrote to the miner, asking him to give some information about himself, and inviting him to come up to London and present himself at the offices of the magazine so they could take him out to lunch. Gully wrote back 'I was educated at Eton, my father is Lt Col. the Hon blah blah in charge of the defence of London, my grandfather is Lord so and so, head of the Midland Bank, and I would love to meet you when I come up to London. Perhaps you would do me the honour of joining me at the Savoy?'

Gully began his career in journalism with an exposé of Greta Garbo, in the days when the press respected stars, his feature based on her legendary, misquoted and misinterpreted plea 'I want to be alone.'

When he was young Dad had a prostitute friend called Doris. He adored her, and said that that was what he really liked, adoration coloured by humiliation, that exquisite feeling. He adored her so deeply there was somehow no question of being able to 'have' her. He said it was like him and Pluto, his dog – Dad used to curl up and sleep on the end of Doris's bed. Gully used to spend time with Doris in her professional capacity, and she was really keen on him because he treated her so well. Gully was in love with Cyril Connolly's girlfriend, but she disdained him, thinking he was too upper class, too polite and gentlemanly. Dad fucked her, but wasn't particularly interested in her, and Gully was desperate to hear about it, burning the backs of his hands with cigarettes in his desperation.

Dad and Doris and the prostitutes of Shepherd Market went to the fair at Hampstead Heath. The girls consulted a fortune teller and were outraged because she asked them what they did for a living. Dad had money; from the attic of his parents' house he had stolen the cash that had been left to him and his two brothers by Sigmund, including solid gold coins received from Marie Bonaparte for her analysis and solid gold coins with Native American heads on them, paid to Sigmund by his American patients; Dad took them a few at a time until there were none left. I asked him if that was why he had been sent to see Dr Hoffer, the psychoanalyst. 'Got it in one,' he said. Doris used her mother as her maid. In the war they used boys but the GIs used to get to them first.

Also talk about Angus and Cerith at the Velázquez show at the Prado. Manuela, Norman Rosenthal's wife, arranged for them to be let into the gallery at night so they could have a good look at the pictures and avoid the eight-hour queue. Cerith told me that Manuela told him the substance passed from child to child in one of the paintings was a hallucinogenic drug. And that in a discussion of the subject matter of another large painting, one showing a large painting within the painting, just off the centre of the composition, Manuela had said that she thought the subject matter was themselves, standing in the Prado at night looking at it.

Dad talking about Leigh, the 'perfect' model. The picture of him as a god luxuriating in the red chair is huge, as yet only filled in round the eyes, the rest drawn loosely with charcoal and some transparent diluted brownish paint showing the form of the upper body. Dad said it was really his first attempt at a mythological subject.

Continuation of talk about his visit to the VD clinic, an anecdote about social disorder leading to Dad on the subject of himself and love/sex. Referred to himself in passing as adolescent in these matters, and talked about 'making love' as a way of showing feeling, creating feeling, as if the act itself existed in an empty space where feelings could not otherwise be felt, communicated or shared. I think he is talking about the thrill of sex in that empty space, where there is nothing else. Not so much a question of expressing love but inventing something out of nothing. And he is inventing it. When he is not theorizing about making love he refers to it as 'having' somebody, as in 'I had her' or 'he had her' but never 'she had me.' Reminded me of the other day when I was talking about getting out of touch with external reality. Dad said he himself sometimes got out of touch with it, for instance 'When I am with certain people I am convinced I am in the company of a horse.' He meant women, I assume in a sexual situation. He really loves horses, but he said of course he never told the person he was with he thought he was with a horse because he knew that would be offensive. He loves horses so much he was happy to eat horsemeat in Paris after the war. And funny to think the word FANCY is used to describe sexual desire and in horse racing, as in 'Which runner do you fancy in the three o'clock?'

Talking about Steve, because THE SUN are going to run a story revealing the hidden secrets of his love children – apparently there are four of them. Dad suggested that Steve give each of the mothers twenty quid a week and then everything would be all right.

Susie arrived as I was departing, she was the next shift.

Had no intention of working when I got home but some ideas began to shift in my head.

Paul McAdam came over in the evening with his new baby, and Pam and Lola and Johnnie. Made roast chicken. I love Pam's children so much, but their behaviour was horrible.

Thursday, 12 April 1990

Dexter's advice about my grief for Sean was not to dwell on it. When I said the result of suppressing it was horrible nightmares he said I wasn't suppressing it, I never stopped going on about it. We had a sandwich in a cafe and he went off to get on with his life and I got myself ready to go to the country.

Lucy and I set off in her car at half past three. Southall in the sunshine, I love it, I must go there one afternoon and have a look round. I went on about it so much Lucy got a bit irritated with me. I said that for me Southall was travelling because I never go anywhere. She who had just returned from Bhutan said it was really very like India. Had a large Bloody Mary on arrival, then a delicious supper of guinea fowl and roast potatoes. Lucy's parents arrived late, and she was stroppy with them. We had an early night. No problem sleeping on account of the bottle of red wine we had shared between us.

Friday, 13 April 1990

Didn't get up until half past ten. Walked round and round the plantation and along the Thames. At supper Lucy's father talked about Miss Freud, with whom he had been in analysis, and Freud's maid, the sweet way that Sigmund used to be nice to her; the maid told him that if Sigmund passed her in the corridor, her eyes lowered deferentially as she went about her work, he would pretend to have mislaid a book so she could have the pleasure of finding it for him. He asked me what it was like, being a descendant of the great man, also about Dad's antipathy to analysis. I said that he was softening up.

Tuesday, 17 April 1990

Picked some budding stems and spring branches to take back to London. Set off after lunch. Lucy dropped me off at Bridges with my bin liner full of greenery and my luggage. Glad to be back.

Told him the dream I had last night about Ali and Sean. Ali dying, yellowish, in the subway or Underground tunnel. I remonstrated with Ali – 'Why don't you go home and look after yourself?' but he didn't want to go home. He smiled and said he wanted to die. Then I bumped into Sean, who had been sleeping on a ledge in the Tube. I asked him why he didn't use the flat Hussein had rented for him and he said that the person he had shared the taxi with didn't realize about the flat and always dropped him off by the Tube. I realized he was going to die, would do nothing to stop himself. Then I met Roger, he hugged me and I

> told him about Ali and Sean. He said to think about all the good things in my life like my mother and that made me feel so bad I woke up. Bridges said this was about my underground envy, I didn't want to go home like the characters in the dream, I didn't want what was good because it was good. He says I am envious of what he has, what I need, therefore reject it, throw it away. Talk of Sean not looking after himself properly.

Waiting for a portion of chips on Talbot Road after an event at the Tabernacle in Notting Hill I asked Sean why he was shaking. He turned away from the saveloys in the hot cabinet and told me it was because of his childhood, beatings from his father that had affected him for life, a revelation of such pain my eyes filled with tears. I had met his father a few times, most recently at Phoebe's birthday party, an event at which Mr Oliver had ogled me and asked me for my phone number. The violence he perpetrated against his own son made Sean vulnerable to further attack, not that we ever spoke about racism, but once or twice when we were watching telly I remember feeling deep unease if a Black character was portrayed on the screen in a soap or comedy programme, *Rising Damp* for example, and utter shame trying to hail a black cab with him when cabs were scarce, white drivers pretending they had not seen us and driving straight past or slowing down momentarily to shout obscenities at me.

I dreamt often of Ali's death, part of my constant fear of losing him, haunted in nightmares and daydreams by needles and wounds and the crack pipe, his eyes rolling back in his slack face when he inhaled or injected himself. In real life he had come close to killing himself accidentally several times after a period of abstinence in prison or rehab, his initial hit on coming out almost fatal on occasion because of his low tolerance, the most dangerous time for addicts, but I don't think he wanted to die, at least not consciously, some combination of tenacity and good fortune saving him from himself in the end, the part of him that sought reckless oblivion pulled back from the edge by the part of him that wanted to live life and take care of his son, a miracle for which we are all thankful beyond measure.

Wednesday, 18 April 1990

At Bridges I was so upset about Sean I said I was craving wipeout, an escape from my feelings, and Bridges said maybe I wanted to be dead too.

Thursday, 19 April 1990

Up at the crack as usual and over to Dad's to sit. Dad gossiping most of the time, about the Astor family, specifically Nancy and her electioneering antics, Bobby Shaw in Soho, Jakey who was a friend of Dad's, the Astor fear of homosexuality, how much Anna Freud had to answer for, and Michael, notorious lazybones and idler who became an MP out of boredom, and his bons mots – to a group of businessmen admiring his special hand-built Rolls-Royce – 'You too could own a car like this if you worked as hard as I have done.'

Another topic Mum and her men. I said she had similarities with Susanna in some ways, particularly the physical self-loathing aspect, and Dad said that must be what he found so attractive. We laughed. Talk of Uwe, also Ginger. Dad said how odd it was Mum managed to find fine qualities in these people. He said he could understand the fancying, the liking, but not that.

Dad said he liked a timetable, hated habits, disliked deadlines – old age and death bad enough without adopting other endings. 'I don't want to stop work at a certain time to get ready to go out.' This in response to my suggestion he might work early then ride afterwards because Andrew Parker Bowles will not get up to ride early enough for him. They used to go riding together often in the park.

Again about Leigh. Last week he was 'perfect', this week he is 'beautiful'. Ib turned up to sit and I set off for home, this diary, and work. I am making progress.

Called in at Angus and Cerith's for tea. Much excited talk about poetry and my love life or lack of it. Angus told me how badly he had got on with his sister in the past, how much she had disliked him, how that if, at Christmas, he had been planning to go up to Campbeltown to visit his parents he would have had to time his trip carefully so it would not coincide with hers. He had seen her in Paris on his recent holiday and she had apologized for being so horrible over the years – as children they had fought on a daily basis, with fists. A resolution had taken place, something very significant, and he seems so much happier. He has recently started work on some poems, using tracing paper to invert quotations from admired artists or writers, the transformation of gathered material into poetry, the form or method perhaps also the subject matter. Went home to bed. Felt happy for a few minutes, the first time for a long time.

Friday, 20 April 1990

Bridges first thing, a resolution here too. Talk about Sean. I am going to make bourride on Saturday night. Yesterday invited Trevor. A bit nervous and excited. Started the first page of DAYDREAMING, many hours of hard graft. Needs more work, but I am glad to have made a start.

Saturday, 21 April 1990

No Frances today – Pat rang to cancel me. Soho for shopping for this evening. The bourride includes mussels, sole, grey mullet and sea bream. Had a cup of coffee and a croissant at Patisserie Valerie then got home and began to get things ready. Pat turned up with Frances in the afternoon for a visit also Jane McAdam and her new boyfriend Kevin. The table looked really beautiful in the sitting room, the white cloth, candles, proper napkins, bowls of radishes and olives, glasses, the white plates with green and gold borders that I bought in Golborne Road.

Angus and Cerith were the first to arrive, then Lucy, Susannah and Trevor the last – I was worried he wouldn't show up. Just as I was getting ready to serve, Pam arrived with three tired children, all hungry and wild after a journey from Glasgow in the aeroplane. Made beans on toast for Lola and Johnnie in the kitchen and laid extra places for Pam and Laura at the big table. Trevor chucking the children about, funny and sweet. Lucy and Susannah left about one, Angus and Cerith about two, and Trevor stayed all night. First we were standing by the fireplace, and I was talking about Sean. Trevor was stroking my arm, comforting me. I put on a Patsy Cline record and we danced. He was holding me in his arms, I was sad, it was lovely. He said we were the perfect height together, dancing cheek to cheek. I knew if we kissed that would be it, we would end up in bed, and I was very unsure how I felt and how he felt, it was all too uncertain, too soon after Sean's death.

We talked about romantic relationships. He said he wanted to be courageous, unafraid of closeness, to be able to put one foot after the next into the unknown, because it was impossible to know how things would develop. This was in the abstract. He said people (meaning women) wanted to make arrangements before anything had even happened, you be my boyfriend and I'll be your girlfriend, but he thought it was better to let things develop. We lay down on the floor by the fire and talked and cuddled. I slept for an hour or so. I made some tea about half eight. I said that if we had gone to bed we would have been going to bed together. He said he could tell by signs that that was not what I wanted, and that to have pressed it on me when I was so sad about Sean would have seemed horrible to him, slipping in when I was open, vulnerable. Two or three times he said that he was glad that it had not happened so I asked him if he felt rejected. He said no. I said that if it had happened we would feel so differently about each other suddenly. He said yes, a sense of responsibility. I said I meant closeness. He left me his telephone number. I wonder what was in his head. Perhaps he just wanted to put one foot in front of the other and see what happened. I felt too fragile to submit.

Tuesday, 24 April 1990

Dad told me about Leigh's instant facelift using gaffer tape. Leigh didn't even use a mirror to get it right. Put his wig back on and went off to a meeting at a health club.

Pronouncement – democracy is bad, equality even worse.

He told me about a young girl he knows who is

going to have therapy because she keeps on repeating herself, one bad situation after another, over and over again, the same problems, the same behaviour. The inevitability of things going wrong. Also of his own relationships – he said that things do seem to go wrong.

Of Paris in the forties, the girl in the beret painting a girlfriend of his who was in the Orson Welles production of Marlowe's DOCTOR FAUSTUS with Eartha Kitt as Helen of Troy. Orson Welles shouting and eating all the time, the first night a disaster – Joan Crawford was in the front row in a fur so glossy it looked like she was wearing a live animal. The girl was cold, unaffectionate, he said he likes them like that. The only time she showed affection was when a friend of hers turned up from England and it was three in a bed at the hotel – then she showed some for the sake of the other girl.

After sitting cleaned the studio while Ib was sitting. Dad frantic, rushing to answer the phone when it was not even ringing. Left at one, felt exhausted, drove Ib home and hung around until it was time to go to Bridges. Bridges strengthening. After that Sam came over. I showed her some old photos of Sean then we went to the Museum Street Café for supper.

Sam told me exactly how Sean died. She came home early from work to look after him because he had had a sickle cell attack, and as she arrived a girl was leaving the building. Brandon, a drug addict, was in the flat. This made her angry. Sean was ill in bed. After a while the girl came back with some heroin and she and Brandon gave it to Sean to relieve the pain of the attack. He became very ill. Sam held him in her arms while he was having spasms. She was not sure whether Sean was having a heart attack or had been given an overdose. She asked the girl but she didn't know either. Sam called an ambulance and got him to hospital. The doctor said he was having a heart attack. Once Sam had got him settled into bed and the doctor said Sean was on the mend she went home. Sean called her in the morning and asked her to come and collect him. She arrived at the hospital but the doctor wouldn't let her take him home. Later that day he had a stroke and another heart attack.

After supper I went home to bed and had a nightmare. I was walking with Gareth and Sean and Sean began to stagger as if unwell. Gareth was supporting him and helping him along when he died. Gareth dropped the dead body onto the floor because it was no longer Sean, just something discarded. I knelt over the corpse and kissed it on the forehead, then woke up. It was six or seven in the morning. I began to cry.

SIXTEEN

Thursday, 26 April 1990

Can't sleep. Dad's early. I had forgotten I was wearing a hairband made out of the cut-off leg of an old pair of tights to keep my hair off my face and Dad decided to use it in the picture. Talk about THE MILL ON THE FLOSS again, how the end symbolized for Dad that rush when things begin to go wrong in a relationship. Everything is going so well, you feel at one with someone, you can tell what they are feeling, then you fuck everything up, an inevitable collapse like the flood, out of control. This led back to the subject of Tuesday, the young girl who repeated her mistakes over and over again. Dad said Degas had talked about repetition but that was different; what he said over and over to his pupils could not be repeated often enough. Dad seemed to be trying to work something out. I hope nothing has gone wrong with Susanna.

He told me how he nearly drowned in the South of France. He disliked the man who saved his life and so when his little boat approached Dad pretended to be coughing in the water, not shouting for help. Later, when the man said 'I saved your life,' Dad said 'Bollocks.'

Memory, how elusive. Dad remembers jumping on the roofs of cars in Paris because he felt so 'animated', then wonders whether he really did this, seeing an angry face looking up at him out of the window of the car he was jumping on.

He showed me a catalogue of his etching show in Paris, the little volume containing an essay that claims he watched the Reichstag burning and saw gangs of looters on the rampage. Dad said he did have to take a detour one day on the way to school because of the Reichstag fire but saw nothing. He said the only gang of looters he knew about first hand was the one he was in when he was eight, stealing chocolate from a sweetshop.

Dad had been to the John Lessore show and really loved it. He said he had seen Mum there and she looked so good, battered but much better than everybody else, and not so shy. I have noticed that she is much less shy with him than she used to be.

Talk of Paul McAdam, his disgruntled outlook. Dad said he should only be half as messed up as other people because he had only half the number of parents.

I can't remember where we were going but we were travelling at speed along Elgin Avenue towards Abercorn Place one afternoon when I was fifteen, the breeze in my hair and the smell of sunshine warming the leather interior of the car, my father quite relaxed behind the wheel until he was forced to slow down because of the traffic. He became agitated, impatient to reach our destination, looked out of the window and spotted a youngish man pushing a pram on the pavement. As the man approached the zebra crossing my father pointed at him and said he loathed that sort of thing, and at first I thought he meant the man's ponytail, but then my father explained he thought a man with a pram looked pitiful, ridiculous.

He didn't say pram-pushing was women's work or too demeaning for men but that must have been what he thought. I was not in the mood for an argument so I shrugged and made a non-committal noise in my throat when he tried to get me to concur, neither with him nor against him. I knew he had never pushed a pram in his life, but I had not realized he believed that for a man it was a pitiful activity – I was surprised and disappointed by the conventional sexism of his attitude when his way of looking at things was usually so original. The young father hesitated at the crossing and nosed the pram forward into the road, very cautiously, expecting Dad to slow down and stop, but my father put his foot down and, sounding his horn, forced the man to jump back.

Thursday, 26 April 1990, cont.

As I was leaving the studio Dad came downstairs to put his car in my parking place to save it for Susanna and said he was going to see Gilbert de Botton to get advice about his will. He asked me what I wanted to do about the McAdams – whether he should pay them off now, ignore them altogether, or include them in the share-out after his death like the rest of us. I said I thought they should be included like the rest of us because that was the right thing to do. He said there was going to be a real lot of money, and a lot of things. At least I don't have to worry about my pension.

My good intentions towards the McAdams make me feel proud of myself now, although in the end my father attached a restricted list of beneficiaries in the letter of wishes that accompanied his will, instructions that I was obliged to respect and the impact of which must have been horrible for anybody who had expectations that were not met. The responsibility he put on me did not feel at all onerous and I was sure that in collaboration with Diana Rawstron, my father's solicitor, whom he loved and respected and allowed himself to be guided by, I would be a fair executor when the time came, my self-confidence raised by his faith in me. I believed in myself not in an arrogant way but deeply, my heart beating with more fortitude because my father was able to recognize and accept my good qualities, my conscientious care for my siblings. I felt legitimated by his choice, not just in my own heart but in the world, publicly, my status no longer as sketchy and subject to his whims as it had been, no longer as precarious. I was high but not too high on the recompense for the discredit of my illegitimacy and the poverty that felt consequential to it, a deficit that had humiliated me as a child, not just no money for school dinners and all those everyday shortfalls that were due at least in part to Mum's romantic approach to her finances, but in my suspicion that my father was responsible for the lack. He always had cash in his pockets unless the gambling was getting the better of him, notes and jangling change he chose to spend on the horses and not give to my mother to feed us. Some children at school had it way worse – there were fifty children in my class in my final year at primary school and six of them were unable to read and write – but our situation felt very painful in relation to my father because we were his children and he didn't want to take care of us in a consistent way, or at least was ambivalent about his responsibilities, making provision sometimes but at other times swept away by his work and his gambling. I am not speaking for anyone else here, but his ambivalence was corrosive for me and made me feel unlovable, as if I were implicated by my personality or my appearance in his lack of commitment, too young to realize that he was just himself and there was nothing I could do about it. The recognition of my good qualities implied in his choice felt like the start of my recovery from all that.

Thursday, 26 April 1990, cont.

Spent the rest of the day and evening working on the

American proofs of SEXUAL INTERCOURSE. Lucy came over to help me because it felt impossible to get it done on my own and the book is supposed to be back in NY by tomorrow.

Saturday, 28 April 1990

Again couldn't sleep, tormenting wakefulness in the small hours. In the morning an outing to Coram's Fields with Frances, Lola, Johnnie and Thelonious and a nanny from a nanny agency. Pam is away. A very hot sunny day. Feeling pretty shaky.

Dexter came over with Maya. She is very anxious and miserable, her face screwed up, eczema in patches, biting her nails. I asked him to come and take her away after swimming tomorrow but he didn't really respond.

Dad arrived to pick up some paints I had collected earlier from Cornelissen.

Maya tried to wind me up about Dexter's new girlfriend. She said that in the future the new girlfriend was going to look after her a lot on Saturdays. I believed her, and said I was pleased for her, but it turned out not to be true. Dexter had introduced her to the woman that morning, but she is going to Japan for two or three months so won't be looking after Maya at all. Poor Maya, she is very unhappy. She got to sleep about ten fifteen and at nine thirty in the morning was so depressed she didn't want to get up. In the end I forced her to go swimming. She moaned and moaned.

Sunday, 29 April 1990

Dexter was supposed to meet us at the pool at eleven but didn't turn up until twelve. He was lying on his towel at a little distance from Maya and me, disassociating himself. She obviously depresses him too. Writing this is making me so angry. I told Dexter I had a lot on but he hung around until five. I think he was unwilling to be alone with his own child, also clinging to me.

I saw panic in Dexter's eyes when I suggested to him that perhaps Maya should stay with me less often in future, afraid as he was that I was beginning to try and separate myself from him finally after our split, and that he would have to find himself another babysitter. I had decided that the best thing for all of us would be to limit contact gradually, but he refused to see the false position we were in, refused to acknowledge that it wasn't doing Maya any good, and was dead set against any change. He wasn't cunning or manipulative, I didn't think he was using me, but I was trapped all the same, worried about Maya and aware of her misery but unable to help in an effective way. I was barely able to think straight because I was so disturbed by her distress but I was certain I had to extricate myself. I am not sure how things would have evolved had I not been so vulnerable, my longing for a child of my own and my complicated relationship with my father adding to my misguided compulsion to hang on and try and fix everything. Dexter and I spoke in the kitchen in hushed voices while Maya watched telly in the sitting room with the volume turned up, and after they left, nothing resolved between us, I lay down on my bed and sighed, overwhelmed by grief.

Monday, 30 April 1990

Bridges, about Dexter and Maya. Decided that I must stand firm and tell Dexter that I am only prepared to have Maya once a month. That is enough. She is unprepared to enjoy anything I offer her, refusing to let go of her grievances. Not that I blame her.

After Bridges I phoned Trevor and found out that he is away in Yorkshire.

Tuesday, 1 May 1990

Up at half six as usual for Dad. The picture is going well. Talk of Freud and the Nazis, Annie, Hamilton Hartford and schoolgirls, Rodin and Michelangelo and the use of hands in their work, and psychoanalysis – I said I thought Freud's work was nearer to art than science or philosophy. Dad agreed.

He told me that any crime or violence he had been involved in when he was young was connected to lack of money, how without money it is impossible to feel all right. I wonder what he thought of the poverty of my life with Mum when we had nothing, Mum working as a cleaner in secret not to upset Susie, me in the Queen Mary Hostel in Hoxton as a teenager.

He brought up the subject of Maya. I told him I was only going to see her once a month from now on. He said he hated her. Then he said he hated Katie. He said Katie was the most horrible person he had ever known, they were never happy, he kept on wanting to see her because they never had a good time, always trying and failing to get that closeness keeping him at it. I remember how terrible life was for him when he was in love with her.

He said he felt that Annie (Freud) liked him less and less. He said when he was seeing Alice, an American artist who was in love with him, Annie fell in love with her and so liked him more, but afterwards her regard for him fell away again. Not for the first time he said Annie said she had no goodwill towards him. I said I knew Annie adored him.

Feeling cross with Dexter. Also tired and so worried about Laura I can't concentrate. Laura is very distressed, Pam is in Los Angeles for work, Steve never home, agency nannies coming and going, me filling in the gaps when the precarious arrangements break down. Writing this is putting my teeth on edge, my head aches, I have to go and lie down.

Wednesday, 2 May 1990

The book I have almost finished I have decided to call ROSE. I am unable to get on with work because I don't want to dissipate my energy and confuse myself by working on DAYDREAMING and ROSE at the same time. I can't work on ROSE until after the meeting with Frances Coady next Tuesday. Tea at Pam's for Lola's birthday, met up with Paul McAdam afterwards and had a drink with him.

Thursday, 3 May 1990

Cindy Palmano's studio for author photo then lecture at the Architects' Association by Robert and Catrina (slides of the Colville Rose looking beautiful.) Angus and Cerith came back with me for an impromptu supper.

Sunday, 6 May 1990

Lunch with Hussein at Kensington Place, then wandered off to Holland Park where Tessa and Andi and Bruce and the children were having a picnic in the sunshine.

Monday, 7 May 1990

Called Trevor in the morning and he said he was just about to catch a train back to Leeds. He said he would love to see me and that he would ring me when he was next in London, whether next weekend or the one after.

Notting Hill in a taxi with Pam and Steve and Angus and Cerith for Sean's memorial at the Tabernacle. Rip Rig + Panic played, obviously without Sean. I was very sad, and drunk. Took some photographs.

Wednesday, 9 May 1990

Dad's to sit. Quite peaceful. Talked about Ned Lambton because I had seen him at the memorial also the ethics of Christianity – Dad professes to admire them – 'So imaginative.' I asked him how that fitted in with his rabid Nietzschean tendencies and he said he wasn't so keen on Jesus, just the ethics. I said that sounded like an Old Testament position, about justice, one of his favourite subjects. He said yes. I then said it wasn't Christianity he admired, but Judaism. He laughed and said he would eat his hat.

Talked also of France. He said there was nothing happening there of any worth, in painting or any of the arts, even the food was going down down down – he said the French didn't even understand apples.

Home, and stuck my photos of Sean's memorial into my album.

Bumped into Helena at Dick Jewell's film HEADCASES. I asked her what Trevor was like in OTHELLO in Dublin and she said that all the other actors were white and flabby, very flabby, then when Trevor came on he looked incredible, black, narrow, straight as a poker. She said everyone knew Trevor in Dublin, when she went out with him and a 'sort of girlfriend of his' they were recognized everywhere. My ears pricked up but of course I couldn't ask for details. Got home in good time and slept.

Thursday, 10 May 1990

Sitting again, as I was leaving Leigh arrived and stripped off in the hall regardless of me, took off his wig and put on a white towelling dressing gown with padded shoulders. Dad and I had worked even later than usual, and I felt exhausted when I got home. This week is a bit of a write-off as far as editing my book is concerned – I need some big stretches of time to work in and some sleep before I begin, although the meeting with Frances Coady on Tuesday went very well.

Oxford in the afternoon with Matthew Yorke to hear Saul Bellow talk about writing.

Friday, 11 May 1990

Dad asked if Susanna could ring me to talk about their relationship because he thought my insight would be useful. She rang me and we talked for a long time.

I feel some unease about telling you this but it is important thematically so I will continue. Dad used to phone me in extreme distress if he was unhappy in love and could not get what he wanted, particularly when Susanna was in Italy; he described the crazy feelings caused by her absence as madness, but felt even more angry and upset on her return. I listened carefully then said that it sounded to me like he was more excited by the distance between him and Susanna than by anything he experienced in her presence. I tried to help him understand his desperation by talking about the fetishization of distance in romantic relationships, an idea that had struck me as very pertinent to him and to myself when I had heard it explained recently in a lecture on psychoanalysis. Dad was not aware that the theory came out of Freud, albeit indirectly, but became calm as we talked, having accepted there might be another way to look at his passion and pain. I was happy to share my newly gained knowledge to lessen his agony although looking back I should have refused to talk with Susanna, or maybe he shouldn't have asked me. I was not impartial nor did I have much in common with her, she was married and had no intention of leaving her husband. She had to protect herself, and I imagine she sensed if she made herself entirely available he would lose interest. Even so, I felt she was a cruel mistress.

Monday, 14 May 1990

Working on the final edit of ROSE. In the evening went to see Frankie Howerd with Susie. His performance was modern, absurd, painful, boring, too sad, not very funny. Susie loved it. After the show we went to the new Häagen-Dazs ice-cream parlour in Leicester Square.

Tuesday, 15 May 1990

Sat for Dad as usual. I am so busy finishing the final edit of my book I can't really be bothered to spend the time and brain cells trying to remember what was said.

Went home, reluctant to work but managed to fight it.

Wednesday, 16 May 1990

Working hard. Diana Ward rang me to talk about a music job. Bridges was sarcastic with me. Watched a documentary about Broadwater Farm. Bent police achieving convictions using evidence forced out of vulnerable young people unable to read their own statements. I especially felt for Mark Braithwaite, a claustrophobic who got life, the only evidence against him a statement made under duress – he signed it just to get out of his cell for a short period. Clearly an innocent man.

Thursday, 17 May 1990

Sitting as usual, discussed the music job with Dad and he said 'I am very anxious that you shouldn't do anything just for the money because I could let you have some.'

Also talk of Jane Bowles, or Janie as Dad called her. He said he really liked TWO SERIOUS LADIES, thought it was really original. I told him about the Broadwater Farm documentary.

He told me that when he was a child he was very interested in sex, not that he wanted to see people having each other as he put it but that he was keen to find out what it was all about. He said he was so protected, longed for danger in the ordinary way, to be allowed to experience danger, and regretted the Jewish carefulness of his mother.

He said he longed for danger in the ordinary way, seemingly having forgotten or chosen to disregard the terror of the rise of the Nazis and his flight from Berlin with his family, real danger but not dangerous enough, or not ordinary enough, or was it his longing for danger that was supposed to be ordinary? He told me that three of his great aunts went to see the commandant to request special treatment from the Nazis because of their status in relation to Sigmund, saying they would rather be killed outright than sent to the camps, and the commandant shot all three of them right there in front of his desk, although it is hard to believe he didn't take them out the back not to mess up his office. I am thinking about my own childhood, which was unsafe in a more local way, entirely lacking in Jewish carefulness, my own want of parental protection not unconnected to his yearning for danger in the face of danger and even his lack of acknowledgement of the impact on him of the Holocaust, the horror and shame of anti-Semitism, extraordinary danger disavowed as if it were even possible that Nazi persecution had not hurt him at all.

Thursday, 17 May 1990, cont.

Then he talked about insufficient weaning. I realized that he thought weaning meant breastfeeding. I told him that insufficient weaning meant a too-sudden ending to breastfeeding. At first he was of the opinion that breastfeeding could not go on for too long, the more the better. Then I told him about Hazel, one of Mum's friends, still feeding her son aged four. I said I thought that a child given enough love, attention and security would get enough of the breast and lose interest quite easily, and want to be separate.

After sitting had lunch in a cafe with Bella and decided not to do the music job.

Friday, 18 May 1990

Useful session with Bridges, about spite and envy, the spite and envy in me and how I disown it. Home, good work on ROSE. Dexter rang at five and said he wanted to come over. Very anxious at the thought of seeing him, I haven't seen him for so long. Anxiety of expectation, the anticipation of hurt feelings, frustration, jealousy. He said he would be over in five minutes. So I stopped working and waited for half an hour.

We had a cup of tea and he told me at length about his martial arts. Then he told me he was worried because he had had 'a few strong words' with a gangster when he was buying weed and he was afraid that the gangster was going to get him. The man was after Serana, Dexter's new girlfriend. Dexter says he didn't really want to start a new relationship, but now he feels like he is in one.

I asked him how he felt about Serana, and he said he was not sure because the gangster aspect clouds everything. I was glad he was not in love and suggested to him that he get out. He seems very anxious and depressed, trapped in some fiasco beyond love and affection, more pain and fear for him. He said relationships make him lazy. He said he might be sticking with Serana to show that he will not be scared off. What a fucking idiot.

Laura turned up as he was leaving. When I took her home the nanny was waiting for Steve to come home so she could go off duty. By ten or so Steve still wasn't home and so the nanny left and I waited with the children until four in the morning.

Saturday, 19 May 1990

To the Saatchi Gallery with Lucy for Cerith's talk about Dad. Very personal, about his experience of being painted. Both Bella and I chipped in out of the audience, about our experience. An American woman brought up the question of possession, whether the artist possessed the model or the model possessed the artist. I said it was not a question of possession but one of collusion.

I felt like an exhibit myself, cross-legged on the floor of the Saatchi Gallery in front of my father's paintings, Cerith inviting the audience to participate in his lecture and me not holding back with my insider comments, one side of me elated to be connected and the other side afraid I might look foolish, making a show of myself and occluding Cerith's viewpoint with my own when it was his time to shine. The American woman wanted to talk about ambiguity, whether Cerith in the new painting of Leigh was lying under a blanket or under the bed or where was he located in space, it was unclear to her what was actually represented in the composition, and Cerith denied the picture was ambiguous, not because he believed that ambiguity was an undesirable quality but just to put her straight. He insisted that everything was perfectly clear, but I said I thought that in fact the picture was a bit difficult to read, I had to squint at it for quite a while to get it to resolve itself. I was aware the talk might be taped and wondered what Dad would think of my comment, unsure whether he had deliberately placed Cerith in some unknowable location or whether the picture had just come out like that, one of those almost mistakes that add to the richness of the work and make you look at it so hard you see things you wouldn't have seen otherwise. Cerith welcomed my contribution although he disagreed with me, and the woman smiled as if in triumph, her hostility in that worshipful crowd almost uncouth, the first time I had experienced bitterness towards my father from a stranger. I think she wanted to topple him, perhaps for political reasons.

The authority of Cerith's address was intensified by his nervous state, a pallor of overexcitement I attributed to his level of engagement, not just in art history but emotionally – everything was personal, everything true to his experience. He made me see the rags in the picture as if for the first time, the Sophie-shaped dent in the rags, once-white sheets from Ratzker's, and Mum's involvement in their procurement, all the autobiographical connections whether known or unknown to the viewer adding to the depth of the work.

I don't know why I didn't write this down at the time but the most astounding and memorable aspect of Cerith's talk was his assertion that when he was sitting he did half the work of the painting himself and was responsible for at least half the outcome. The audacity of this claim made me think about art and about myself, my humility, a condition that persisted in spite of my growing confidence in myself as my father's executor, the chosen one, perhaps because I was afraid he might demote me at any point if I let him down.

It's not that I never felt important, most of the time I knew I was loved and useful to him, the studio a home from home when it was my turn to be immortalized, when I felt able to submit, or when I was washing the floor, another way of being close to him. The intense light and the smell and the rags and the embrace of the brown sofa, the whole private world, felt like a place in which I might assuage my longing to belong and be parented by him, but I was bound to him by his focus on me with such force I lost track of myself outside his perception of me, how he saw me and how he wanted me to be. I had learnt by instinct since I was small how to please him both in the studio and outside it, but my sense of self was eroded by my determination to be lovable.

And of course the temporary increase in value I experienced under his gaze triggered in me some kind of vertiginous delusional rise above everybody else because he wanted to paint me at least in that moment, he wanted to paint ME, when in reality I am not sure I felt all that important as a subject because there were so many sitters, so many sisters. I am not sure whether his regard for me was conditional or not, sometimes it felt conditional and sometimes stronger than that, more permanent, a deep true feeling of love for me as his daughter that cut through all his uncertainties. That does sound wonderful, but even now I am not sure what he felt, the polarity of my imagination in relation to him pulling both ways – of course he loved me, he bought me a flat, he never told me he loved me, maybe he didn't love me, of course he loved me. He painted me, but it had never occurred to me that I might equal my father in the creation of one of his paintings, just by being there on the couch in my stillness with all my thoughts and my feelings, not exerting myself in the way he exerted himself – *art is wrought* – but making my own contribution to the project in my own way.

SEVENTEEN

Saturday, 19 May 1990, cont.

After Cerith's talk Lucy drove me home, I made some flapjacks, Mum and Laura came to tea. Mum brought me some beautiful roses from her garden at Medina Road and helped me rearrange the sitting room. I am so glad she was much better.

Sunday, 20 May 1990

Swimming, Susie came to lunch, washed the kitchen floor. Laura and Johnnie came over for pancakes. Read the papers. Pam rang from Cannes to get a report on Steve and the children.

Tuesday, 22 May 1990

Didn't have to sit today because Dad cancelled. Didn't see Bridges as he cancelled also. Good work on the book, then to a party at the Waldorf Hotel. Talked to Francis Wyndham about the Krays because we had both seen the film. He thought it was rubbish, as I did, and was very funny, imitating Violet Kray on the train back from prison (they used to go together to visit her sons) and talking about her airs and graces, snobbishness, he said she was terribly grand.

Kirsty's boyfriend talked a lot about how drugs would help me with my writing, and how Kirsty understood him chasing other women. Jeannette, Gareth, Andi, Angus and Cerith, Celia. We decided to go to Freds, Susie very upset in the taxi. I took her back to my flat and put her to bed.

Wednesday, 23 May 1990

Swimming with Susie, she is very unhappy. I got some good work done, spent the evening at Pam's with Angus.

Thursday, 24 May 1990

Insomnia last night, worried about Susie, then up at half six to go to Dad's. Talk of Francis W, his friendship with the Krays, his fondness of Ronnie and Reggie. Tellingly Dad said that Francis always chooses people who will not or are not able to reciprocate. Dad said he assumed that the twins ended up ditching Francis, letting him down. Also of asking Lulu Norman to sit, and Mum and her new cheerfulness. He received a letter from her today saying thank you. For the children.

Oh Mum. He should have been thanking her. Although I am glad she was grateful.

Thursday, 24 May 1990, cont.

After sitting went to Ib's, it was horrible, she was nasty to me and I lost my temper. We tried to talk but didn't get very far. She just wanted to make me submit to her point of view and wouldn't listen to me. I don't know why she can't accept I might see things in a different way. Winning the argument was all that mattered to her.

Then Bridges, an extra session to replace Tuesday, and much needed. Lucy and Clare came to supper. Isa and Kalifa so sweet. Slept suddenly at about eleven but somebody rang up at one in the morning, woke me up, and put the phone down without saying anything. The same thing happened very late last Saturday.

Friday, 25 May 1990

To the John Lessore show at the Nigel Greenwood Gallery, and had to force myself to work when I got home. Dexter phoned and I felt a stomach-churning anxiety of jealousy, anger, fondness, irritation, disappointment.

Sunday, 27 May 1990

Dexter and Maya came over and we had a picnic at Coram's Fields. Very hot and sunny. I felt surprisingly detached.

Monday, 28 May 1990

Another bank holiday. Swimming at nine, felt very low, went back to bed. Visited Angus and Cerith, felt miserable, in the evening visited Pam. Missed a call from Angus, inviting me to supper. Felt miserable.

Tuesday, 29 May 1990

Sitting, got onto the subject of the FRED magazine, Dad said it was like shit, all stirred up, with maybe a chance of something good in it, like a coriander seed undigested that might grow into a tree.

This scatological talk reminds me of a story Dad told me about a dinner he was invited to at the elegant London home of a man he didn't know very well. The lift attendant escorted him up to the top floor, my father was admitted to the flat by the butler and noticed with some surprise when he entered the drawing room that all the guests were male, and dressed in formal attire, some of them even wearing cummerbunds. Drinks were served, the men took their places at table and after the innocuous first course a team of young boys appeared in the dining room and presented each guest with a dish under a domed silver cloche. The host struck the rim of his glass with his knife, the room fell silent and the boys lifted the domes. Each dish contained a lump of fresh shit produced recently by the boy who had delivered it. Steam rose from the shit, and all the men tucked in apart from my father, who dropped his unfurled napkin on his plate and pushed it all away, not with a dramatic gesture of disgust but gently, almost surreptitiously, just far enough towards the middle of the table to remove it from under his nose. He didn't say anything to me about disgust and I imagine that he felt compelled to under-react, not to gag or throw up, not wishing to appear gauche or judgemental in front of his fellow guests or his host, who had chosen to invite him in the hope or suspicion he might share his tastes, maybe because of his paintings. The young waiters, in little grey trousers and white shirts like schoolboys, formed an ornamental human frieze against the back wall of the dining room, their pink cheeks and slouching postures providing visual stimulus to accompany the consumption of their faeces.

On a similar theme he described a weekend he spent in the country with a family who kept a small pack of hunting dogs. The host, as an entertainment for his guests, inserted sausages into the anuses of his six children, ordered them to scamper round the drawing room on all fours and set the dogs on them. The host and his guests laughed as the dogs ate the sausages.

`Tuesday, 29 May 1990, cont.`

`Without a prompt from me onto the subject of MAMA DRAGON, a Black Theatre Co-operative production of`

1980 starring Trevor Laird. Dad went to the show because Bella worked for the company before she went to Italy to study fashion. He said Trevor was really good in it, he was that rare thing, an intelligent actor, but then wanted stardom so much he would play in anything. I stuck up for him, and told Dad about his recent success in the Dublin OTHELLO, and that after that performance he had doubts about continuing to take bad parts for the money. Dad said that was right, playing Othello should do that to you. I understand T's desire to make money, not to be out of work.

Dad knocked over a shallow square wooden box that stands on one end in the studio. The box fell onto a canvas and made a gash in it. Dad was upset. Susanna's dog's puppies were born in that box, including Pluto. Multipurpose. I remember a picture Dad painted while standing on it. He said what he would really like was another room in which to store canvasses. I have often suggested he should have a rack built but he doesn't like the idea, thinks it is so good to work in a rectangular studio, when you can see the rectangularity of it, unobscured. I know what he means, I too am like that about rooms, seeing the corners. While I was sitting I felt low, thinking about my row with Ib, about shit. Home, feeling very tired, overcame reluctance to work, made some good progress on the book.

At Bridges talked about my reluctance to work, caused by a voice in my head telling me my book is rubbish, everything is rubbish. He said the voice is an internalized authoritarian father figure, telling me off, criticizing me, telling me I am not good enough. When the voice starts up I have to overwhelm it, grapple with it, smother it. HARD WORK. And this figure gets projected onto Bridges himself, and then I can't speak to him.

Wednesday, 30 May 1990

Back to work, fighting a horror of what I have done so far. Began to feel really pleased, a fleeting feeling but maybe one I will be able to cultivate. Worked straight through the day, Bridges at six fifteen, then the Embargo opening party with Lucy and Cerith. I am so glad I decided not to work there. Dexter was on his first shift. On his break he told me that Maya's mum is going to live in Amsterdam with Maya. He said he was very pissed off. On the way back Cerith and I got a cab with a phone in the back. Cerith phoned Angus and we all had a chat. Stayed the night at Lucy's. Sleep disturbed, some nightmares, but better than insomnia.

Thursday, 31 May 1990

Sitting. Dad talked about Ali, the unease he felt with him sometimes, Dad's reluctance to open his wardrobe full of suits in Ali's presence in case Ali felt envious, although Dad said he knew it was all in his head.

I said Ali was probably still having quite a struggle to keep himself together, and that he too probably felt uneasy, thought Dad was thinking bad things about him, things that they hadn't discussed. Dad said that their relationship was always 'easy and casual' and that there was no history of that type of conversation, it was hard to start now, meaning hard to start talking about painful subjects.

Dad on Flaubert and the punch of the novel, how long it takes the reader to recover from that punch a measure of its success. Also Flaubert's adoration of THE GOLDEN ASS, incense and urine mixed. His love of dung in art, like James Joyce.

Beau Brummel, the crowd of admirers on the pavement applauding on a daily basis as he emerged from his house. According to Dad he used to allow chosen young men the chance to watch him select his clothes and get dressed. When the soldiers came back from the Napoleonic Wars he was ruined by gambling; they were loaded with spoils and the stakes went up. He fled to Calais and fell in love for the first time in his life with the daughter of the Mayor of Calais. He was a ruined man, and was refused.

Of Leigh, who doesn't like the idea of his mother, but likes her in fact. Dad said he loved the idea of his mother, but didn't like her very much. He laughed. Then of Leigh getting caught by his mother as a boy having sex in his bedroom with his friend. Caught his mother's eye through a crack in the door while he was sucking his friend's penis.

I felt very angry because Dad was so nasty about Lucy, deriding her for her desire to do what is right. Stifled my anger, wanted to get up and walk out. Then he talked about Lavinia. I said I thought she was fucked up, Dad said not. I reminded him of his young friend who was going to have therapy because she was always repeating bad relationships, always getting abused, and said I thought Lavinia was similar. I think he understood that. Delicate subject. I want to talk to him about Mum, her choices. I want him to understand, although he would rather view things more romantically, people can't help who they like, Lavinia is so feminine . . .

On Courbet, his self-pity imaginative, like his

vanity, both traits unattractive generally but not in him. Dad said self-pity made him feel sadistic – 'I'll give him something to feel bad about.' He said in prison Courbet painted a fish, clearly a self-portrait. On Tuesday he said writers could write in prison but no good paintings were ever done there. He was talking about materials and equipment, the difference in needs between a painter and a writer.

Again Dad was imagining what Bridges would say in relation to certain of his antics, mainly his obsession with Rebecca Abbott, a woman who wrote to him recently to offer herself as a model. He said to me 'OK Jon, what do you make of this?' Then did an imitation of what he thought Bridges would say – 'Don't trouble me with such trivialities.' He said he was becoming obsessed with Rebecca, and rang her several times while I was there, but no answer. He said he didn't want anything to mess up or complicate his life, meaning he didn't want Susanna to find out and get upset with him. Said only once had he ever got a model by post. He can't resist the temptation. Wants me to find out about her through my literary connections, because she is a senior editor at Collins.

Then about birth, the enormous effect birth itself has on the personality. This came about after talk of star signs, because Rebecca Abbott mentioned in her letter that she is a Pisces. Dad said the doctor who delivered Courbet was so proud of his head, the lovely roundness of it, like a sculptor admiring his own sculpture. He said it was your birth that determined things for you, and the way your mother was with you, your upbringing, not the stars. He didn't refer to the father's part in all this, although he did mention when we were talking about Ali that he himself was in some way part of the rehabilitation process. No, really?

I said I was a forceps birth, and Dad said that was very common. I am not sure what he meant about birth having such a great effect on the personality – maybe he meant the trauma of it. When I tried to get him to elaborate he just talked about the renowned and beautiful roundness of Courbet's head. He said if he himself was feeling particularly vigorous tonight he could father four children, all of whom would be born in nine months' time. Would they all be the same? In spite of Rebecca Abbott he is obviously not a great believer in the zodiac.

Tuesday, 5 June 1990

Woke up with a crushing feeling of misery, something that happened in my dreams. Dad's fairly quiet, painless, more talk of Flaubert, Baudelaire's review of MADAME BOVARY commenting on the male side of her character. Dad said that Madame Bovary was the first literary representation of women's lusts and ambitions centred on a realistic character rather than in witches or mythological figures. Hmm. Becky Sharp, Lady Macbeth, Cleopatra . . .

Friday, 8 June 1990

Feeling overwhelmed by recently unravelled mental confusion and the exhaustion of having unravelled it. Made a cake for Lola's party tomorrow.

Saturday, 9 June 1990

Lola's party with Maya and Frances, so many noisy children, none of them actually mine.

Friday, 15 June 1990

Bridges as usual, then delivered the bound manuscript of ROSE to Rachel Calder. Feeling pleased.

Saturday, 16 June 1990

Susannah came to supper and we watched the World Cup. John Barnes played very badly.

Sunday, 17 June 1990

Beginning to enjoy the strange lightness of living without the pressure of an unfinished novel weighing me down. There will be a short gap before I begin to get anxious about the next one. I have written nine pages of it. Calls from America about SEXUAL INTERCOURSE. Exciting. And nerve-wracking.

Wednesday, 20 June 1990

Bridges then Lucy's, then to a party. Gareth asked me how I was feeling about Sean. Feeling very upset and anxious about tomorrow because Mum is coming over also Susie, to spend some time with me on the first anniversary of Robert's death. I am too sad about Sean.

Thursday, 21 June 1990

Didn't sit for Dad so I could be with Susie. In the studio on Tuesday when I told him I wanted to cancel for today he looked injured, as if I had just slapped him in the face – the shock of being considered less important.

Susie arrived at about ten and got into bed. Mum came over for lunch. Robert's sister Tessa collected Susie at three. Mum had a good moan about her analyst. Her life with Tom sounds pretty boring, she is run by his jealousy. I didn't know he was like that. Fetched Lola from school in the pouring rain. She made a cake, her favourite activity. Speaking to a man from INTERVIEW magazine on the phone from New York.

Saturday, 23 June 1990

Took Frances to a lunch party at Susannah Clapp's for Francis Wyndham. Met Carmen Callil, who seemed to like my book ROSE, although very sceptical about the title – she told me it was a mistake.

As well as telling me my title was a mistake Carmen said my next book must be VERY BIG as well as good, which I remember was very unsettling and did not help with my confidence.

Monday, 25 June 1990

Pam, Laura and I went out for supper at Museum Street Café. Pam made Laura cry.

Tuesday, 26 June 1990

Dad's as usual. Remembered from last Tuesday the strong smell of scent in the flat, a couple of empty half bottles of champagne, evidence of something going on. Dad loathes scent and nobody who knows him would smother themselves in it if they were going to spend time with him. Mentioned the smell in passing and Dad said he was amazed at my nasal perspicuity. He said he had been seeing somebody the night before.

Talk of Leigh's new club, a search for a name. Dad suggested he call it At Home as in smart invitations, or after a sign Dad saw outside a theatre in the war – Folies Bejeebers. Also of Leigh's new electric teeth, his cheeks pierced to accommodate the wiring.

I told Dad about the electricity privatization

scandal involving Cecil Parkinson, and the British Airways/Rover sweetener scandal involving Lord Young, neither of which events had come to his notice in spite of the fact he buys at least five newspapers every day. He loathes Cecil Parkinson, and thinks the Sarah Keyes scandal was disgusting – how can a man run the country if he can't even run his private life properly?

Then he spoke of love, the amazing random illness of it, the madness. He doesn't recognize the difference between the illness of obsession and love itself. I couldn't bring myself to talk about love with him because he continues to regard people caught up in compulsive destructive relationships as star-crossed lovers or whatever. He doesn't want to hear about women (or men) who love too much.

He described David Mlinaric as a boring, unprepossessing goody-goody who married a beautiful young girl twenty-two years ago, and told me with genuine amazement that they are still in love. Unaccountable! Then he expressed animosity towards Anne and Torquil as a couple, Anne eccentric, Torquil ghastly. He said, 'More cruelty has been perpetrated in the name of duty than in the name of more conventional types of cruelty.' He said that the supposed Astor queer phobia was caused by the queerness of the half-brother, Bobby Shaw. Then reported a dialogue between himself and Nancy Astor.

NA: 'What are those cigarettes you are smoking?

LF: 'Gauloises, they are French.'

NA: 'I loathe the French, are you French?'

He then told me that one of her children said to her 'You say we were conceived without pleasure and born without pain. Is that why we are all so odd?'

Also of THE STEPDAUGHTER by Caroline Blackwood.

No art, that is the problem, although there are good things in it. Postcard of a rearing horse on Paris waste-ground, of its beauty, 'so beautiful, without art.' Art required in novels, but appreciated when absent in photographs.

Then the Janet Green saga. Dad said 'The woman is engaged to be married to Gilbert de Botton, who is young and rich. Why should she take an interest in an old man of seventy?' I imagine it is something to do with her passion for art.

The picture is progressing. Dad says he wants to take out the head of Leigh in Leigh's picture, rub it down and start again. He had better not do that with mine. It would kill me.

He gave me a break and we went in the kitchen. I made some coffee. Dad said he was feeling low suddenly, a wave of blueness had swept over him. Then he told me about two lies his mother had told him. One was when he asked her about the function of the bidet in their house in St John's Wood. She told him it was a footbath.

The other was much worse. At Dartington he spent all his time riding or in the stables with the local farmer, a man who was charged with looking after the horses that belonged to the children at the school. (Dad ruined a good horse by toughening one side of its mouth. Even now, he says, he has to remind himself not to pull too hard on one side.) According to Dad the farmer took him for one of the little people, a small adult rather than a child, and because of this misapprehension felt comfortable telling him all about his marital problems. Dad and the farmer grew very fond of each other and Dad spent as much of his time as possible in the stables until suddenly his parents told him he was sacked from school and had to move to

Bryanston. Dad felt really betrayed by the farmer, somehow associating his dismissal with treachery on the part of his friend, but in fact it was Dad's parents who were 'treacherous'. Dad recently found correspondence between his parents and the school that made it clear his parents had removed him from Dartington by choice. He feels they betrayed him.

Last Sunday night Dad rang me to talk about Annabel, he said she really needed somebody to talk to and asked me about psychotherapy, an almost unbelievable turnaround on his part when he has been so suspicious of it. I rang the Tavistock and they gave me the numbers of two doctors to get in touch with at the Maudsley, near where Annabel lives.

After sitting went to Shepherd's Bush Market to get a wig for Lucy and some jewellery to go with my sari for the Normans' fancy-dress party at Far Park on Saturday. Then drove home feeling tired. Bridges going very well, aggro, the impending onset of the holidays, trying to learn how to take the pressure off myself. It is important for me to live in the present and not in anticipation of the future, in fear of what might happen or the hope that it will be better. Home, watched England v Belgium on the telly, very exciting, England won at the last minute.

Wednesday, 27 June 1990

Trying to stop bossing myself about.

Friday, 29 June 1990

Another good (tearful and painful) session with Bridges. Afterwards spent most of the day in bed.

Went over to Lucy's about eight to go to the country. We set off about nine. At Bridges we had talked about jealousy and spite, feeling your feelings rather than postponing or repressing them. This helped me with the motorway. Bridges said it was useful to be aware of these feelings, in fact to fear them. The fear real and useful rather than panic. Arrived tired but pleased with myself.

Saturday, 30 June 1990

Cold swim, lunch, reading the papers, long walk, sitting on the croquet lawn in the shade of an ancient tree. In the late afternoon we set off for Cirencester, the Normans' party at Far Park. It was much further away than I had imagined. Our twin room at the nearby pub was horrible, the loo behind a little formica screen in the corner, one of the beds on a dramatic slope, hideous carpet, grubby candlewick bedspreads, a spindly lamp that toppled and knocked over my cup of tea. I changed into my sari and Lucy put on her blonde wig. The leering amused publican grinned at us as we set off, his facial expression like the man in THE TEXAS CHAINSAW MASSACRE. The party was lavish, four hundred guests, the whole thing a bit of an ordeal. I was in touch with my feelings and didn't like what I felt, the lack of a partner.

I was too humiliated to mention this in my diary but for the first four hours of the party I was pursued by some bearded arse whose interest in me was persistent to the point of coercion. He was a rigger (not that I have anything against riggers) and wearing a red Jethro Tull T-shirt, proud to have erected the marquee, and would not take no for an answer.

The party theme was Movie Moguls and Starlets, a bad start, and the young Old Etonians in their loud suits and comedy ties were not friendly to Lucy and me, probably because we were too old and it had not occurred to us to try and look sexy. In her blonde wig Lucy was magnificent but more Charles II than Brit Eckland, and I was wearing so much fake gold from Shepherd's Bush Market I felt weighed down, clanking as I walked, my sari showing my white midriff. I thought I was side-stepping the misogynist dress-code and making a statement of solidarity with Bollywood in my beautiful costume, the concept of cultural appropriation not having reached me or any of my friends at that point in history; we were all comfortable wearing the same clothes whatever our skin colour when we were young, many of our outfits made of African fabrics or English shirting and cut to African versions of English Edwardian patterns, most of the clothes designed and made by Clare Thom. I did not stop to wonder if anybody at the party might have been excruciated by my stupidity, and in fact nobody was affronted in the least. Every single person was white, including the band.

Towards midnight I managed to shake off the rigger, but the taint of his relentless pursuit had ruined me for the rest of the night, the smear of his bearded breath still in the silver threads of my sari, still on my neck. I felt shamed, demeaned and demoralized, and in my depleted state the party arrangements were disorientating – I was no longer able to work out where I was in relation to any known architectural feature in the dark terrain, although I knew Far Park off by heart – as children we had spent many holidays with the Normans, playing billiards and listening to Little Richard, the whole family sharing with us the lavish gift of their hospitality.

We enjoyed not only the grassy rides down to the river in the private wood, the smell of wild garlic underfoot, the edible sorrel and hosts of wild daffodils, the shallow river pools under the trees in which we would swim when it was hot, but also the snow at Christmas, the giant tree reaching the ceiling of the double-height sitting room, the mountain of presents, Anne like a spare mum or godmother all year round when we needed her, none of the

Norman children showing any resentment towards us however needy we felt ourselves, however thin on the ground our own riches, not just material but psychological and emotional. At the party I felt confused by the decked access tunnels linking the marquee to the house and the pool house, all the unfamiliar entry and exit points, straw bales and crowds of people blurring the corners and edges, the present laid so thickly over the past I lost my special connection to the house and the family, to the landscape.

Then by the pool I met Caroline Garland, a family friend, and sat with her for a while at one of the small tables, the chlorine fumes from the water making my eyes smart. I didn't tell Caroline about the rigger because I felt implicated in his pursuit by my failure to convince him to leave me alone, as if he could tune in to my weakness. Every time I knocked him back he just came at me stronger, my resistance ineffectual like one of those nightmares you are trying to scream and nothing comes out, the same feeling I remember when I got raped, the paralysis of the shock of the attack, self-blame and the complete loss of hope of a good outcome. Caroline had recently trained as a psychoanalyst so I might have felt a bit better had I confided in her, but instead I asked her if she knew Bridges. I shouldn't have nailed her like that but I was clinging to her not to drown, and even as we spoke of this and that some of the female guests stripped off and dived in the pool, bikinis under their party outfits, full of strange confidence, while I clutched my sari round myself, dying to go home.

EIGHTEEN

Monday, 2 July 1990

Angus rang. Had a cup of coffee with him then swimming as planned. Spent hours catching up on this diary then made a start on work. Bridges, he was pleased at my achievement of the weekend. Just getting ready for bed when Susie rang and asked if she could come over and stay the night. Happy to take care of her.

Tuesday, 3 July 1990

Left Susie in bed and set off for Dad's. He is making each sitting last a little bit longer now at both ends, so I start earlier and earlier and rarely leave before eleven. Maybe I should just submit and accept that I won't be able to get to work until after an early lunch. Unless I fight with him to the death over this he pushes and pushes me.

Now he wants me to come on Sunday as well as Tuesday and Thursday because the picture is going so slowly. I absolutely can't. Although he NOT ONLY asked me if I needed any more money – he said just to ask rather than get a job as soon as the need arises because it seems to him I am getting into a really good rhythm of work – BUT ALSO offered to get me a new car if my old one (1969) fails the new MOT regulations on exhaust emissions. Very generous. He very much doesn't want me to do anything apart from writing so more time for myself, more for him.

Discussed with him an idea for the cover of ROSE and gave him a copy to read. I asked him if he would make a drawing in colour from that anonymous School of Fontainebleau painting in the Louvre of two sisters from the waist up, naked, one tweaking the other one's nipple. Ideal, and eye-catching. Dad had a good look at the reproduction of the painting and thought he could do something with it. In fact he seemed quite excited.

Much talk of the Queen, whom Dad met when he received his CH. He saw her at a party at the French Embassy recently and he was thrilled when she waved to him. She didn't look very pleased on another occasion when he introduced Esther to her. Talk of 'medals to be worn' at the Chatsworth Ball, Dad has lent his medal to Janey so she can wear it. He said everyone would be wearing medals. He told me not to tell anyone.

Leading on to talk of Matisse, who won a medal for one of his pictures. Dad said that an art collector, visiting Matisse's studio in view of buying a picture, inevitably chose the one for which the medal had been awarded. Matisse said he couldn't sell it because of the medal. The man was delighted that he and the medal shared the same taste. Dad commented that people set so much store by medals that they even think medals have opinions.

Susie was waiting for me when I got home. Felt

really irritable and mean and I just wanted to get on with my book.

Told Bridges how I had left Dad's feeling bad, a niggling feeling that I had made a mistake in a conversation about Kafka because I called Kafka 'Frank' and not 'Franz'. Bridges said this was me attacking Dad, mentioning Frank, Frank my brother the son Dad doesn't see very often, and that was why I felt bad.

Thursday, 5 July 1990

Sitting for Dad as usual. He bombarded me with chat. Not easy first thing in the morning. He is on page 60 of my book, he stayed up until half past four to get that far, he thinks it has similarities with ULYSSES in that the reader is fully absorbed. Although he has found three lines he thinks should be excised.

He asked me about one of the characters in the book – who was Veronica? – and I said I was unsure whether or not I had made her up, although I knew she was based on a woman who travelled with us on the ship, possibly a girlfriend of the mate. Veronica was real, but I might have invented the closeness between us. Dad seems to believe everything.

He took a romantic interest in Veronica because in the book I made her so lovable. His attentive questions pleased me because I was proud I had made her seem real, although my pride was mixed with the familiar puke-making pandering feeling I experienced when something I said about one of my friends or acquaintances aroused his curiosity, inadvertently or with some intentionality on my part, often on the lookout as he was for someone to paint and/or become involved with romantically or sexually.

Verónica received the full beam of his attention even though I had invented her, and the sexual element of his interest made me wonder suddenly if the real Veronica had been the other woman on the ship, not the mate's girlfriend but Uwe's side action. I asked myself if the adults on board were much more intertwined than I had envisaged them, not that there had ever been any evidence, and felt disloyal to Mum and guilty about demeaning her, if only in my thoughts.

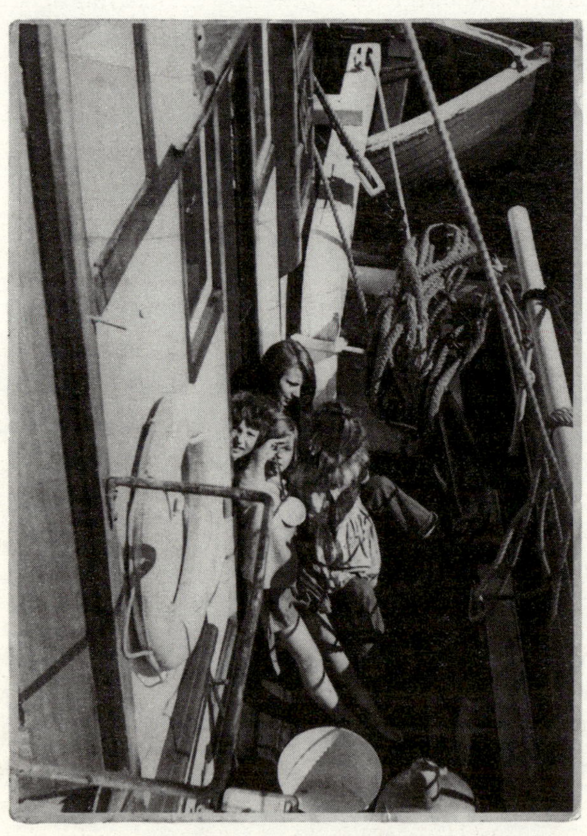

On Inga with Veronica
Photographer Unknown

Dad asked me if Veronica was as attractive in real life, like he wanted me to sell her to him, and I had to choose between taking Mum's side or pleasing him; it was my fault he was captivated. I hope I didn't tell him about my suspicions, which I am sure were unfounded.

I said I didn't know what she was like in real life and he was quiet for a moment. Then he asked me if I distrusted conversation when I was growing up, if I had made a deliberate choice not to take part, and I was surprised by this version of myself, not having been aware of my reticence until he reminded me of it. He said I was a silent child and I took his word for it, convinced not just because he was so convincing but because I experienced during that conversation the same pressure I used to feel when he appeared in the kitchen at Mum's and regarded me from the outside with his searching eye, making me up in a way that made me shut down to protect myself. My cheeks were hot, although on that occasion I was not cowed deeply enough by his scrutiny to lose myself. I might have smiled at him, I don't know whether I smiled, but I looked up and said maybe back then I was too angry to speak.

He stared down at me from his vantage point in front of the easel, neither of us entirely registering the implication of my inadvertent retaliatory hypothesis, at least not consciously, and he just kept on going where he wanted to go rather than pulling back from the conversation or asking me what I was talking about. He remarked that he used to wonder what was going on with me when I was quiet like that, and I wish he had asked me back then, when I was nine or ten, if only he had asked me instead of just looking at me, inventing me, not that I would have been able to explain. He said he came pretty close to assuming the blank face I turned to the world was an indication of internal blankness, my silence the evidence that nothing was happening. He was measuring the angle of my eyebrow with his paintbrush when he said that, squinting at me in all innocence as if that quiet child was no longer a part of me, and I just smiled defensively and looked blank, not wanting him to go any further, waiting to see how far he would go.

He scraped some paint off his palette with his palette knife, wiped the blade on the wall, cleaned it on the rag he had tucked into his belt and compared me to a little pot plant, a simile that was disparaging but ambiguous coming from him, fond as he was of the Zimmerlinde and the other plants that he nurtured in the studio. He said he used to think I was a little pot plant when I was a kid, and expected me to be amused, not to feel he was picking on me, although I am sure he was picking on me. The little pot plant was wishful thinking on his part. He said he had thought I was blank, but now it was clear to him from the first sixty pages of my book that he had been wrong – he understood suddenly that in childhood I had observed as acutely as anybody. I said if I was quiet maybe it was because I didn't trust anyone enough to engage in conversation with them, and Mum was always crying in real life, which wasn't very encouraging. What could I say? I didn't want to explain to him that I was unable to speak only in relation to him when he turned up at Mum's, a child paralysed in his presence by Mum's self-conscious smiles and his own uneasy demeanour, my fear of his judgement. He didn't know how to read me, and I would have loved to be understood, nothing required of me in return. And now I was asking him to read my book, to see my early life and the part he played in it through my eyes instead of his own. No wonder he needled me, perhaps uneasy still in himself to discover that not much had got past his sharp little daughter. He was afraid of what else I might have remembered, what else I might say.

I assume I must have been on tenterhooks since I gave him the manuscript, but my fear of his reaction did not find its way into my diary, although I know at the time I had my doubts about hurting Mum. Is it possible I was unafraid, proud of my achievement and relying on him to love my book because I felt loved by him, totally unaware he might be upset by the contents? I have no clear recollection either way, but I trusted him artistically, he had read my previous novel in an early version and was very helpful, even correcting a grammatical error because although English was not his first language he had a very good ear. I believe now I gave him the manuscript of *Rose* in almost complete confidence he would admire it, and admire me.

Tuesday, 10 July 1990

One of the worst days of my life. Went to Dad's and left feeling suicidal. He began by saying he had finished my book and felt uneasy about it. Then he attacked me. He said my book was fuelled by resentment and should be called BABY'S REVENGE by Nora Titsoff. He suggested I put it in a drawer for a few years.

I broke down, lost all sense of right and wrong. He convinced me the book was like a grenade in my hand, with the pin pulled out, ready to lob at Mum and Kai. I decided to give up writing because the book I am working on now is just as bad if not worse and I don't want to sit in my work room trying to invent something innocuous to write about. Without writing my life no longer seemed worth living.

He was shouting at me and we did not have that sort of relationship. He had never shouted at me before – I did not feel he had earned the right. He wheeled away and stomped across the kitchen towards the fridge, turned back to me abruptly then spun away again, so angry he didn't know what to do with himself. His contorted face was white. I had never seen him like that before. I sat down at the table and bowed my head, waiting for his rage to subside, not sure that it would ever subside.

The fridge shuddered loudly and the noise startled him. He stopped shouting, leant back and stilled himself against the white rectangle of its door, the paint on his chef's trousers all the colours he saw in Ib and Susie and me. He didn't want to be angry with me.

He admitted that the problem was 'amour propre' on his part, repeating it three times, perhaps hoping his confession would sound better in French, less embarrassing. I did not feel comforted, and had to look up the expression in the dictionary when I got home, not wishing to stop him mid-flow and ask him to translate – I didn't want to give him any further cause to despise me.

I didn't understand the explanation for his rage in the moment but guessed that my depiction of the misery and poverty of my childhood made him feel ashamed of himself, and he didn't want people to judge him on that account, particularly his grand friends; he was afraid of exposure. He appears very little in the book, and maybe that hurt too. He was careful to explain to me that back then he had little or no money, even though when he appears in the book he is driving a Bentley. He insisted that any time Mum asked him for money he got some for her. He said the book made it clear that most of the time she was with somebody else anyway. He felt that that let him off the hook. He was oblivious as I was that his anger at least in part was caused by his realization through my cool prose that his inconsistent behaviour had had a profound impact on his family, a possibility I am pretty sure had never occurred to him before.

I was too shocked and upset to speak. I was glad of the respite in the silence between us when he stopped excusing himself, we both were, but once we started work he got going again, he couldn't help himself; there was no question of not working on account of the upset. He claimed that I had always had a battling relationship with Mum, and that I had never got on with Ib, neither of which things were true, and asked me whether I thought I was detached, his way of saying I wasn't detached, detachment an aspect of personality he thought I might do well to cultivate. He was trying to undermine me, my confidence in my ability to make relationships, and I am wondering now whether in his fury he was having doubts about my position as executor, if only to punish me, although I didn't think of that at the time.

He could see that I was devastated by his reaction and he wasn't proud of losing his temper. So to make amends and in spite of his rage he told me he thought *Rose* was a good book, interesting and well written, and that the fact that there was no possibility of taking anything out of it proved to him it was good, whole I suppose he meant, like a poem, no further mention of the three sentences he thought should be excised from the first sixty pages. I said I thought it was impossible for a book to be good *and* fuelled by revenge and he said no, it was possible, but he couldn't give me an example. I said the subject of the book in part was resentment and he said maybe.

Then he talked about his relationship with his own father, how he had felt so protective towards him. It was the first time I had heard him talk about Ernst. He was suggesting that I should feel the same way in relation to him, I should be protecting him from myself, not betraying him by making his private life public. He said this was not a question of aesthetics but of family feeling. Family feeling! He said he had never used that phrase before. We were both quiet again momentarily after he spoke, marvelling together over the irony. I smiled through tears and he admitted that his mania for privacy was wrong and unreasonable and neurotic so he did not feel he could bring it to bear in the argument. At one point in the row I remember he said 'Publish and be damned,' but not with his whole heart, employing the same voice he used when he quoted a favourite maxim of his – 'Never apologize, never explain' – in both cases aware of the preposterous pomposity of his phraseology and not wholly convinced he could get away with it. He was shocked by the violence of his outburst and admitted he might be spreading his own horror of publication onto Mum and Kai. I was shocked that he had attacked me with such vehemence and distressed that he had read my book with no sorrow whatsoever for me, for what I had suffered. I was angry he failed to acknowledge my suffering. He showed me no sympathy.

Tuesday, 10 July 1990, cont.

Before I left he said he would grin and bear it if Mum and Kai saw it before publication and felt all right about it.

It is my fury making me feel ill. He patted me on the head as I headed towards the door and told me not to worry. I said that was impossible. Tears falling as I descended the stairs. Scraped through the day then saw Bridges and had a good cry. Lucy came over late evening and I talked things over with her. She is going to read the book before I proceed.

Wednesday, 11 July 1990

Still in a state of extreme upset. I am having a complete rethink, not that I am able to think clearly. Spent the day feeling miserable then went for a swim at four. Am trying to decide whether I want to go on writing or whether it is too tough for me with all this aggro to contend with. Yesterday I told Dad the next book was going to be even worse, about a young woman and her relationship with her father. Got through until the evening then went to Bridges and he helped me a bit but not enough. I feel angry with him too, that he doesn't help me more, and because of the holidays coming up. Still I have managed to regain confidence in my book as a book and feel less frightened of its power to destroy the lives of my loved ones.

I was supposed to be meeting Celia but she didn't turn up. Ib, Pat and Frances came over for supper and I talked to Ib about the book. She was very kind and helped me to feel calmer about it.

Thursday, 12 July 1990

Back again to Dad's for more grief. I was silent

and smiling until he brought up the subject. He said if I published the book people would always be guarded with me.

Then proceeded to tell me about a three-hour argument he had had with Susanna about Arthur Scargill, Susanna accusing him of putting Scargill on a pedestal then conducting a witch-hunt against him. Dad said like all arguments this has more to do with him and Susanna. Also him and me I reckon. Dad talked quite a bit about my book. When I said I didn't exactly come out immaculately he said he thought by the end in a way I did.

Also today and the day before yesterday much talk about the voluptuous perfection of little girls. This may be the key at least to some of his unease.

What was I trying to say?

It must have been painful for my father to read about Uwe's behaviour towards me, although as I recall he didn't condemn him strongly enough, nor console me for what he had done. He should have been angry with him and not me.

My book had opened my father's eyes, the child Rose more real and more vulnerable than the little pot plant, his version of me, but even so, in full knowledge of all I had been through, the voluptuous perfection of little girls was the subject he chose to examine over the course of the next two sittings, hardly the most propitious choice under the circumstances, under any circumstances. He was uneasy, but what about me? Had I been perfectly voluptuous? He might have offered to kill Uwe for me. So what if I had been perfectly voluptuous.

My father's interest was purely aesthetic but he was perplexed by the connection in his head between his pleasure and my misery. He was unsettled maybe because it had dawned on him for the first time that the way he looked at people might be uncomfortable for them, as if to be stared at was what they were for. He wanted me to see through his eyes, not through my own, to understand his viewpoint and give him my blessing. He remembered his own childhood but never quite understood children as sentient beings. He stood on his head to make us laugh, clowning perhaps an upside-down way of being himself, of distancing himself.

Much later, he used to say that my daughter Stella was so feminine, an observation intended as a compliment, but he found it distasteful when I showed off to him about her vocabulary. He said small children were just parrots. Just parroting what adults said. He shut me down and I heard irritation in his voice against me as a proud mum, and against my wonderful daughter. He complained to me that one of my sisters did the same, crowing over her own child. He said he really hated that sort of thing.

He was profoundly upset by my book, but gave the manuscript to Frank Auerbach for a second opinion, perhaps in an attempt to get over his distress. I was affronted he had not asked my permission, but understood he was trying to help. This high-handed action might have misfired had Frank hated my work, but he read the book and declared it 'a small masterpiece'. His admiration helped my father recover. He was no longer angry with me, which was a relief, and suddenly even proud of his daughter the novelist. Frank said that the mum in the book was a heroine, which I remember was very annoying at the time, a complete misreading on his part of my intentions, although now I suspect if I reread the book I might think differently. He wrote me a letter to congratulate me and I was delighted he took me so seriously.

Some time after publication I tried to speak to my father about Uwe's behaviour, hoping he would express outrage against him since he had had a chance to process his own feelings, but it didn't go well. He mumbled something almost defensive in response as if I might have been accusing him by association, his demeanour a bit sad but not sad enough, the low-key reaction normalizing the abuse that had been perpetrated against me. Then six months after my mother's death, tears in the eyes of my bereavement counsellor because I told her that one of Ali's friends had raped me in my own bed before I left home, when I was fourteen years old – not that I had been able to name my experience nor to speak of it at the time – I remembered in my fresh grief a conversation I had had with Ali many years after the rape, when I tried to make him understand what his friend had done and he made the same type of mildly uneasy response as my father, just sort of *shit happens* and not even unfriending the perpetrator on Facebook.

After the bereavement counselling had finished and with the proliferation of the #MeToo movement I began to reframe what had happened to me, my new consciousness I had been raped making me feel entitled to claim Uwe's behaviour towards me as abuse, in spite of my parents' normalization of it. I dared to see more clearly once Mum was dead, no longer constrained by her vulnerability. Women were speaking out. I phoned the Rape Crisis helpline and was understood. My experience was not minimalized. I was offered weekly sessions with a rape counsellor, another step on the road to more therapy. Nobody asked me whether it was *rape* rape or just rape, as if a category of rape exists that doesn't hurt very much.

Thursday, 12 July 1990, cont.

Talk of Mum and her problems, her personality, her murderous streak.

Afterwards felt a bit better, although unable to get on with my life. Also my chest is bad. Perhaps I picked up some germs feeling low and going to the dentist on Monday. I feel like blaming that on Dad too.

Susie came round for tea then Angus and Cerith for supper and together we all went to Leigh's new club at Zenon. Somehow I forgot about Dad and the book.

Friday, 13 July 1990

Bought some wool and a pattern to make a romper suit for Ib's baby. Knitting, early night.

Saturday, 14 July 1990

Angus and Cerith for supper. Angus cooked. Very enjoyable.

Sunday, 15 July 1990

Annie came over in the evening and we had a serious talk about Dad.

Monday, 16 July 1990

Must contact Mum so I can talk to her about the book. I feel very angry with Bridges for not having confidence in me and it. I was angry and upset in my session, but in the end I think I managed to make him understand. He brought up the picture of me as a child, silent, angry, crying to myself in my room. Angry tears.

What is real doubt about my book and what is angry destruction of the good thing I have made? At least I know I am angry.

Tuesday, 17 July 1990

Dad said that there was something clear in my book that had never occurred to him before – Mum doesn't like herself very much. Also he said that he of all people should understand my predicament. I said at least he asked his subjects before he worked from them.

Dad used to refer to himself as having been King Leared by Annie when they fell out. Today I mentioned the play and he said, 'Oh, isn't that the play about that horrible old man?' And we talked about imagination. Dad defines imagination as the ability to feel what somebody else is feeling. That's funny, because I have always thought him singularly skewed in that ability.

He told me something about Annie. He said a while ago she spent ages apologizing to him about borrowing an expression she had got from him to use in one of her short stories, a phrase that turned out to be an insult Dad had heard used by one of the porters at Covent Garden when the flower and fruit and veg market used to be situated there, namely 'you bottle-nosed prick'. Dad said he wondered what all the fuss was about. Nothing compared to the fuss about my book.

Francis Bacon, his claim to be working with accident and sensation. Dad says no longer. Then talked about abstraction, Frank's view of it as subject matter. I said I thought it was a question of degree. Dad said that colour is drawing. We were discussing the green velvet piping round the collar of my jersey. At first he tried a vivid green colour but thought it was too much 'a touch of colour', something he wants to avoid in his work although he likes it in other people's work.

AIDS. Dad said it was unimaginably horrible to have it, but even worse to give it to somebody. Talked about sex and death, Dad said they both occupied the same area of the brain.

I knew Leigh had AIDS and tried to break it to Dad in a tentative way, but he wasn't having any of it. He loved Leigh and loved to work from him, and mourned him tearfully after his death. The paintings of him are some of the best, most magnificent and tender and celebratory, but in spite of his love or tangential to it he chose a very snide name for the double portrait of Leigh and his wife Nicola, his choice of title revealing the invasive assumption he made about the nature of Leigh and Nicola's relationship. He called the picture *And the Bridegroom*, from the A. E. Housman poem 'A Shropshire Lad', which when I looked it up made me feel very sorry he was unable to see the meanness in his gesture, the transparency of it.

Lovers lying two and two
Ask not whom they sleep beside,
And the bridegroom all night through
Never turn him to the bride.

Tuesday, 17 July 1990, cont.

A return to the subject of painters in their late years, the few whose work improved – Matisse, Velázquez, Titian. Said Rembrandt levelled off or stayed the same, a variation on our last talk about Rembrandt. Dad keen of course to number himself amongst those whose work gets better, and it does, it is becoming more human. About a show soon to open in Edinburgh of Poussin. Dad really wants to see it. He is almost as bad at travelling as me.

Also about his Companion of Honour, the excitement of receiving it. Francis Bacon bad-mouthing him about it. Dad said, 'They say a Jew loves an honour.' Jo, Dad's cousin, of Francis – 'He must be so unhappy.' Dad said Francis was one of the happiest men he ever knew, positively ecstatic.

Wednesday, 18 July 1990

Went to the Café de Paris for the last night ever before it shuts down. Straight to Dad's at half seven without having slept.

Thursday, 19 July 1990

Sitting, not feeling too bad, longing to get home.

Snoozed in the afternoon, Kai came over in the evening to discuss my book with me and said he really didn't mind at all. Early night.

Friday, 20 July 1990

Mum came over for an early supper. We had a good talk about the book and she was very supportive and encouraging. She is going to read it.

Saturday, 21 July 1990

Subterranea with Dominie. Met a man called Daryl who invited us to go to a party with him and two friends. The party was in North London. I was the navigator. Slow dancing. He drove me home and stayed the night. On Sunday morning I made him a lovely breakfast.

Until then he thought I was strange but my very clean flat and skills in the kitchen brought me closer to the lovely conception of womanhood he had in his mind.

In the evening I had supper with Angus and Cerith and Lucy. Talking of conception, I told Daryl I was afraid to get pregnant and he said he would be careful.

Monday, 23 July 1990

Went to the doctor for the morning-after pill. Had my photo taken for Associated Press. They were supposed to come on Friday but cancelled because the Stock Exchange was bombed and all their photographers were deployed to cover that story. Bridges, and in the evening had supper with Francis Wyndham at the Museum Street Café and afterwards watched Cerith's film on the telly. It looked very beautiful.

Tuesday, 24 July 1990

Sitting from the usual time until half twelve, dozed a bit for the first time. Then we had lunch at the River Café with Jo, Dad's cousin from New York, and Bella, Esther and Susie. A happy occasion. I drove Jo back to St John's Wood – she is staying with her brother Wolf in a house Dad used to live in with Kitty when he was young. Sat in the garden for a while with Jo and Molly, Wolf's wife.

At Bridges was too angry to speak.

Wednesday, 25 July 1990

Rang Mum to ask her about the book. I was worried she might have killed herself on account of it so I was very pleased when she answered the phone. She said it was beautiful, devastating, and too important not to publish. Good old Mum. What a relief.

After publication she told me that one day she might sit down and write a riposte to my version of what had happened, meaning that I really didn't understand what she had been through, and although she sounded a bit bitter and hostile I encouraged her to fulfil that ambition. I wish she had told her side of the story.

Dad was slightly in awe of the grandeur of her early life – I am not sure how much of that I made up and how much I gleaned from Mum's stories – and Mum was shocked and dismayed she had cut Ali and me with a sharp knife and mixed our blood when we would not stop squabbling, blood brother and blood sister, an incident that never happened. In reality she just made us spit in a saucer and mixed our saliva together with a spent match. I thought she was going to make us eat it but she spared us the torture of that.

Both of them believed every word and told me how they felt in relation to what I had written but neither of them saw fit to apologize to me for what I had suffered. I don't know what I was hoping for. It might have helped had they acknowledged it would have been better for me if they had been able to look after me a bit more carefully.

Thursday, 26 July 1990

Gave Dad the 'good' news about the book – Mum and Kai don't mind about it. He almost apologized to me about the uproar he had caused and said he would begin work on the cover shortly.

Later I rang Daryl and made a date to meet him on Wednesday. He found this all a bit boring. He wanted to come over right away. I told him that Lucy was coming over at six to go to the theatre. I said I wanted to get to know him, to talk, and to go home on my own at the end of the evening. He seemed to think this was outlandish but complied. He said, 'I want to make love to you over and over again,' like he has been listening to too many Luther Vandross records.

He did say that if he was married and his wife was unfaithful to him he would give her one warning then if she did it again he would hit her. He said that that was the way some women liked to be treated. I protested, and he said I was making him out to be some sort of a freak.

The argument was brief, and in the diary I failed to remark on the way Daryl turned it round on me after I protested, like I was rude to make him feel freakish. I didn't ask him whether he would slap or punch his unfaithful wife, if that was enough punishment, or if he would take off his belt. His claim that some women like to be hit reminds me of my father's assertion that there was no point in a woman leaving a violent relationship because she couldn't help her sexual preferences. He always used to say that people don't change, they never change, but I don't believe that. Even he changed. His problematic position in relation to women (not just to women) became untenable as we grew up and he learnt from us what he had been unable to learn without sisters. He loved his daughters and was too caught up not to be changed.

Thursday, 26 July 1990, cont.

Lucy came over and we went with Tom to see THE ILLUSION by Corneille and afterwards to Leigh's club. Dominie turned up, and Cerith, and Dad. Lucy and Tom sat quietly. Didn't stay all that late because it is the last Bridges session tomorrow.

Friday, 27 July 1990

Bridges, the fond farewell. I was supposed to be meeting David McAdam for a drink but rang him to cancel and stayed in.

Saturday, 28 July 1990

Mum came over for breakfast and to drop off my book. I made bread rolls. She was repressing all her bad feelings about her analyst, who has gone away. Some venom leaked out in my direction. This made me feel anxious and miserable.

I had a row with Pat when he came to pick up Frances because he was so impatient with her he made her scream. I slammed the door on him. Half an hour later he rang up and apologized. If it weren't for the fact that Ib is about to have another baby I would tell him I needed a break for a few weeks. Susie came over and I made some spinach soup.

Tuesday, 31 July 1990

Dad's as usual, talk of Freud, Dad's admiration for his Moses book, the idea Sigmund had that Moses was an

Egyptian. And psychoanalysis, Dad's aversion to it as an American parlour game. He proposed the idea that there are two types, the parlour game and a treatment for people who are really ill. He said, as he always does, that it is out of scale with the lifespan, it takes so long. A misunderstanding based on the idea that life is on hold until analysis is over. Also, he doesn't take into account that people who are very disturbed often don't have much of a lifespan.

He said that Mum is a very strange mixture of the unrealistic and the practical. He expressed some worries about Ali, he said he sounded so odd on the phone recently. Dad still fears he will go back on drugs. I said he is bound to be strange, the numbness of years of drugs wearing off, real life, also Mum's hostility, her dim view of his life in the City. Talk of Narcotics Anonymous people, their lack of abandonment. I said that that was necessary for them, not to let go. Dad said it made them unattractive, meaning sexually.

When Ali was still taking drugs Mum told me that given the choice she would rather he was a drug addict than a policeman; the son of one of her old friends had become a detective in the Met and Mum preferred his twin sister, who was glamorous but chaotic, her substance abuse and other difficulties impacting on her relationship with her children and with Mum's friend. I said it was a matter of life and death, not about lifestyle, and Mum opened her eyes wide in response as if that information was news to her. She backed down, almost grateful to me for putting her straight.

Dad often used the word 'abandoned' to describe a young woman open about her own sexual desire or eagerness for frequent submission to his, whether or not under the influence of drugs or alcohol, somebody careless about keeping herself safe in relation to him. A young girl who was lovely and manifested this type of behaviour was irresistible to him but only for work and sex and companionship, his attitude towards her and her availability an uneasy balance of marvelling amused admiration and intolerance, her loveliness always devalued for love in his eyes in the end by the keenness of her affection. I am thinking with love and compassion of various young women who got caught up with him in genuine ardour on their part, either temporarily or for years and years, and wondering about the connection between abandoned behaviour and feeling abandoned, perhaps the lack of self-care having been caused by a previous abandonment or several abandonments – women who have been abandoned might act abandoned as a consequence, the abandoned woman condemned to a life of abandonment, getting abandoned over and over again until she can find a way out.

Tuesday, 31 July 1990, cont.

Talk of Dominie, how she used to edit herself as a lesbian who only went with men for money rather than as a whore. Dad thought this was a good idea, more alluring.

Whatever his relationship status Dad was always hoping to meet somebody new. During a party at Northwold Road to celebrate my birthday I looked up and saw him in the doorway; he had just arrived and was scanning the long narrow sitting room. I waved at him from the back by the kitchen door, pleased he had made the effort to cross town. I had just had my hair cut in a new style and my home-made dress of silk crêpe felt slippery but not too slippery. He waved back, smiled, looked a bit puzzled, then his face cleared as he recognized me. Afterwards he told me that for a minute he had thought I was a girl, he had mistaken me for a girl, meaning someone he might hit on.

Tuesday, 31 July 1990, cont.

Sitting extended again. Had to ask to leave after half past eleven (the sitting is supposed to finish at half ten) to get back in time to meet Jo (Dad's cousin) for lunch. Made it with ten minutes to spare. Showed Jo the old Freud photos from St John's Wood Terrace.

Then Dad phoned. We talked for a bit, ordinary conversation, then he slipped it in about his new arrangement with Leigh, who has been sitting after me every Tuesday and Thursday. Leigh is to come later so Dad can work later from me and get on with my picture. Not so much as a by-your-leave, I will have to talk to him about it on Thursday.

Wednesday, 1 August 1990

I have time on my hands because Bridges is away, and my day feels much less pressurized, although I miss him and will miss him more if I get very upset and lose touch with him in my mind, something I am guarding against. He says I am attracted to danger, mental as well as external. I am supposed to be going out with Daryl tonight except that he hasn't rung me to make a plan. If he doesn't ring I may well heave a sigh of relief. Spent the day reading and waiting for Daryl to ring but he didn't ring. So when Ib asked me over to supper I went out to get away from the terrible feeling of waiting. So I don't know if Daryl rang or not. If he did, he didn't leave a message. Had a lovely evening at Ib's.

Thursday, 2 August 1990

Remembered something Dad said a while ago – 'I force people into a corner, make them behave badly, then I have a reason never to see them again. So avoiding grey areas.'

Also talk of his mother's cooking, good cooking, as his father liked it – 'Stodgy and greasy, you know, good homely cooking.' He said his father always liked a proper meal with meat, as he does himself.

He said that when they lived in Berlin they always had a cook, so his mother was very excited when they came to England and she was to do the cooking herself. Remembered Jo telling me about Anna Freud – 'She had no clue whatsoever about ordinary people, human beings, their feelings.' Talk of Guy Hart, his meanness, and Victor Chandler, his Hoxton gangster grandfather in his big house with servants.

Dad's plan to paint Ib and the new baby with Cerith and Leigh as attendants. He was feeling very low in spirits, the weather getting him down. Not at all keen on the summer. He has begun work on my cover from the nipple-tweak painting.

Tuesday, 7 August 1990

Dad told me that the hand of the artist is not as important as people make out in painting – he said look at the late Matisse cut-outs, the chapel at Vence and late Sickert, those things hardly made by the artist at all.

On the same subject, the brilliant films of Andy Warhol made by Paul Morrissey, and yet the films Morrissey made without Warhol behind him were rubbish. Dad's theory on the Marlon Brando case, the daughter's baby was fathered by her brother. It transpires that Brando orders rum and raisin Häagen-Dazs by the ton, literally, and eats it for breakfast by the bucketful.

Dad says the incest theory is the only one to explain the details of the case, the fact that Brando declared his family 'cursed'.

After sitting a phone call from Daryl. He asked me whether I was pregnant and I said no, you will be glad to hear I am not. He said he was not glad. He said a little half-caste child with me would be lovely. I said I would not have a child unless I was married. He said he would come over on Friday.

Wednesday, 8 August 1990

Over to Ib's to give her a bottle of champagne and a big bunch of roses for her birthday. Mum was there, giving me funny looks.

Thursday, 9 August 1990

Dad's as usual at half seven, sitting until twelve now, it's a killer. He talked about women and their attitude towards their body. Told him about Mum giving me daggers. He said all the women he had been with were funny about their body, disliked their body – he named Katie, Celia, Mum and Susanna. I said, 'That says more about you than about them, kiddo.' He said, 'I know.'

Friday, 10 August 1990

The big Daryl day. Cleaned the flat, clean sheets, even ironed the pillowcases, then went swimming, it was luxurious, then when I got home there was a message from Daryl saying he would not be able to make it tonight. On the message he said to ring at ten for an explanation and so I did but his machine was on. That is that. I can't be bothered. There is nothing he can do or say to make me change my mind.

Saturday, 11 August 1990

Subterranea with Dominie. First thing that happened Daryl grabbed me. I shrugged him off and told him I didn't want to talk to him. I felt very anxious after that, the damp air choking me, the bass making the cavity of my chest vibrate. Tried to go outside but the bouncer wouldn't let me. Turned round and there was Daryl again. Talked to him for a while, not very impressed by his excuse, something about a drunk dog. I was not able to sustain much anger against him, just talked a bit, brushed him off a bit but not final enough, he asked me when he could see me, make love to me, but I had lost interest. He asked me whether he could touch me and I said NO. He tried to convince me that I was unreasonable, that if I really liked him I would understand that he was just overworked and a bit disorganized. He said life was dynamic, things just happened, I couldn't always have things my own way. He left. After he had gone I felt relieved, cross, disappointed. After the club shut walking with Dom up the Portobello Road, she was really pissed, barefoot, got a cab home, Dom raving, got to bed.

Sunday, 12 August 1990

Not feeling too bad when I woke up, then the phone rang, somebody crying desperately, thought it was Mum, then relieved to find it was only Debbie. She was in a terrible state. Went round to see her at Pam's and put her to bed. Two abusive men in one week. She wanted to come over but I said I was going to bed and went to bed. Read LEAVES OF GRASS and slept from nine until nine in the morning.

Monday, 13 August 1990

Had a cup of coffee with Pam, who has just returned from Spain, and Debbie, who was feeling much better and on her way to the doctor's to enquire about psychotherapy. Pam gave me a bottle of Femme, the scent I wrote about in ROSE. The scent was nice but not as nice as I remembered it. Glad Pam is safely home.

So after getting some good work done on DAYDREAMING and beginning to feel the possibility of getting somewhere with it the phone rang and it was Daryl, wanting to talk, wondering when we can meet up. I said I would call him. He asked me how I felt about him when I saw him on Saturday. I said angry. He asked me how I felt later, when I had simmered down. I said choked, holding in the anger. He said he was getting hard just thinking about me.

After I put down the phone I realized I had torn up the piece of paper on which he had written his telephone number. Then I realized I had copied it into my telephone book. I tore the Daryl page out of my book and threw it away. So now I can't ring him even if I feel like it.

Tuesday, 14 August 1990

Dad's as usual at half seven. Esther was there for breakfast, Dad dished up three cold grouse but I didn't want to eat grouse first thing in the morning. I had a peach and a banana with my tea. At last he has something to show me for the cover of my book. I really liked what he had done, although he was unsure, wanted to work further on it. Ink drawing of the nipple tweaking with curtains, coloured in in chalks, different shades of red, pink and pale grey. Spiky, very satisfactory. Sat until almost twelve.

Much talk, about Dad and his ability to pick up girls. Grew out of a discussion of Sean and his amazing ability to attract women. Dad said it was because women were not afraid of Sean. He said girls were always afraid of him, even when he was a young boy. He would always get women, hard-bitten ones, or ones with the clap.

He told me an anecdote about waiting in Marseilles for a boat to go to Greece, he couldn't understand why nobody was interested in a beautiful girl hanging around the bar, he went with her, boarded the boat and when the symptoms began to appear discovered why nobody else would go near her. He said that on the boat he had filled a little notebook with drawings, one of those rough ones with rounded corners and blue gridded pages, pictures of the Greek sailors and the volcano island. The radio operator was a poet who couldn't speak English but knew Eliot off by heart – 'Let us go then, you and I,' in a heavy Greek accent.

Talk about men and women getting together. I told him about Debbie, who woke up on Sunday morning to discover that the man she had picked up on Saturday had disappeared in the night, while she was asleep. Dad said he really enjoyed it when that happened to him, he spent a night in Paris with a beautiful girl and woke up to find the bed empty.

He was quiet for a few moments and then said almost wistfully, as if to comfort himself, that he loves it when, after drinking tea in the kitchen with a girl and saying goodbye to her, he returns to the bedroom and discovers that she has made his bed. He said he finds it so touching. 'Domestic bliss,' I said.

Spent sitting time quietly puzzling out some DAYDREAMING problems and unravelled a few mysteries of how to progress. After sitting went home, a little sleep, got some work done, read, rang Tessa P. Rang Neneh and arranged to meet on Thursday.

Thursday, 16 August 1990

Dad's. I said 'Imagining people rather than perceiving them is aggressive,' and he said 'I am always doing that,' and I said 'I know.'

Went over to Neneh's, picked her up and had lunch with her at the Museum Street Café. Drank some wine, continued to talk about imagination versus perception. She said that was exactly what Jeannette did to Andi. She told me how hard it was to give sometimes, how few real friends she had, how out of the habit of giving, how she hid her real self. I was touched she confided in me.

NINETEEN

Tuesday, 21 August 1990

Sitting as usual at half seven. It was ten to one by the time Dad had finished with me. I felt explosively angry. He spent a large part of the sitting talking in detail about some poor girl he had fucked recently.

Drove home and met Dominie at the pool. Still angry. Dishing out support and advice makes me angry. Dominie like a child trying to get a smile out of Mummy. When I got home I had to have a lie down. Debbie came over with a huge bunch of flowers. Made me feel a bit better.

In the evening went to Lord Goodman's 77th birthday party. Bumped into Angus and Cerith on the way. They are on the wagon, like Debbie. Met Dad at 2 Brydges Place, had a drink (dying for a drink) then to Lord Goodman's.

On the way up to his flat in the lift Dad talking about getting fucked up the bum, the prostate gland, how for queers it takes a while to get a taste for it, Francis Bacon on the subject, and Leigh, who claims most men make do with wanking and blow jobs. Dad loves to talk about that sort of thing.

At the party he held forth about hate, art, the impersonality theory, his loathing of journalists, his admiration for good burglars, all his favourite topics. He admitted to one of the guests that he was making it up as he went along. He said that his ideas came out of prejudice. Nobody mentioned the war that was just about to break out in the Middle East.

When I got home I spoke to Debbie on the phone, she is attending a daily detox clinic, then Pam rang from Ireland, feeling low, then Lucy.

Wednesday, 22 August 1990

Mum coming to supper. Made some spicy lentils for her also stuffed some small pickled peppers with tuna and mayonnaise for a first course. Began to dread her arrival but once she arrived things were all right, she seemed all right. I don't know exactly what I dread. Her attacking me, some kind of explosion, too much anxiety.

Thursday, 23 August 1990

Enjoying not sitting. Dad has put off my sitting until tomorrow. Great feeling of freedom. Early phone call from Debbie, she was irate. This is day four off the drink for her. Went swimming with Kai – he is working at Pam's on the bathroom. I did some good work.

Friday, 24 August 1990

Early morning meeting with Derek Birdsall at Dad's about the design of my book cover. I made kedgeree and Derek drank a half bottle of Louis Roederer '82. Not much said really, but he went off happily with Dad's drawing of the nipple-tweaker.

Sitting, talked about dreams, the meaning. Dad seemed to connect them more with the digestive process than with the machinations of the unconscious mind. I told him about the censorship of the unconscious, the distortions caused by its effort to repress wishes and desires. This was news to him.

After sitting went home and went to bed. THE NEW YORK TIMES phoned me for an interview.

Saturday, 25 August 1990

Lucy came over for supper. Tomorrow she is going to South Africa for her sister's wedding. Pam is going back to Ireland for work.

Monday, 27 August 1990

Dreamt I was selling my flat because Mum and Tom were moving in downstairs. I did not want to let the flat go but saw I would have to get rid of it and them. Mum ruining my life. I had to give up writing and get a job.

Carnival with Steve Noble. We sat on the top deck of the bus, some girls on the back seat singing 'Silly Games', recently rereleased (version.) Got off at the Gate and made our way down through the back streets to Powis Square where Andi was performing. Got there just as she was going on stage. Great performance. She sang 'Bad Like Jesse James'. A triumph.

Tuesday, 28 August 1990

Worked late. Mark Marvell rang from INTERVIEW magazine to interview me and for his final question asked me if I had ever had sexual intercourse with my father.

Wednesday, 29 August 1990

On the way to the pool this morning met Angus and Cerith who were drinking coffee outside a cafe in Museum Street. Today or tomorrow is the seventh anniversary of their first meeting so I invited them round for an early supper tomorrow night. I am seeing Celia anyway. I think I will buy some grouse and make brown-bread ice cream. My breasts have swollen up to way beyond their normal size because of the morning-after pill.

Thursday, 30 August 1990

Sitting. Dad received an estate agent's booklet about a house in the country. Talk of ancestral homes. This was a leasehold property in Dorset with some obligations to repair. I said I thought it would be better to get somewhere freehold, although this place did look very nice, particularly the kitchen and scullery and laundry, for me those functional rooms often the most desirable.

Talked about Debbie's driving ban. She is planning to get hold of a new driving licence. She will end up in Holloway. Dad ordered me some grouse from Allens.

Home, cooking. Celia, Angus and Cerith at seven. Everything turned out perfectly.

Friday, 31 August 1990

This is the heaviest period in the whole history of womankind. Woke up covered in blood although I was wearing a tampon. First hour of the day changed tampon four or five times. Unable to go swimming. Put grouse bones on for stock. I am going out with Matthew tonight to Freds and Quiet Storm and Fat Tony's new club. I wonder whether I am going to bump into Daryl.

Received a dozen red roses from David Rosenthal as an apology for the muddle over the publication date of SEXUAL INTERCOURSE. The note that came with the flowers says 'Blue Skies from now on.' When I saw the delivery man mounting the stairs with the flowers I assumed they must be for somebody else. The bouquet arrived in a good quality but hideous vase that I can give to the church fete. We have finally got a cover that is acceptable to all parties so that is a relief. Publication has been put back until October and so has the publication of the paperback in England.

Saw Bella outside Quiet Storm, trying to get in. Some friction between her and Matthew, he had been telling me earlier that Bella had almost run him over on Blenheim Crescent, Bella told me later that the incident was two months ago and grossly exaggerated. At Quiet Storm saw Mario, Daryl's friend. Mario said 'The thing about Daryl, you just have to give him some space.'

Sunday, 2 September 1990

Swimming, Derek Birdsall's for ROSE book cover, I am very pleased with it. Hoxton to see Eileen, then Pam's. I ate some fruitcake, some mandarin oranges with cream, drank a glass of Bailey's Irish Cream and felt a bit sick, not very surprisingly, then went home and went to bed. Suddenly felt as I did in the West Indies when I was nine – hot, helpless and alone. Frightened.

Monday, 3 September 1990

Bumped into Angus and Cerith and Debbie outside a cafe on Museum Street. Had a cup of coffee with them before work. Debbie angry and rude.

Reworked much of the third chapter. B spins in the revolving door and emerges as a different person in the eyes of her father. So far I have twenty-nine pages to work with. Lucy rang, she is back from South Africa. Good.

First Bridges session, felt so angry I nearly killed a traffic warden when she gave me a ticket but managed to restrain myself. Was grumpy and ungrateful in my session. Told him I felt he would just put me down if I told him my problems, particularly my problems about men. Feeling ridiculous.

Lucy came over for supper. Made a pasta dish with spinach and anchovy. Received a card today from Mark Marvell in New York. My penfriend. Maybe he will turn up in London and we will fall in love and get married.

Tuesday, 4 September 1990

Dad's reluctantly. Having told Bridges yesterday how much I hate sitting made me feel a bit more able to endure it. My spirit has been broken and I just do what I am told. The half past ten deadline we agreed on has been pushed back and back. Dad is taking advantage of my pain and weakness following his anger over my book. I don't get away until twelve or one now. I feel I have no will left with which to fight him. I don't even have the pleasure of giving him the time, being thanked for it, because he just takes it from me.

Talk of the new facial expression Norman Rosenthal has adopted perhaps because he has heard a rumour that he will be knighted. Dad said Norman's appearance is like Eric Blore 'my favourite actor' playing a conman baronet in THE LADY EVE. This fantasy knighthood occurred to him following his private visit to the Royal Academy to see the Monet show. He met Norman at the gallery in the early morning, before it opened to the public, and said the Monets didn't do anything for him, he said he left feeling exactly the same as he had felt on arrival. He said 'In great painting every inch of the painting is equally important, in Monet's pictures every inch seemed equally unimportant. Too flawless, but then Vermeer is flawless and I like his work. I did like the Monet pictures of London, I like everything about London. I find London so exciting even though I live here.'

Just recording his words like this is making me feel fucking angry. I sat on condition my delicate feelings and my writing be taken into account. I made this clear before we began. The very fact of me making this clear stimulates him to get one over on me. He has received a silk cravat from Paul McAdam as a present.

Home, Pam rang. She was devastated because Steve has said perhaps it would be best to admit defeat. This has completely thrown her, because up until now he has been begging her to take him back. He is turning everything round, trying to make her feel he has left her. Which in effect he has.

I put down the phone and Lola rang up. I rushed round the corner to give her a cuddle. She and Johnnie and Laura gave me a pair of castanets, a souvenir from Spain.

I hardly had time to think before it was time to go to Bridges. Talked about work, and the dramas taking place around me. Also the pressure of time, sandwiched between Dad and Bridges, the little bit of day left in the middle all that is left for my work.

Pam woke me about eleven or half past. I talked to her until midnight then went back to bed. What can I do to help? I love her but my involvement is stopping me from sorting out my own problems. Talked about this with Bridges. Also talked about pressure, what makes it so hard to face work. Pressure the pressure of repressed feelings.

Wednesday, 5 September 1990

Early phone call from Pam, who says she can hardly carry on. She has to carry on, because she is in the middle of producing her first feature.

Freds with Lucy. We bumped into Steve, who said I looked beautiful, and would not shut up about it. I went to the bar and in my absence he told Lucy that he and I used to have anal sex, which is not true. Then he said he was going out with John Barnes on Wednesday and would I like to come. He said he was using John Barnes as a carrot to get to me. Cocaine psychosis. In real life he doesn't even fancy me.

The Vintage launch party my two lives collided – the party was at the Milk Bar, Spike and Neville on the decks, very loud and a free bar. Lucy wanted to go home so I left with her but came back five minutes later because I didn't want to go home. I had to plead with the bouncer to let me back in.

Saturday, 8 September 1990

Went with Ali to see a flat. He was angry, finding it very hard to be wrong about anything, not as stable as he might be, and I felt quite worried about him. His hands and face were less carefully clean than his usual high level of cleanliness. I didn't much like the flat, so that didn't help. I said he should set his sights higher. He is questioning everything, including NA.

Pam's to collect Frances from Pat. Pam's parents arrived from Basingstoke and we all went to Highbury Fields together. Pam very upset and anxious, desperate to get back with Steve and yet knowing he will continue to treat her like shit. Her dad was very tense, driving dangerously through anxiety. Little Johnnie very clingy and apprehensive, afraid everybody is going to leave him. Heartbreaking.

Took Frances home about five and she crashed out. Neneh rang me. We had a long talk about Tessa, who is in a bad way. Angus and Cerith came over for supper, and Kai later for a drink. I made grilled courgette salad, grilled aubergine and grilled mushrooms, followed by chicken with roast mini onions and roast spuds with gravy and watercress, then apple tart on yeast pastry for pudding. To bed about three.

Sunday, 9 September 1990

Had been thinking of going to the Kiss FM party at Highbury Fields but decided against it because Dexter rang and said he was going with his new girlfriend. I was feeling too manless to endure meeting her.

Tuesday, 11 September 1990

Dad's at seven forty. Told him I thought he had painted one side of my chest flat and the other side busty. He hadn't noticed this flaw in the picture so now he's got to work on my jersey some more. Still it can't be much longer I don't think. I asked him for a cheque for Bridges (two hundred and eighty-eight pounds) and he wrote one out to me instead. Four thousand pounds!! Result.

After sitting drove to the toyshop on Elgin Crescent and bought a Teenage Hero Turtle rucksack for Johnnie – it's his birthday today. Home about one, Tessa phoned to ask me about giving up heroin. Talked to somebody at the NA head office, phoned Tessa back and gave her the information. I am the expert because of Ali.

John's party. Felt depressed. Went to Bridges at half past six – he had moved my session time, which turned out to be convenient. Talked about distortion, corruption.

Back to Pam's after my session to say goodbye because she is going to Ireland until Christmas. Debbie was laying into the champagne and talking about love. Pam said the ending with Steve is so painful she would rather get back with him and put up with anything, but Steve doesn't want to be with her any more. I was quite cross and told her to get help.

Feeling of doom, Debbie the sickest, talking about two types of men, kind and weak or nasty and strong. She mentioned her violent relationship with Pete the Murderer and how she no longer had violent relationships. She no longer has relationships as far as I can see. She was encouraging Pam not to let go of Steve, talking about the sanctity of marriage, the strength of love.

Friday, 14 September 1990

Sitting, the usual, can't bear it much longer. The worst thing about Dad is the nose-picking, for which he seems to need an audience. It makes me feel like I am going to vomit.

Met up with Debbie at Freds. She was a bit drunk but not too bad, although still smarting because Pam had been horrible to her in spite of the fact that Debbie has been looking after the children all week. Well, it's a long story. Pam arrived totally unexpectedly and I had a row with her. Quiet Storm. Saw Daryl briefly. Pam went off into the night with Phil Dirtbox.

I walked home and put the machine on and unplugged the phone. When I woke up there were two messages from Pam. She rang again, in a complete state. I told her to come over and rang the doctor. She came over, got into my bed and stayed there for the weekend, only waking to talk to the doctor and make a few phone calls. Pat came over with Frances. Debbie and I took her and Pam's children to Phoenix Park. Frances slept in the afternoon and by a process of memory and detective work I found Daryl's number. In the evening left Pam in bed and went out with Susannah Clapp. Respite.

Sunday, 16 September 1990

Trying to talk sense to Pam. She is blaming things on Debbie that are not Debbie's fault. I want to say sorry to Daryl. Suddenly I feel so sorry. In the evening helped pack up kit at Pam's, Carol the nanny driving the children to Ireland in the morning, Pam having gone ahead. Planning a good day of work tomorrow.

Monday, 17 September 1990

Call for help from Carol first thing, another fiasco, the car uninsured and so the journey has been postponed. Swimming, and now I am sitting here in front of my word processor. I am tired out and my head is full of rubbish. I can hear Lola and John outside in the street. Yesterday Laura told me that when they were on holiday she had looked through the keyhole and had seen Steve with another woman. Lola and John are confused, clinging on, begging me to come to Ireland with them. Amazed I was able to work.

Bridges, afterwards rang Daryl and left a message for him to ring me. Lucy came over for supper. Daryl rang and we had a good talk and that made me feel better. He said to ring later when Lucy was gone so we could talk more and I did but he was asleep.

Tuesday, 18 September 1990

Dad's as usual, sitting went on for ages but now we are on the home straight I'd rather get it over and done with. Afterwards went down to Shepherd's Bush and bought some fabric. Hung about at Bella's for a while then rushed to Bridges. Horrible session. I felt worse afterwards than I had before. I thought he was cruel and didn't understand anything. I still feel angry now.

Writing cards to Lola, John and Laura in Ireland. Celia came over, I burst into tears, partly a release of the anger I had been feeling also such upset about Pam's children. Feel heartbroken. Celia nice and kind.

Wednesday, 19 September 1990

Phone call from TC whom I bumped into at Highbury Fields the Saturday before last, asking me out for a drink. He was in a call box, his money ran out, he said he was going to ring back later.

Progress on DAYDREAMING although pestered by horrible doubts. Then Bridges, had a go at him about the grief he gave me yesterday. When I got home there was a message from TC saying he would ring soon. Talked to Lucy for a long time then TC rang again. He said he would call for me so we could go out for a drink. Went to the Plough. Then back to mine and sat up talking into the night. About his girlfriend and two children. I said he should go to Relate. He tried to kiss me. I said 'If you kiss me you will never leave.' He said that that was what he wanted. I said I had to look after myself. We embraced briefly in the hall and he went.

Thursday, 20 September 1990

Sitting, talked to Dad about poetry, managed to escape at half eleven. Letter from Mark Marvell enclosing a copy of INTERVIEW and a photo of himself. Took my mind off TC. Mark Marvell is proposing a meeting in the spring. Couldn't do any work today, my mind so full of longing, desire, confusion. I have two tickets for Soul II Soul in Brixton on Saturday.

Lucy dropped in about seven to have a look at the photo of Mark Marvell. Watched a bit of telly, tried to write a letter to Mark Marvell in reply to his letter, failed, couldn't get it right, either too surface or too agonized.

Friday, 21 September 1990

Wrote a card to Mum and posted it. Just wanted to say hello.

It's TC's birthday today. I can't ring him because he said not to although he gave me his number. But as I am definitely not going to go to bed with him at least while he is in his present situation and don't want him to get out of his present situation on my account and not sure whether I would go out with him anyway even if he were properly single and not just sleeping on the couch I don't see why I can't ring him at home as a friend but he said no.

Read 'Ode on a Grecian Urn' and 'Ode to a Nightingale', also HAMLET. Debbie came over for supper. Early night.

Saturday, 22 September 1990

TC rang up. It is his birthday again today. Turns out he was born at midnight. I said I would meet him at Freds after Soul II Soul – it was too late to invite him. Tom arrived while I was still getting ready, we had a drink and he drove us over the river. Soul II Soul joyful and uplifting.

TC turned up at Freds, back to mine and talked all night. He left around six or seven. He says he wants to marry me. After he left reading 'The Other Garden' by Francis Wyndham, slept most of the day. TC rang at six and told me to look up at the lion's head on the right above the front door when I went out so I got dressed and went down and there was a rose in the lion's mouth. He must have climbed up.

Monday, 24 September 1990

Unable to get out of bed. Wrote to Mark Marvell, saying I looked forward to meeting him in the spring. Bridges, he really helped me, really tried to understand.

Tuesday, 25 September 1990

Sitting, Dad talked about Degas, how Bruce thinks that he is one of the greatest painters of all time. Dad says he loves Degas but that he has limitations, although he didn't go into the nature of the limitations. He said it was typical of Bruce to say that Degas is one of the greatest because of his own enthusiasm. Dad says, as he always does, that there are absolutes in art, but obviously it is he and not Bruce who gets to decide. After sitting visited Lucy. She is sick in bed. Strained relations, she talked about my feeling for TC as if I am ill or something.

Bridges, another good session, then when I got home TC rang. Met him in a pub in Islington opposite the cinema. We had a quick drink then went to see WILD AT HEART.

Wednesday, 26 September 1990

I find it so hard to end things it makes me afraid to begin. Good work today. Mark Marvell rang me from America again. Bridges, managed to stay on an even keel.

Thursday, 27 September 1990

Sitting, home about two. Had a rest, TC rang, Mum came to tea, TC rang again. He had to put the phone down suddenly because his family were coming downstairs after EASTENDERS. That made me feel really angry and upset. I went to bed, Lucy rang, we had a long talk, we are not getting on. My fault. Then slept, Dad woke me up, slept again. Not sleeping very well, partly because I get cold in the night.

I am very glad I didn't ditch Tom at the last minute and invite TC to the gig in Brixton instead, an act of disloyalty to the brother of my best friend that would have been yet another thing for me to feel bad about, although I may well have gone for it had TC not told me not to call. Lucy was very disapproving of the whole situation and told me that no good would come of it, and of course she was right, although at the time I felt scolded and judged, completely failing to understand how she was able so definitively to foretell what might happen. I thought I was in with a chance, and besides, I *was* trying to stop myself. I was concerned for his family, those poor children deprived of a father, but teetering because I believed only his children and their mother were at risk, unaware I was at risk too and should have been trying to save myself.

I am not proud of myself but he was so keen and I was ineluctably drawn in, not little by little, the two of us getting to know each other over a quiet drink to build trust when I didn't trust anybody, but all at once, in the Plough, by no means the most propitious location for a first date, not that it was even a proper date because he was committed elsewhere. I remember that when he referred to his girlfriend while we were talking I thought for a moment he meant he had a girlfriend as well as an ex-wife and two children, but it turned out he had never been married, he called the mother of his two children his girlfriend; he told me they were separated. The separation must have been so recent he wasn't yet ready to call her his ex.

He sipped his half-pint with eyes downcast (he was driving) and I looked at him sideways with so much unwarranted sympathy I felt doomed to respond, condemned suddenly by the look of him hunched over his drink at that dowdy bar, not my heart pierced with love by his scrubbed manly profile and his unlined duffel coat, the coarse buff-coloured cloth so threadbare the warp and weft were discernible in the sleeve creases and other areas of high friction, not much protection from the unseasonably foul weather, but my precarious sense of self-preservation threatened by some mildly depressing corrosive romantic illness that had started up in my head.

I feel embarrassed and shamed by this episode but am no longer horribly lowered by it because I have some compassion for myself now I am able to understand my behaviour in context, the impact on me of my father's complicated attitude towards fatherhood in relation to me and the consequential intensity of my longing, neither of my beloved parents setting a great example of how to love, not that I blame them for everything. My behaviour was influenced by the power of my longing, TC was unavailable, if only I had been able to recognize that. The pain was so familiar. I could see how my father operated in the distances between himself and other people but was unable to recognize in myself the same difficulties with real intimacy.

TWENTY

Friday, 28 September 1990

Bridges, all about my envy, my jealousy, my feeling that I am no good. The difficulty of dealing with TC, the fact he hurt me yesterday, I might get hurt badly. Find it hard to believe he would hurt me, that blindness a warning. He said he would look after me, he won't hurt me, but yesterday he did. I feel angry with him and got upset in my session and Bridges was brutal with me again. At least I am feeling something other than confusion. My life is unfolding, and I don't know what will happen next. Thinking about what Lucy was saying last night. She asked me if I could respect a man who deals with people in the way TC deals with his family. I said I don't want to sit in judgement. I said look at my father, how he has behaved, and I still love him. She is warning me to watch out.

Fragile after my session, and dying to talk to TC. Argos to buy a birthday present for Frances. Chose a nursery rhyme Wendy house and a tea trolley with plastic tea set, both perfect.

TC rang, I told him how bad he made me feel when he put the phone down on me. He said sorry. He said he would ring again later.

Making a cake for Frances's birthday tomorrow. Waiting for TC to ring but he didn't. Full of bad thoughts and feelings. Why am I putting myself through this? Managed to console myself, drank some Jameson's and went to sleep.

Woke up at a quarter to five after a nightmare about Ali hitting the bottle. I felt furiously angry, so unhappy, alone and bleak in the dark. Before I woke up I shouted at him - 'My whole life is weighed down by the anxiety of you and your habit. When you gave up, I felt like you had got off my back. Now the crashing weight of worry and depression has returned.' I was frightened in bed but I managed to save myself. Nothing matters, I am free, I am me – and went back to sleep.

To the supermarket with Ib to get supplies for the party. Frances was very naughty, probably due to the imminent birth of the new baby. Back to Ib's and made a large quantity of sandwiches. Dad arrived with a little dress from The White House in Bond Street, beautiful fine creamy white wool with smocking and hand-worked pink rosebuds, absolutely breathtaking in its loveliness. The receipt was still in the bag – the dress cost three hundred pounds. Ib decided to return it to the shop and change it for something more practical.

After the party drove home with Susie. She came in for a cup of tea. There was a message from TC saying he would ring again and he did, at half past six. He said he would come over later, as soon as he could disentangle himself from his family. That took ages – he was much later than expected. Susie and I drank whiskey and danced and she left shortly after he arrived.

TC and I went to Leah Kharibian's party at Chatsworth Road. We had to run to catch the 38. My shoe fell off at the top of the bus stairs and tumbled down. TC nearly fell off trying to rescue it. That made me feel embarrassed. The party was supposed to be a barbeque but it was pouring with rain. Strangely hot outside, the rain falling onto my best dress. The artist Rita Keegan turned up, in a Chinese wig, and we reminisced about the Hot Sty. Left at three and walked back to the Angel. TC asked me if I would run away with him to Gretna Green. I said no. He asked me if I wanted him to come home with me and I said no. I marched off on my own and caught the night bus.

Sunday, 30 September 1990

Lucy came over for supper, then Angus and Cerith rang up and I invited them over as well. Made pizza. Cerith brought some cheese back from Holland for me. He has been attending a video festival there. Lovely evening.

Monday, 1 October 1990

Spent hours working on my book then lost all my new work in the computer and couldn't retrieve it. Horrible feeling of loss.

Tuesday, 2 October 1990

Sitting for Dad, talk of Leigh, Dad repeating private things Leigh told him about Angus and Cerith's relationship. I said to Dad that Angus would really hate the idea of Leigh talking about him and Dad telling me everything.

Also of the dynamics of queer relationships in general according to Leigh – 'Most couples like to take a third party to bed with them, in the hope that he will be a man, because, as you know, ninety per cent of queers are passive sexually. So a couple go out to pick up a third party, and the threesome ends up as a man and two girls.'

Dad talking about his own childhood, his horror of being understood. I said that being understood was being listened to, not having your mind read, that invasion of privacy.

Tonight Jock Scott is reading some of his poems at Freds. I was supposed to be meeting Paul McAdam tomorrow so I have brought that forward to kill two birds with one stone.

Dad rang, having received a letter from Paul asking to meet to discuss a loan for a business plan. Dad plans to send him a cheque for two thousand pounds and to enclose a letter saying he is too busy to meet. Dad said Paul has asked him to make a regular commitment to see him. Dad said 'I couldn't even make a regular commitment to see my wife if I had one, in fact I can't even make a regular commitment to see myself.'

Then talk of the tarot reader who is very popular at the minute. Dad said he wants to go and see him 'just so I can tell everyone about it.'

Bridges helpful, about money, then home, Debbie came round for a bit, then set off for Freds and to meet Paul. Andi was there. Jock's poetry–

Went to the Wag,
Picked up a slag,
Went home for a shag,
Smoked a fag . . .

Afterwards had a drink with Lucy and Tom and everybody. As Paul left he said, 'Next time I want to get you on your own.'

Wednesday, 3 October 1990

TC rang at ten and asked me if he could come over at lunchtime. We went to the Marlborough to see Frank's show. We kissed. After Bridges I had supper with Debbie. Early night. Dreamt I was pregnant also that I went to Ireland on an aeroplane. Tomorrow TC and I are going to go on a train.

Thursday, 4 October 1990

I told Dad I saw a young woman we both know mauling men at Freds, hands everywhere like somebody in a Carry-On film, all the other female characters hating her because she is after their men.

He said that that is the type of girl he would like to meet. Then he changed his tune and said those kinds of girls started early, getting between their mother and father, the little girl saying 'Oh you have let yourself go, haven't you, Mother,' and getting on the dad's knee. I said he was describing the Oedipal impulse, to come between a couple and try and have what you can't have. Exactly what I have been discussing at Bridges.

Home, fried eggs on toast, TC rang. He made me feel anxious, talking about his family. He has decided to go to Relate to try and sort himself out. He said 'I want to get out but feel I ought to stay. Also in the mornings when the kids are bouncing about I don't want to live without them.'

He said he would be round at four to go on a train. Yesterday we were so close the journey felt manageable. He made me feel secure. Now I remember that he might get back with Michelle I feel frightened, although it would be a relief. I don't know what I am doing, planning to travel with him. It's like we have made a plan to make love.

I got some work done in spite of all this stuff in my head. TC showed up on time. I said I thought we should stop seeing each other. I knew I could not go on the train unless I got out from between him and Michelle. This was unpremeditated, but felt right. Bought tickets, mounted the steps with trepidation, excitement, horror. The fear of getting stuck in a bad place. Obvious connection to getting stuck between TC and Michelle.

On the platform I began to feel worse and worse, about myself, my life – a crumbling feeling of nothingness, hating the way I am. Used the coping strategies copied out of my phobia book. They calmed me a little. Then read 'Ode to a Nightingale'. That helped me relax. Three quarters of the way through the poem the train came. Once it set off I continued to read the poem. When we got to Hampstead Heath I was jubilant, ecstatic.

We went to Keats' House and stood by the garden wall. Full moon, the lawn was shadowy. Then we took the train back. On the return journey I felt no fear, just a heightened sense of myself. I feel I am no longer limping. I was planning to cook something when we got home but couldn't. TC went home. I was alone, feeling good about the train and my decision to get out from between him and Michelle. He is going to write to me one day. When he is single. If ever.

Friday, 5 October 1990

Gleefully told Bridges about my train journey and my decision not to see TC any more. My instinct to disentangle myself overcame the voice telling me to get stuck in and hang on.

Saturday, 6 October 1990

Received a confused and confusing letter from TC but managed to retain some of my equilibrium. Pat came over with Frances, went to the British Museum, the park, then met Lucy for lunch at a dim sum place in Chinatown.

I wrote a reply to the letter from TC but I don't want to post it because of all the letters Pam has shown me from the other women to Steve. While I was writing it I kept on imagining what Michelle would think and feel if she opened it. Once the letter was finished I continued reading POETS IN THEIR YOUTH about Berryman and Lowell.

Tuesday, 9 October 1990

At five in the morning Pat came round to drop off Frances because Ib had gone into labour. Frances was in an exuberant mood, ate a boiled egg with bread and butter, then we went back to bed. Got up again at eight, had a bath. I was worried in case anything happened to Ib or the baby – I could not trust that everything would be all right. Bridges says my worries are due in part to my desire to kill Ib anyway. Unconscious, obviously. Frances joyful and miserable. TC rang from a call box to ask me if I had received another letter from him. I said no. He said he had had about the worst weekend ever. When I asked him about it he said he would tell me later.

I rang James Kirkman's office to ask them to get Dad to ring me because I was supposed to be sitting today. Dad rang, but said he hadn't been expecting me. Very odd. Then he rang back to ask me if I would clean the studio. I said I would do it on Monday evening. Then at ten past two Pat rang to say that Ib had just given birth. A girl, eight pounds four ounces. I woke up Frances and Pat told her on the phone while she was still half asleep. Then we got a cab to the hospital. Utter joy, also sadness I have no children.

Pat had to go to the electroplater's and once Frances had met her new sister he took her off with him. Ib and I talked. I held the baby until Mum turned up, then handed her over. Ib had to get a bed wash from the nurses so Mum and I went for a cup of tea. Mum seems to be shrinking, holding herself like a grandmother, a little powdery and frail. I felt like a giant.

Bridges, had a good cry. In the evening Debbie came over and ranted on about Pam with no concern for my feelings. As soon as she left I went to bed. I dreamt about the letter from TC. It was a pink cardboard heart, shiny, like a Valentine's card, with a drawing of a telephone inside and some romantic message.

Wednesday, 10 October 1990

Swimming, the letter from TC arrived. It made me feel angry. I wrote part two of my unsent letter, telling TC I would never be a bit on the side. Got on with work, then Bridges. Spent the evening at Ib's, holding the baby and helping out.

Thursday, 11 October 1990

It has come to my notice that I am not sitting for Dad any more. He has not made an announcement to this effect but it's over. He just finished the picture and didn't tell me.

TC phoned from a call box. I talked to him for a while then agreed to meet up with him because it seemed so silly to talk on the phone when he was just round the corner. Walked to the river and along to Blackfriars. Walked on the bed of the Thames, on the silt of brick, flint, glass, bone and the white stems of clay pipes. Then to the Tate to see Richard Long, slate and clay and flint on the floor, all the Rodins cleared out to make way. Walked to St James's Park and sat on a bench. TC told me about his horrendous weekend. I wanted to offer comfort but afraid of getting too close. Walked to Soho, Bar Italia, then went off on my own to Freds to meet Lucy. Meard Street for the opening of Pat's show.

Friday, 12 October 1990

Bridges first thing, I left feeling so angry and upset I slammed the door and stumbled off down the road to my car wondering how I was going to get through the day. Spent the rest of the morning with Pam, looking at houses for sale, then went on a train with Lucy, reading Keats' letter to his brothers on the disquisition he had with Dilke about negative capability.

Saturday, 13 October 1990

Two more letters from TC. Not really communicating with me. Spent the day at Ib's looking after Frances and the new baby so Ib could get some rest. I was lying in the garden with the new baby asleep on my chest and Frances tipped a mud pie over us both, saying 'Would you like a slice of my cake?' In the evening Pat came over to turn off the water supply to my washing machine – it had leaked through the floor and all over the Verde sisters' kitchen.

Sunday, 14 October 1990

With Ali to see a nice flat at the top end of Gloucester Crescent. Ib's briefly for a visit. Ali left while I was in the loo, without saying goodbye or thank you to me, and I was stranded. Luckily Kai turned up and gave me a lift home.

The Verde sisters started a row with me about the noise they say is insufferable when children play in the sitting room. Went to bed feeling miserable. Had a nightmare – dead babies, the police, investigation, shame, hiding the truth, Ali. I drove my car into the canal.

Monday, 15 October 1990

Swimming, very bad headache, neck-ache, shoulder pain. Wrote five pages of DAYDREAMING when I got home from the pool then realized I was very angry. Absolutely dreading going to Dad's to clean the studio. So I went to Bridges in a fury and told him how angry I am, looking after everybody, the pressure in my head, no babies of my own, TC, and nobody looking out for me. Decided in the session not to go to Dad's to clean the studio. Went round to Lucy's instead, had some pasta and salad and went home. Dad rang up. I told him I had a headache. He wasn't cross, in fact he was kind, solicitous.

TWENTY-ONE

Not always but quite often when I told him that I was worried or upset about something he would become acutely attentive unexpectedly to what I was trying to say, his listening ear cocked for my benefit, the depth of his concern a heady and incomparably luxurious experience. I never told him I suffered from anxiety because of the shame I carried about that aspect of myself, but if luck was on my side when I confided in him about some practical difficulty he would say 'Please don't worry' rather than judging or berating me, the words pronounced in a voice so unusually pleading and courteous it was as if he had borrowed it for the occasion from Trevor Howard in *Brief Encounter* or some other intensely pained hero of the black and white films everybody watched at the end of the war. He did not sound insincere, far from it, although this rescuing side of him mostly came out on the telephone, hardly ever in person, perhaps his solicitousness more easily sparked by my disembodied voice than by my physical presence, the ether on the line between us more dreamy and richer in potential for gallantry than the sight of me in the flesh. He phoned me, I talked, and suddenly my troubles were too painful for him to ignore. Or at least he felt that the pleasure to be gained from a grand gesture might outweigh the pain and the inconvenience, not forgetting he was already paying for my psychotherapy, for which arrangement I was very grateful but that had its drawbacks for both of us, not that cash was the only way he was able to express his affection for me.

I suspected he had it in him, what I needed from him, but still I was always surprised when I brought it out of him so successfully in my distress without even trying to manipulate him, always aware I was not the only one of his children who might need help to get by, just the one he was most caught up with in the moment of his munificence. I could not help smiling into the receiver, even through tears, grateful and thrilled he was so loving and full of responsive kindness all of a sudden, ready on the other end of the line to step up like the ideal parent, something about the nature of my difficult situation stilling his desire to distance himself, maybe because he could see a way to help me that would work for me and not make him feel obligated, not make him fear I might begin to expect even more from him on a regular basis. He was keen to offer assistance when it suited him but did not want any of us to rely on him too heavily, afraid he might let one of us down if he was lacking in the wherewithal, financial or otherwise, when he was called on for help.

His gallantry came out in unexpected ways and his motivation was not always uncomplicated. I am thinking of a series of events that began in the autumn of 1976, somebody started a small fire in the Queen Mary Hostel next to the music hall on Hoxton Street and I was out on my ear suddenly with my big suitcase. It pains me to come clean but the person who lit the fire was my boyfriend at the time, who lived in the flats round the corner. My friend Eileen felt bad about what had happened and told me that a friend of her brother-in-law had just moved out of a bedsit on Englefield Road, the room more than likely still empty. The landlord, a Jamaican called Mr Mullings, didn't live at the property but drank in a pub nearby – I was to go and ask for him at the bar and tell him that Duncan had sent me.

Mr Mullings was amused, perhaps by my youth – I was

seventeen – or my haircut. He showed me the room on the first floor, the big window overlooking the yard at the back, a Baby Belling and sink in one corner, then took me downstairs to view the shared bathroom. The walls were painted purple and the floor fully carpeted, a short brown pile that did not show the dirt but as it turned out was always a bit wet round the tub and the lavatory, the hot water not included in the rent – you had to put money in the slot meter, ignite the pilot light with a match and wait for the blue flames to snarl and roar in the open mouth of the gas geyser. The door was slightly too small for the doorway, fastened by a flimsy hook, but I was undeterred by the facilities and soon to discover only a short walk along Englefield Road towards Dalston you could take a hot bath safely in a private cubicle in the public bathhouse for less than the price of ten cigarettes, and do your washing by hand in the public laundry off the main lobby, alongside the neighbourhood women toiling elbow to elbow at the giant sinks. The building is now a derelict Vietnamese community centre.

A young woman called Jenny occupied the room underneath mine, a few years older than me but keen to make friends. She left piles of magazines on the stairs for me when she was done with them, the romantic stories quite mild in the first few weeks of my tenancy but the language used to describe the behaviour of the protagonists and the behaviour itself becoming more and more pornographic as time went on, the action occurring between covers that were deceptively innocent-looking, the heroine gazing up at the chiselled chin of the hero in loving respect.

The stories were compelling but produced in me a sickness of guilt or depression that became so intense I had to stop reading them. Hard to say whether Jenny was breaking me in one step at a time to the extensive collection of titles already in her room, testing me to see where I might baulk, or if, as she became inured to mere suggestions of violent conquest and submission in the earlier stories, she felt compelled to go out and make further and more shameful purchases from the newsagent round the corner, hankering after stronger material and offloading the new magazines onto me once she had done with them, regardless of their content, perhaps in order to manage the guilt and shame of her longing to read about coercive sex and other forms of violence against women by getting me to join in. She never mentioned the magazines, but once I stopped picking them up she got the message and stopped leaving them out for me. I asked her to take back the ones I had read but she would not, so I threw them away.

Jenny kept her room beautifully clean, her teacups smelling of bleach, and was very sharply dressed, skirt suits of lightweight brown or beige woven fabric with big lapels and wide-collared blouses in pale yellow polycotton. She received no visitors from outside although held down a job in an office, her life ticking over quite nicely until her grandfather died in the Caribbean and she found herself haunted by this aggressive relative, an elderly man in a homburg who sat in her chair by the window of her room and would not let her sit in it. She tried to engage him in conversation but he shouted her down and she was taken away in an ambulance to the German Hospital at Dalston where she blew up like a balloon on the ward and was sedated so heavily she could barely find her mouth to feed herself. There was nothing wrong with her bladder but they catheterized her anyway for the convenience of the auxiliary staff, two men in scrubs who said they were way too busy to take her to the toilet every five minutes. The catheter bag, fixed to the front of her dressing gown, filled up in plain sight as I tried to converse with her. I visited twice then never went back. Women were screaming out of the barred windows. I was too frightened. And all alone now in the house with Mr Brown, the other tenant.

Mr Brown told me he was an Anglo-Indian. He went out to work every day like Jenny before she was hospitalized, and kept himself to himself, inhabiting his respectable mustard-brown blazer and striped tie with pride and anxiety to ward off racial attack; we were polite to one another if we passed on the stairs but didn't make friends. He lived in the biggest room in the house, next to mine but at the front, two curtained windows overlooking the street. I had never entered it, although I did peep in from the landing once or twice when his door was open and noticed a white bucket in the corner, half full of yellow liquid.

I owned a record player and three LPs. Every night I stacked up the records on the spindle and allowed them to play me out as I tried to sleep. Sometimes the music cut out, maybe a loose wire or something, an intermittent fault it never occurred to me I might be able to get fixed. If the music stopped I banged the record player a few times, replaced the needle in the groove and the music continued.

One night Katie came to see me and missed the last bus. We were stretched out on top of the bed, still dressed, Billie Holiday bemoaning the meanness of her lover and both of us joining in occasionally, Katie's voice low and melodious, both of us trying to wind down. She had cut off her brown ringlets for punk reasons, not just for punk reasons, and on her feet was wearing a long pair of black training shoes she called her banana boats, the ugliness of the shoes and her shorn head doing nothing to reduce the devastation of her allure. The music cut out and I had to lift the needle and bang the record player. I didn't think the knocking noise might disturb Mr Brown in the next room. The knocking was rhythmic, and perhaps sounded too insistent through the wall – I had not thought that he might be listening.

I can't remember whether he opened my door or perhaps he knocked and I opened it for him. Anyway, he was out on the landing in his vest with a big butcher's knife in his right hand, shouting at me incoherently about sex and insisting on his high status; he called me a whore and demanded the respect due to him as an Anglo-Indian. I listened to his rant and began to understand he thought the knocking he heard through the wall was my sex noises. He said I was too hot. Every damned night! He could stand it no longer!

I cowered in the doorway as he waved the knife at me, hearing him out and very slowly backing into the room until I was able to slam the door and lock it. He banged on the door and continued to rave on the landing, his blows not forceful enough to break through the panels but loud enough to express his intent. He said he wanted to kill me. I felt shamed by his sexual allegations but didn't tell Katie about my shame – I possessed inadequate resistance to humiliation because of my past experiences but couldn't have put my sense of myself into words. When my boyfriend stayed over we made no noise. Mr Brown's rage was not about anything that happened in reality. Katie and I felt trapped, but after a few minutes he was done suddenly, no more banging and shouting, perhaps coming back to himself and feeling bad about his behaviour.

I waited for ten minutes and opened the door, only a crack – he was no longer on the landing. We couldn't hear him moving about next door but could feel him on the other side of the wall with his big knife, maybe subdued after his outburst, or taking a breather before launching his next attack. We had to get out.

Katie and I gathered up our stuff, opened the door and ran, not stopping to lock the door behind us. Once out in the street she suggested she call my father from a telephone box, not something I would have considered had I been on my own – I am not even sure if I had his number at that point. She dialled and spoke to him with such confidence I felt confused by the easy display of her power and wondered whether she knew she was lording it over me, flaunting her assumption he would drop everything for her and come running.

He turned up surprisingly quickly, entered the house and took the stairs two at a time, Katie and I lighting up and watching his urgent ascent from the other side of the road. From where we stood we could hear wood splintering, the sash windows rattling in their frames, thuds and shouts of anger and pain. I ran to the pub to fetch Mr Mullings, hoping he would restore order, but, unable to find him, returned to the house. My father burst out of the door and skipped down the front steps, followed by my neighbour, still waving the big knife, roaring now and dripping wet – Dad had picked up the white bucket and doused him with the contents.

Mr Brown was bellowing, seriously murderous. My father took off his belt, a giant bunch of keys attached to the plaited leather, and spun belt and keys round himself at speed, ingeniously protecting his head and chest from the blade of the knife without hurting anybody. A mounted policeman appeared at the end of the street so again I went to get help, afraid my father would receive a fatal wound or lose his temper and do Mr Brown some proper damage. The policeman kicked his horse and moved at a sedate rising trot towards the incident, Mr Brown continuing to shout and brandish the knife as we approached, me trotting beside the horse and Dad light on his feet, dancing fearlessly, still spinning his keys in self-defence.

Mr Brown lowered his weapon when he saw the policeman and became pitifully aggrieved as he tried to explain himself, the big blade pressed to the side of his leg in the vain hope that the policeman would not notice it. The policeman chose not to dismount. He took our side against the Anglo-Indian, unsurprisingly, although my neighbour wanted him to arrest my father for assault. Dad, smiling and acting patrician suddenly in front of the policeman but wearing paint-covered chef's trousers and a torn shirt, fondled the horse with deep love and showed his equestrian knowledge, endearing himself to the confused officer, although my father despised the police and was not always civil towards them.

Nobody was arrested. Dad had been heroic, pouring the piss bucket over my neighbour because he had threatened Katie and me, and we were both quite grateful to have been avenged with minimal hurt to either party and impressed by Dad's skills in street combat, although now I am wondering why Katie chose to ring him in the first place. As long as we didn't re-enter the building we were no longer in danger. What had she wanted from him? I had gone along with her idea and felt rescued but in a slightly false position, troubled by his spectacular response.

Mr Brown had been thinking about me in a sickening way and I was permeated by his sexual disgust in spite of my punky self, also sorry nobody understood what it was like for him to live without the respect he was due. I lost my home, although that turned out much better than I could have anticipated, because my father arranged for me to take over the flat at Clarendon Gardens that I was to share with Bella when she came up to London, two bedrooms, sitting room, kitchen and private bathroom, the lease held by an old friend of his who was no longer in need of the accommodation. I knew the flat well, because Katie had lived there until recently, I had visited her there several times and hardly even bothered to envy her the big rooms and high ceilings, the safety and civility of the comparatively deluxe neighbourhood, not dreaming even for a second I might end up taking possession of it.

The flat was perfect, although Katie had left one of her pets behind, a live eel, two feet long and about the same girth as an erect penis. I left it alone for a few days to slide up and down in the bath where it lived, its body muscular yet lethargic in captivity, washing myself in the basin when I needed a wash, then fished it out and released it into the canal.

Katie had given up the flat of her own volition, under no pressure from my father to vacate, a decision I found inexplicable but which was obviously very much to my advantage. I don't know exactly what was going on between them at that time but looking back I imagine she assumed her occupation of the property was dependent on her willingness to be with him, not necessarily very often, just as long as she was available sometimes, and maybe she was trying to break it off. Anyway she had moved out and he arranged everything for me with one phone call. I was astonished and grateful to have been so beautifully provided for but couldn't help wondering would he have come to the rescue if it had been just me in trouble in the bedsit, just me on my own and no Katie, his dream girl always in two minds about him and maybe even prepared to be won over by his display of heroic agility, the gallantry of his measured violence? Would he have come just for me? Of course he would have come had I been able to summon him. But I would not have summoned him. Might he have come if I had? I will never know the answer to that impossible question.

TWENTY-TWO

I met Bella and Esther for the first time in Islington, the two of them playing in Milner Square, somewhere we hardly ever went, the tall gloomy houses occupied by multiple families renowned in our neighbourhood for violent crime, particularly towards strangers entering their territory. Islington was very different in those days.

I don't know how they came to be there – they must have been staying with somebody locally – but I understood they were connected to Dad as we were connected to him, not necessarily more tenuously although not definitely with a closer bond. It's possible as there were so many of us they felt sidelined, like we were his main family simply because we outnumbered them, our mother more forgiving of him than their mother, but that thought did not cross my mind even for one minute at the time because they were so irresistibly dinky and cute, so plainly adorable.

Maybe Bernadine was in contact with Mum and between them they had arranged something. We ran over Liverpool Road and came into Milner Square off Barnsbury Street, crossed the mossy surface of the play area on our way to the swings and there they were, two small dark-haired children sitting on the rusty play equipment between the blackened houses that loomed over the dank little park, just looking at us with tired eyes that were not baleful exactly but not expressing much enthusiasm.

Stepping back from his easel early one morning in 1990 he measured me with his thumb and told me wistfully that I too was small and thin once, before I had my tonsillectomy. I can still remember my convalescence from that operation on general surgical because there were no empty beds on the children's ward, the doctor in his heavy black glasses telling Mum I would have to stay put with the old people unless a bed became vacant, red and green paper chains suspended above his head between the pendant light fittings as it was Christmas. I was three or four, enjoying a diet of ice cream until my throat healed, each yellow portion wrapped in greaseproof paper, in my mind the bricks of dreamlike sweetness prescribed by the doctor not just for medical reasons but as a reward or consolation for my acute pain.

In my father's studio the light was pale grey, perfect for his purposes, and he was painting my nose while he reminisced with some regret about the earlier version of me, one of those sly smiles on his face of knowledge he shouldn't be saying what he was saying but unable to help himself. His voice was playful and light but as he spoke I knew he liked me better then, when I was ill all the time, a feeling I was reminded of when reading bell hooks recently, the feminist writer describing a time when she was loved as a small child, before the people who loved her turned away.

He painted Ali and me when we were six and seven, two little figures in the bottom left-hand corner of the picture of himself as a heroic modern artist, my brother and I occupying an ambiguous space in front of the mirror in which he was reflected, perhaps as an afterthought to strengthen the composition or enhance the status of the main subject like the hunting dogs, symbolic vessels and other possessions displayed in traditional portraits. Or maybe he had it all planned from the beginning, a proud father keen to acknowledge us both in his own way.

I can't remember much about that sitting apart from the floor-boards and the windows at Gloucester Terrace, although that memory might be taken from the portrait of Harry Diamond standing legs apart on a red carpet in the same studio, or from the one of Ib, who hated sitting so much she screamed when my father came to collect her and had to be coaxed or dragged away, her screams connected in my mind with the way she was portrayed in the painting, a girl child lying on the floor of the studio under a large plant in her vest and no knickers. Nightmare. I can't even begin to imagine how that came about. No wonder she screamed.

Not long after Uwe jumped off Tower Bridge my father decided to paint the view from the window of Ib's bedroom at 9 Barnsbury Terrace, the subject of his painting the industrial building opposite, a mica factory with a tall chimney that emitted plumes of chemical smoke. He chose to work from Ib's room not only because that was the best angle, the top floor of the house the right vantage point, but also because it would have been easier for him to work round Ib than round Ali, who had the other room at the front on the top floor and was fifteen at the time. I felt proud we lived across the road from such an important landmark.

A woman used to come out onto the metal fire escape in the course of her work, carrying unidentifiable burdensome items in her arms, some of the bundles wrapped in brown paper. My father said she reminded him of Flo in *Andy Capp*, a cartoon strip that appeared in the *Daily Mirror*, and as he made the comparison I recalled the shame I had endured when he caught me gazing with the fascination of a twelve-year-old at the depiction of the marital strife of Andy and his wife in the back of the paper. He looked at me and I wanted to disappear, agonized by his presence because I had assumed the antics of Andy and Flo were too low for him. I had thought I was alone in the house. He must have let himself in.

I turned over the page and studied the football at the back, not even raising my head, afraid he would judge me, not that he said anything, and I can't remember how we passed the time after that, if we managed to communicate until my mum returned from the playground with my brothers and sisters or if I continued to read the sports pages and he looked out of the window. It was not until a year later that I heard him talking in the French Pub about the unparalleled genius of Reg Smythe and learnt that all my discomfort had been for nothing.

This mistake was in some way similar to my misunderstanding of the Communists, politicians who disappointed me bitterly when I found out they looked just the same as all the other men who wanted to take power, in conventional suits instead of revolutionary T-shirts and headgear like Che Guevara, adults in the adult world always unpredictable in their affiliations and enthusiasms. Andy and Flo were embattled like Punch and Judy, Flo on the receiving end of Andy's constant disparagement and disrespect, although occasionally she floored her feckless husband with a well-deserved right hook. My father was thinking he might include the woman on the fire escape in his painting and asked Ali to take some photographs of her and the factory for research purposes, which was unusual for him, but in the end he decided against it, perhaps suspecting she might edge his picture too close to social commentary, as if he were trying to say something about poverty when he wasn't interested in poverty.

Ib was dislodged from her room during working hours and it was strange for me to return from school and find him at home, the sound of his footsteps advancing and backing away from his painting over and over again, the low voice of concentration as he muttered encouragement or berated himself, the door slightly ajar and the smell of oils and turps and white spirit emanating tantalizingly from behind it, almost like he had moved in.

He liked to get people to do things for him, not just me but friends and family he regarded as trustworthy and in possession of the appropriate skills, his confidence placed in those of his circle who were either suitably humble in relation to him or so eager to please that any question of status flew out of the window. He demanded and inspired a very high degree of loyalty but of course not everybody was delighted to be co-opted like this, and resentment sometimes built up towards him if his demands went over the top, the annoyance generated by his high expectations expressed behind his back for the most part but occasionally blowing up in his face.

After university I moved from Northwold Road to live with Lucy at Notting Hill Gate, her house a short walk from the studio at Holland Park, the distance between myself and my father about the same as the distance between his studio at Thorngate Road and the flat I used to live in with my boyfriend on Elgin Avenue when I left home. Since I was nearby he asked me to clean for him twice a week, not the studio itself at this point but the other rooms, a little job to pay the rent while I was working on my first novel. It was hard work, and I remember how puzzled I felt when Bella said she wished she could do it instead of me.

He loved not only the results of my labour but also the process, the smell of bleach and the sight of me in my bare feet handling the deck brush and mop bucket, skating across the wet floor with clean rags underfoot to absorb the water once I had scrubbed the white lino in the kitchen. Only when he questioned my cleaning methods did I feel put down, not that I allowed him to see my abasement, not that he was able to read me. If my cheeks burned scarlet when he humiliated me he just remarked in passing how well I was looking and went back in the studio.

I stood at the big Belfast sink in his kitchen, elbow deep in suds, and heard him say he thought washing up was disgusting, he had never really been able to make himself put his hands in the dirty water. He held up his hands and looked at them as if to prove his point, the veins blue and prominent through the skin, his square palms and muscular fingers not dissimilar from my own. I dried and put everything back in the cupboards and he continued to riff on the subject of dirty dishes, describing with fondness the young Lucian who refused to clear away his own plate after lunch at some prep school he attended where the boys were expected to clean up after themselves, still proud he had refused to cooperate. I asked him how he had got away with it.

'There was nothing they could do,' he said. 'I told them I was made for greater things.'

He used to refer to me as a bouncer when I worked on the door of the Café de Paris, a description that felt like the last nail in the coffin of my femininity, and when he sent me to the Midland Bank in Bond Street he told me before I set off that to help the manager identify me he had described me to him as an Amazon, my Amazonian daughter is on her way to the bank with a green carrier bag to collect cash. He addressed me laughingly but became conscious as he heard himself speak that I was excruciated by the disloyalty of his description, I saw in his face he knew he had hurt me. I don't know whether it would have been easier for me had he acknowledged his cruelty and said sorry, but he let it go as I was expected to do; he was not going to apologize.

Once I had located the bank I stood in the banking hall and waited for the manager to come out from behind the mahogany door of his office, my head held high but thinking the man would be thinking my own father was ashamed because of my size he had fathered me. The brass plate bore his name and had been polished by a cleaner on the early shift until it gleamed and her wrists ached. I imagined the manager was adjusting his tie behind the door before he came out, preparing to disguise his curiosity about my physical self, maybe despising my father for trying to find common ground with him at the expense of his own daughter, or intimidated by his wealth and fame and more than happy to smile on the phone with him over his description of me, unable to recognize the misogyny because it was too ordinary for both of them, a shared currency. Although Dad called himself a feminist when he got old.

I was feeling demoralized on Bond Street, also hating my father with some mercy for the insecurity and vulnerability he betrayed in his wish for camaraderie with the bank manager, his attempt to collude with him against me motivated by his desire to belong somewhere, the longing for acceptance and respect coexisting uneasily with the anarchic side of his personality, not that I regard personality as an immutable substance. I was wearing a stylish outfit, my skirt home-made and my blouse from Hungary or Romania, white embroidery on white cotton, brought back from his travels for me by my ex-boyfriend. I wondered if the bank manager would be disappointed; I was an average size and only five foot nine in reality, quite tall but nothing to write home about, nor had I chosen to have either of my lovely breasts surgically removed to make it easier for me to wield my spear, should I wish to employ it to destroy anybody.

The manager looked tired. Our eyes met and we shook hands, his attention remaining on my face, his mild interest in my physiognomy avuncular rather than invasive, his glance letting slip nothing of what had passed between him and my father – had he been expecting a more warlike and magnificent woman he did nothing to betray himself. He showed me into his office, made polite conversation, handed over the cash and turned away as I packed the wads of notes into the carrier bag, fiddling with his pen and glancing once or twice at a bad painting over his desk of a limp young woman on a swing, just somewhere safe to rest his eyes instead of looking at me.

My father was often uneasy in himself, and I was never very relaxed in his presence even in adulthood, always on guard, although I don't think he intended to make me uncomfortable. I registered and absorbed his impulsive slights without comment, and even though his small acts of aggression were few and far between I was undefended against him out of eagerness for his good opinion when they came, always very alert to how he saw me, my sense of self abraded by his assumption and assertion of his superiority.

Not long after I had signed the legal documents that committed me to my responsibilities in relation to his estate he began to consult me about his own conduct as well as talking about his will, knowing I would dissuade him from following through if for example he was working on the text of a letter intended to devastate the recipient, perhaps finding satisfaction enough in reading me his final draft and hearing me wince down the telephone.

I did my best to keep my head straight but as a result of his wishful thinking he began to exaggerate in his mind my integrity and other assets. He was unable to accept any ordinary confusions and delusions on my part, his new version of me almost without defect. I enjoyed the elevation although my pleasure was undercut by the fear I might fall from the height to which he had elevated me, aware at moments of extra precarity between us he might not be able to resist the desire to take me down. Even as a teenager I can remember him insisting I was so strong. I didn't question his appraisal of my strength but wondered why as a strong person I felt such weakness. I tried to be strong rather than working out what was really going on.

He expected too much of me after he had chosen me, and of course I tried to live up to his unrealistic ideal, the most surprising aspect of the appointment my ability when the time came to execute his will successfully. He was right all along! The success still feels like a miracle of trust and love, credit where credit is due to all of us. I was delighted by the responsibility but took care to ask for help not just from lawyers but from my siblings when I needed it. They were all very helpful and patient. And I tried not to swagger, aware my brothers and sisters would find me too annoying in my self-importance if I got on my high horse.

His papers and other items from the basement, including a large number of drawing books, were offered to the government in lieu of death duties, and I had the very important task of deciding which institution should be the recipient and keeper of the archive. I talked with David Dawson, my father's studio assistant and great friend, and he agreed with me that the National Portrait Gallery would be the best place. I found it hard to let go of everything all at once, and in the large black handbag I had bought myself when my father was first diagnosed with cancer, a receptacle capacious enough to contain everything we needed on our daily trips to the hospital for his radiotherapy, I secreted one of his early letters, a huge sheet of paper with illustrations as well as text in both German and English, a missive to his mother from Paris that I took out and read over and over again to comfort myself until I was ready to give it up, afraid it would fall apart if I didn't stop unfolding and refolding it.

Some of his letters were applications for funds, and his childish dependence on his mother and father, quite a long way into adulthood, made me feel better about my own needs in relation to him. I found myself checking the dates of his communications and calculating his age on my fingers, amazed and reassured he was not independent nearly as quickly as I had assumed, this realization allowing me in reptrospect to feel he might have minded less about my own need for cash at the time of the painting of 1990; he had been the same way with his parents.

After lunch at the Wolseley about a year before he died he began to address me in German, a language he professed to have forgotten long ago quite deliberately, an act of denial of his fatherland, and I wondered whether he had got confused for a minute and was thinking of his mother. We were seated at his regular table, between us on the white cloth a pot of mint tea, two long silver spoons and the remains of an amandine, the sundae he ordered so often it was renamed in his honour and that I still order sometimes for old times' sake, a trio of pistachio, hazelnut and nougatine ice creams served in a silver cup with whipped cream and a substantial fan wafer, butterscotch sauce on the side. The restaurant was busy, and the staff, who all loved my father, were extra kind to us as always in spite of the crush, everybody genuinely glad to serve our whole family. My father asked for the bill and as we waited for it to arrive he flicked pellets of bread at the balding head of a middle-aged man sitting opposite an elderly woman at one of the central tables, her hair in a neat bun, grey and soft in texture, fastened with wavy pins, the paisley shawl draped over the back of her shoulders the same shades of orange and yellow and brown as the curlicues on the dress worn by his mother in *The Painter's Mother Resting I.*

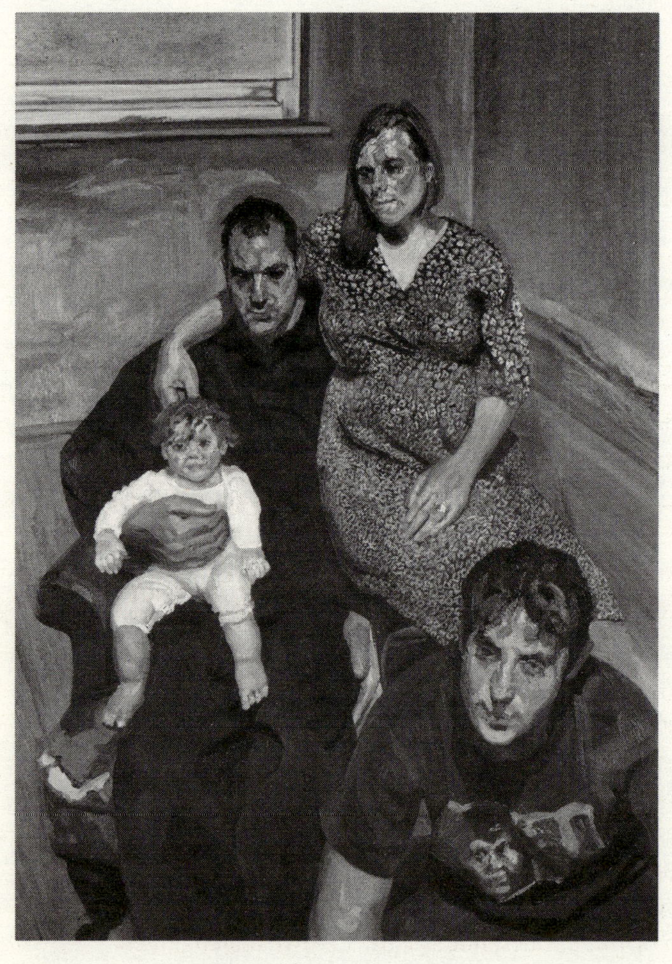

The Pearce Family (1996–8)

LUCIAN FREUD

TWENTY-THREE

I wanted to get married and have children myself almost beyond anything but such a substantial part of me believed that type of happiness was out of my reach it was very hard for me to imagine how I was going to make it happen. I didn't know any suitable candidates but was always on the lookout, even in the supermarket – there was no time to waste. I no longer felt unlovable but I didn't know if I could love anybody available and safe. By the time I was in my early mid-thirties I reached such a high level of frustration with myself I decided to swear off going near anybody who did not seem like potential husband material, however intensely I felt drawn in.

Susannah Clapp was in hospital following an operation, and rather indelicately over her bed in the gynaecological ward I met a man called Mark, an old friend of hers showing up for a visit the same time as me. She had been close to his wife, who had died about a year and a half earlier, and had spoken to me about him two or three times, not as a prospective match, unless I was being particularly dense, which I might have been, but just bringing his good qualities into the conversation in a casual way, something about her wonder as she described his extraordinary constancy encouraging me to get my hopes up before we had even met.

Mark left the ward to pick up his son from school. He said goodbye and loped away between the beds, his walk so unselfconscious it was clear he had no idea we were watching him. Once he was out of the way Susannah turned to me and asked if I thought he fancied me. The anaesthetic must have worn off, although she had only recently come out of surgery. I said yes, I do think he fancies me.

Mark and I coincided several times on the ward after that, hoping to bump into each other, our hospital visits probably more frequent than they might have been otherwise, both of us astounded by the other's kindness, not that we weren't kind, the partially unconscious motivation behind our attendance not entirely devaluing our devotion to our invalid friend. Susannah healed fast enough but not so fast that Mark and I were deprived of the opportunity to see each other three or four times at our best, or at least at our kindest, one on each side of the bed as Susannah chatted and dozed, our gifts of grapes and flowers luminescent on the wheeled cabinet in a beam of soft light from the window like a still life, the pair of us smiling at each other slightly surreptitiously and enthroned in the visitor chairs, the second chair borrowed from a patient who never had any visitors.

One time he was late and arrived with his son Alex in tow, both of them carrying motorcycle helmets, the child's cheeks reddened by the wind, having ridden pillion on the bike from South London, and I was moved by the care Mark took of that bereaved child. Mark wrote to me, I phoned him, and on our first date I asked him if he was one of those men who had no intention of getting married again or having any more children, not that I was proposing to him but I just didn't want to start something if there was no hope. He didn't even laugh. He said he wouldn't rule anything out and proposed to me a couple of months later. I didn't accept immediately but said to ask me again once we had got to know each other. It was not just Mark's heart that might break if I bailed, finding myself unable to go through with the commitment, but that of Alex, the stakes raised from the start, although of course it was reassuring that Mark was already a father, and had been with his first wife since he was nineteen – I saw that he was able to keep steady in all eventualities. I trusted Mark, a whole new experience for me, and was not afraid of his grief, but in relation to Alex I had to ask myself if I could be a good substitute for his real mum, if I could be reliable. It was a lot to take on.

I remember seeing Mark's motorbike parked outside the hospital before my third or fourth visit, thrilled by the sight of the machine that was his but not him, even the empty parking space when he parked elsewhere charged with his absence. The longing was brief because he was so quick to act, so sure that he wanted me, and although I didn't miss the agonized wait by the phone and all that messing about, I did rather mourn the lack of distance between us at first, deprived of the longing that feels like love, all that excitement. He loved me properly and I had to adjust consciously to the newness of closeness and trust, a combination that turned out to be far more potent even than the familiar deprivation of love misery.

My father refused to shake Mark's hand when they first met and if he phoned my flat when I was out and Mark answered the phone he refused to believe I was not at home. He used tell people 'That bloody man won't even let me speak to my own daughter.'

He paid for our wedding and came to it under mild duress, happy to appear at the party but, until I persuaded him otherwise, didn't think it would be necessary for him to turn up for the ceremony.

Nor did he want to be in the photographs, although he is visible in a couple of the group pictures, skulking at the back in the doorway of the register office, unaware he is in shot.

I remember him and Frank standing together afterwards and talking over the noise of the jukebox in the crush in our sitting room, both still hunched in dark overcoats like they were planning a quick getaway. Dad was trying to make himself heard and getting annoyed he could not hear Frank properly, gesticulating in frustration towards the Wurlitzer but lacking the know-how and cheek to pull out the plug.

It took some time for him to come round, but once he had met Mark a few times they began to get on – he trusted Mark and Mark was always happy to help out when my father needed his boiler looked at or anything else of a practical nature. Once, turning up for a family gathering, Dad peered down the end of the garden where Mark was standing under a tree looking dappled and tanned in the sunshine and asked me 'Who is that big spade?'

Not long after the wedding he wanted me to sit again, and I agreed but only if Mark could sit with me. I didn't want to spend too many evenings apart from my new husband, didn't want to subject myself to the undiluted intensity of my father's scrutiny again and knew he would curtail himself in Mark's company.

So Dad agreed to paint the two of us. I chose to sit on the arm of the chair and encouraged Mark to sit in the seat – at that time he was training to become a primary-school teacher, an exhausting experience for anybody, and I didn't want to worry about him feeling uncomfortable. I was used to sitting and he wasn't.

After what felt like innumerable evenings I made a joyful announcement – I was pregnant, what I had always wanted, and feeling so happy I could hardly contain my happiness. My father shouted 'FUCKING HELL' loudly and looked horrified for a few seconds when I told him, because of the threat to his painting, then he was pleased for me – he must have guessed I always wanted a baby, although we had never discussed it. In the picture I am wearing a capacious wrap dress I made for myself out of washable crêpe de Chine, a miracle of forward planning, the crossover design with long sash fully expandable just in case my dream came true.

My decision to perch on the arm of the chair began to seem less and less tenable as the pregnancy progressed, but it was too late to change the composition. I sat right up until the birth, then not long after I came home, extremely fragile after almost a month in hospital and attached to my new baby with such anxious love I could not put her down, my father began to telephone frequently, trying to persuade me to return to work. At first I was outraged by his persistence and asked for time to convalesce after my illness, but then I felt ready. He understood that baby Stella would have to be in the painting – I would not and could not leave her – then I explained that Alex would have to come too; I wanted him to feel part of the family.

Back in the studio Mark held Stella on his lap and Alex sat on the floor at the front, understanding the immense importance of what was happening without being told, which touched me deeply, and wearing his Jimi Hendrix T-shirt, Hendrix another person my father embraced uncomplainingly and was able to make work for his picture.

Dad and I sang to keep Stella entertained – she wriggled a bit but was spectacularly good-natured, patient and cooperative. I found sitting so much easier with my own little family because I could use Stella as an excuse to take a break when I needed a break, lying down with her on my father's bed in the privacy of his bedroom when I needed to lie down, and Dad could just get on with painting Mark or Alex in our absence. This freedom diminished the anxiety of being trapped alone with Dad, utterly powerless, literally unable to move.

Then when Stella was nine months old I had another announcement to make – I was pregnant again! This time my father was delighted. He diluted some reddish-brown paint with turps and painted a baby curled up inside me with the umbilical cord puffy and floating in amniotic fluid like some rare species of sea life, half flora and half fauna, then got on with the rest of the picture, which was finished not long before my son Vincent was born. We all felt completely celebrated.

TWENTY-FOUR

On arrival at his retrospective at the Pompidou Centre in Paris my father turned to me, waved his hand at the magnificent paintings and asked me if they were all his own work. I said yes, and he said 'No wonder I feel so exhausted.' The legacy he left behind, his life's work, will always speak for him, even if the shine comes off as he is reassessed. At his 2022/23 show at the National Gallery I was so moved to see the extreme tenderness portrayed in the depictions of male couples, in particular the double portrait of Angus and Cerith, in which their love for each other is completely undisturbed by my father's gaze.

My daughter Stella, who is an artist, used to say that she didn't want to leave anything behind, an impulse to tread lightly, no need whatsoever to immortalize herself. I have seen how complicated it has been for her to negotiate her grandfather's influence, and how affected she is by the fact that I am writing this book. We have transcended the fear of exposure together and we are proud of each other. She is my star. I have learnt much from her about the truth in art, what else it can be.

At the Cromwell Hospital for a blood test an inept nurse laid him out on a high trolley and, trying to find a vein, stabbed him over and over again in his left arm until he was shouting in pain. The nurse wanted to have a go at the other arm but I asked her to stop and find someone more experienced. She went to get help, leaving us alone for a few minutes under the bright lights, my father closing his eyes in exhausted resignation, too done in even to get up and walk out in disgust, both of us knowing the ordeal was not over. I wanted to take his hand but was too shy. I took his bony old foot instead and held onto it while a phlebotomist in a white coat entered the room and found a vein without inflicting any more pain. Afterwards, back home in bed, my father told me he felt like he was trying to hold open the lid of his coffin with one hand.

After a light lunch at Clarke's the following Saturday Dad climbed slowly to the top of his house for his afternoon rest and I followed, glad to keep him company, glad to get some rest myself in the peace of his bedroom. I renewed his morphine patch, he divested himself of his trousers for comfort and lay down in bed, still wearing his shirt and the scarf he rarely took off, head propped up on a couple of pillows and his diminished body almost flat under the covers. I was reading *Middlemarch* to him – we were about halfway through the first chapter, my chair between the bed and the window, the book angled to catch the afternoon light coming through the top leaves of the trees in his back garden. The trees had grown tall and thin, reaching up for the white sky to stay alive, and diagonally behind me, in the shadow the other side of the fireplace, the Bacon painting *Two Figures, 1953* took up nearly the entire wall, the grappling men ceaselessly grappling while my father rested under the fawn blankets and the white matelassé bedspread edged with white crochet lace.

I like to read aloud but remember on that occasion I was careful to enunciate every word to the best of my ability because I lacked complete confidence in my voice, the shape of my vowels in particular, my mother having taught me to say 'how now brown cow' to correct my accent but undermining me unintentionally with her edicts against the way some people pronounced or even just employed certain words and phrases. She really minded any contravention of her mysterious system, was helplessly pained if we said *either* with a long *e*, although she had discarded nearly all the other social niceties or otherwise of her own upbringing.

I had picked up the fat paperback of *Middlemarch* from a pile on the floor and begun from the beginning the previous day, pretty sure my father had not read it before, wondering whether an excursion into a world so far from his own might take his mind off his illness. He listened intently and I took a breath after a few pages. He was still wide awake, agitating slightly under the certainty of the authorial voice, not lulled by it as I had hoped. I asked him what he thought of the book and he said what struck him most about *Middlemarch* was George Eliot's extraordinary method, the woman telling the reader exactly what to think and feel about each of her characters. It was clear to me he was not prepared to take her word for anything and wanted to make up his own mind. The next day I dipped into *Man With A Blue Scarf*, a book by Martin Gayford about sitting, and read out a long passage, the author quoting my father holding forth about art. Dad began to smile and nod his head in delight, not realizing he was listening to himself. 'I couldn't agree more,' he said.

I lay beside him on the bed, not believing he could die, not wanting him to die, also wishing for his sake it was all over. I was able to hold his hand now he could no longer judge me.

Dr Gormley arrived and I questioned him about the ethics of my father's care, surprised that he didn't feel obliged to set up a drip and keep him alive for as long as possible. I thought the preservation of life was fundamental to the Hippocratic oath. It was outrageous. We were just letting him go.

The doctor told me that for him there was no moral dilemma, he was certain that no further intervention was the right way to go under the circumstances. I was convinced by his moral certainty and his love for his patient but still I remembered my father telling me that although Dr Gormley was a good doctor and a good friend he could get mildly annoying sometimes with his welcoming attitude towards death, his philosophical acceptance of the inevitability of it. My father said it was all right for him, he had his faith. Dad didn't want to die, was not resigned to what was happening to him, he wasn't ready, and wondered in a half-joking way if his doctor was putting up enough of a fight.

Nobody tells you that one or both of your parents might dehydrate and starve to death, nobody warns you. I am warning you now if you have parents.

After Sean died I suffered anxiety day and night, debilitating physiologically as well as psychologically, and Bridges wondered why I should be surprised to feel like that, having lost a beloved friend – he told me that loss and anxiety were connected, and I have always carried that knowledge with me.

I was expecting to feel the same way, my father bedridden and unable to speak, I was dreading the anxiety of loss almost more than the loss itself, but I surprised myself – I felt almost unbearably sad, for a long time, but hardly felt anxious at all, perhaps because I was well prepared for his death, it was time and everything felt settled between us. I was proud of how impeccably we had pulled together as a family and handled his care.

My father had changed as his passions waned, his loving kindness in old age erasing from my memory the selfishness that had driven him when he was driven, before the decline of his energy. This amnesia was transient but made my care of him in old age much easier, the act of forgetting consolidated by all the lies I had told about the impact on me of his selfishness, assiduous as I had been my whole life until now to protect his privacy not just from journalists but from any other interested parties, one or two of whom chose to fasten on me in my bereavement and take advantage of my vulnerability to screw me for information. You know who you are.

The palliative-care nurse listened to his breath and told me he was trying to die but would not allow himself to go in my presence. Her pronouncement gave me hope. I asked her if I could keep him alive for ever if I never went home. She told me that would be cruel.

The children were asleep when I got home and my husband set off almost immediately. We had got used to this brief changeover, me spending my days with my father and Mark staying the night in case he was needed. Kai was already there when Mark arrived, or turned up shortly afterwards, and the two of them kept him company, one on either side of the bed, the nurse coming in and out of the room to keep an eye on everybody.

I cleaned my teeth and changed into my nightdress and got into bed, so weary I hardly even felt sad. When the phone rang a few minutes later I got dressed again, phoned a friend and asked her to sit with the children and went back, my friend's husband driving me and collecting Ib and Susie on the way.

That was the first time I had seen a dead body apart from once as a teenager in New York when Anthony d'Offay took me to a night club and a young woman was brought out in a body bag. My brothers and sisters and I kept the news of the death to ourselves for some time, most of us gathered together and wanting to possess the fact of his death and his dead body for as long as possible before we went public. People were always trying to take him away from us when he was alive. Dr Gormley said he would come in the morning, allowing us some private time. I talked with Esther about the funeral. In my grief I felt hostility towards the McAdams, and was convinced that they should not be allowed to attend; I just could not countenance grieving with them. I was desperate for privacy to grieve, and I believed they had been mean to Dad and did not care about him. My position was utterly inflexible until Esther made me see I was wrong and I was saved from myself. She said we couldn't just ban them from the funeral of their own father, and I will always be grateful to her for her wisdom and kindness.

The undertaker came the following night, parked the unmarked van on the pavement against the front door and loaded the body into the back. He told me unless we followed this protocol my father would get papped as they brought him out, nobody wanted to see his dead body on the front page of the *Daily Mail*. I remember hearing the announcement of his death on the ten o'clock news and thinking of Auden's 'Funeral Blues' –

Let aeroplanes circle moaning overhead
Scribbling on the sky the message 'He is Dead'.
Put crepe bows round the white necks of the public doves,
Let the traffic policemen wear black cotton gloves.

At 31 Lonsdale Square when I was small he held me in his arms at a narrow window overlooking the street. I was aware of the lure of the window for him, the view into the square of broken railings and rose bushes, a few children playing out. I can't remember who else was in the room, if my mum was cooking the supper, her back turned, but he was dancing with me in his arms, holding me tight, and singing to me as we danced, an amended version of the Al Jolson hit, the altered second couplet obviously more truthful than the original in relation to me as far as he was concerned, although I doubt he changed it on purpose. He rocked me from side to side and sang

Oh, you beautiful doll
You great big beautiful doll
Let me put my arms around you
I'm so glad I found you

and the original reads

Let me put my arms about you
I could never live without you.

TWENTY-FIVE

My mother's maternal grandfather was called Ernest Stevens, a saucepan manufacturer who made his fortune and endowed various institutions in Stourbridge, the place of his birth. Ernest wished to set up his two sons as gentlemen, and to this end he drove round the West Country in his Rolls-Royce in the company of a land agent he had engaged to show him suitable properties, my great-grandfather looking for a big house with a lake, his sons both keen to keep waterfowl. A house was found, and Uncle Ron and Uncle Bee were installed in their new home. The land agent spoke very highly of Ernest's generosity and dignity in the essay he wrote about him, a document I found on the internet.

When my mother was ill I thought it would amuse her if I read her the land agent's description of her grandfather's search for a property, with all the period details – the shine on Ernest's hat, his sons' friendship with Haile Selassie, the purchase of all the Heal's furniture with which the house had been staged for the sale, the previous owners having removed all their ancestral Chippendale and Hepplewhite, Ernest and his sons too new to wealth to possess anything suitable. My mother listened to the land agent's story with a mild frown of discomfort, a facial expression I put down to the pain of her cancer, but when I asked her if she would like a copy of the document she said she would rather not if I didn't mind. I was puzzled by her displeasure, then came to understand she was not happy to be reminded of the saucepan factory of her antecedents, her insecurities exacerbated by the shame of trade, how recently her family had risen from humble beginnings, although she herself had sold old clothes in the shop in Upper Clapton and on a market stall in Islington, albeit in a very ladylike way. When I was young I asked my father if Mum's family was upper class, having only recently been introduced to the concept by Katie, and was glad when he said yes, he supposed so, not immune myself to the abstract consolation of poshness in the face of the shame of our low status, having been exposed my whole life to the drip-feed of both my parents' acute awareness and irrational and sometimes conflicted high regard for high status.

Talking of shame, when my children were small we used to drive past Pentonville Prison once or twice a week on our way to meet Lucy and her children at the park or the zoo, the nursery-rhyme tape blaring in the cassette machine and the children cocooned in their car seats, both of them having their childhood how it was supposed to be lived; I was doing my best to look after them properly in spite of my own difficulties.

On the pavement opposite the prison one morning I saw a young woman hold up a baby so that the child's father, behind bars in one of the upper windows, could see his daughter and wave at her over the top of the high wall. The woman's arms were strong, her loose sleeves falling back. She wanted to show her man how the baby was thriving, how well she was turned out, and I found myself thinking about the arrangement they might have made so that he was ready at the window of his cell right after the baby had been fed and changed, the unpredictable timing of it, or was he just standing there all day, waiting on the off-chance to catch a glimpse of his loved ones, the little family all he had left. I was moved by the young mother's optimism, her generosity, but felt sad and anxious every time I drove past those prison walls because Ali was in there, my beloved brother, serving a sentence for bank robbery.

I don't suppose he burst into the bank with a gun, terrifying the poor counter clerk, a balaclava over his head or his face hidden behind a tan-coloured stocking, the nylon mesh flattening and distorting his features. No, I suspect the truth was less dramatic, maybe more shameful in a way for our family, a white-collar offence, or perhaps he just sidled into a bank with a stolen cheque book and tried to withdraw money that did not belong to him, pushed out in front by his partners in crime because he was foolhardy, the poshest, collared attempting to commit a theft that carried an unexpectedly long custodial sentence. I don't know, I have forgotten the details, but after his release, housed in temporary accommodation arranged for him by the probation service, he found an almost untouched hamburger in a bin in the street outside King's Cross Station. Not very hungry at the time and hoping to warm it up a bit, he stashed the burger behind the radiator in his room and forgot about it. Two weeks later, drawn by the smell of cooked meat, he found it again and devoured it. No harm came to him. Just one of the gleeful stories he tells about himself when he was a drug addict.

I made some unstable choices myself in my life, some of which I regret, and it costs me to admit to the everyday abasements I suffered as a young woman, unequipped as I was with much sense of my own value. I regret I told my mother to look after her own children when she needed help, but I was only fourteen and I forgive myself. When Stella was a teenager Mum told her how awful I was at the same age, not laughingly but with deep bitterness, and I asked her to desist – it was not open season on me even decades later, my teenage years not an easy subject for any of us.

Mum was hostile towards me when she felt angry and miserable, almost regardless of my behaviour, or that was my experience, the proximity of my body and soul quite enough to spark her envy or rage however hard I tried to efface myself, but of course that's not the whole story. We had some memorable times when she was happy, even in my teenage years, at the Rainbow in Finsbury

Park and at Hammersmith Odeon, Bob Marley and the Wailers in concert, two unforgettably joyful mother-and-daughter outings that will always be extraordinarily important to me. Both times I felt young, a child on a special treat with a beloved parent, but at Hammersmith also that ambivalence of adolescence when you are the boss and have to make sure no surging youths in the thick of the crowd snatch the tickets out of your mum's hand when you are queuing to get in, even if she would give them up willingly. We both knew those young boys had more right than us to receive Bob's uplifting message of freedom and love and redemption, the right not to remain on the street and miss everything apart from the bass through the walls of the auditorium, angry to have been shut out, but I was keener than Mum to put myself first in spite of my knowledge, to stand up for myself, one of the differences between us.

My favourite Gregory Isaacs record is called 'No Speech, No Language', and the first time I visited the speech and language department of UCLH with my mother I heard his wonderful voice in my head, wondering what the song might mean and wondering why the department was so named, wondering if they could do anything to help her. The speech and language department was adjacent to head and neck oncology. I had not thought of my mother's cancer defined in that way until I saw the welcome sign when we came out of the lift, the department embracing her even if I felt she might not belong. I noticed that nobody had bothered to remove the embossed metal plaques fixed to the window frames of the waiting room – *Patients must not throw cigarette ends out of the window* – although of course smoking was no longer allowed on the premises, men and women on drips in hospital gowns lighting up out front in spite of everything. In the waiting room I stared at those signs and I thought about smoking, the ease with which my mother had given up as soon as she received her diagnosis, wishing she had given up before it was too late. I gave up when I was twenty-eight, having read *Freud and Man's Soul* by Bruno Bettelheim and understood suddenly I was killing myself.

After a wait of four hours the department nutritionist asked my mum if she had ever eaten an avocado pear, expressing his enquiry with great care not to make her feel bad if such an exotic fruit were outside her range of experience. Sometimes the wait was so long free sandwiches were handed round the waiting room to keep everyone going. Most of the patients were unable to eat sandwiches, but their family members and carers were grateful for the sustenance.

At the end she was admitted to St Joseph's Hospice for a brief stay, the palliative-care team planning to adjust her pain medication and send her home in a few days. Kai stayed with her every night, sleeping in a big chair to keep her safe and comfort her if she woke up. Her room was bright and sunny, overlooking the car park, and every morning at eleven a drinks trolley did the rounds, a volunteer from the local community offering gin or vodka to visitors and patients at no cost. The jingle of the trolley was welcome, but we never availed ourselves of the alcohol.

We were still bringing soup when she no longer wanted to eat soup, and gave the extra to Moses and Abigail, a couple who had moved into the hospice not as patients but as visitors, son and daughter-in-law of an elderly man who was dying in a room along the corridor. They slept in the visitors' lounge, and were fed three times a day on the leftovers from the patients' food trolley, untouched meals and buttered bread, supplemented when necessary by our soup, which was nutrient rich, laden with calories.

In the early days when it still seemed inappropriate for me to witness or help with my mother's personal care the nurses would ask me to leave her bedside so they could get on and I used to flop in the lounge, bedding still spread on the sofas or rolled up in the corner behind the telly, the curtains drawn and a pale nature programme flickering on mute in the half-light. Moses talked about letting his father down and failing to capitalize on all the opportunities that had been his for the taking, breaking his father's heart, and Abigail complained that he was infantile. She told me her daughter had been taken away and would not come back to her now even if she was allowed by the local authority, the child unwilling to be reunited with her real mum because she was angry and believed she was better off in foster care. They were amazed and grateful anybody even troubled to take time to sit and talk, ashamed as they were of themselves, both of them having failed in so many ways to live up to expectations. I told them not to be silly and enjoyed the camaraderie of impending bereavement, their heartbreaking accounts of themselves, and talked about losing my own father, unsolicited hints and tips that they may or may not have found helpful. Their car was parked in the car park and contained their clothes and other belongings, and once I saw them preparing themselves for an important meeting, Abigail wearing a miniskirt, high heels and white tights and applying spectacular make-up in the rear-view mirror, the car door open and her bag and some other kit spilling out onto the tarmac, Moses fixing a skullcap to the back of his head with hairgrips.

Possibly because of the circumstances of my mother's initial admission I was still thinking she might recover somehow or at least keep going even after she lost her swallow. I took her down to the garden in a wheelchair for some fresh air and we parked up under a grim bower of honeysuckle, in the shade, her depression so intense I could feel the danger of her mood, the inanity of my desire to point out the spring flowers and the birds singing, the terror for both of us of her anger and hatred.

A nurse removed her drip in the night and when I turned up in the morning I was outraged, explaining to him that without receiving the water it contained she would die, failing to understand that to embrace death was the whole point of the hospice service. The nurse replaced the drip to humour me, and in my presence the doctor asked my mother if she would like to be transferred to UCLH and fed through a tube into her stomach, not as a real possibility of action Mum might choose to keep going but in the expectation that she would refuse to go back there. Mum shook her head conclusively, faltered for a moment then turned towards me as if she thought she must ask my permission, the question in her eyes brave and pleading with me to let go, her voice almost indecipherable, although I had no doubt what she was asking me. I was sobbing, but nodded my head.

She was blissed out once they introduced an intravenous anti-anxiety medication to her drug regime, and I remember thinking it would have been kinder if she had been given that earlier on in her illness, earlier on in her life. She reached up and touched the face of the young nurse who was leaning over to moisten her lips with a small pink sponge on a stick, the same pink sponges we had used to nurse my father, and told her she was a beautiful angel. The nurse was concerned I might be jealous and tried to explain away my mum's expression of love as a side effect of the drugs, morphine a disinhibiting substance and the other stuff even more powerful. I only felt glad my mum was happy in that moment, in heaven temporarily under the influence, released from her cares. I remembered one time her looking at me and telling me I was beautiful, when I was in my fifties.

I sat by her bed with a couple of sentences on the back of an envelope I wanted to tell her before it was too late, my last chance to resolve everything, and she accepted my apology I was a bad teenager before I left home. She was unable to speak by then, but wrote a few words about my teenage years on the pad she used to communicate with us – I said I knew I had been difficult to cope with and she said we were all up to it, meaning we managed, and she was smiling, which was not how it felt at the time but I was glad that's how she remembered it. I thanked her for taking care of us all whatever happened. And I was grateful. I am grateful. She never let us go.

Acknowledgements

With thanks to George Morley, Rosie Shackles, Connor Hutchinson and all at Picador, Diana Rawstron and David Dawson at the Lucian Freud Archive, Pilar Ordovas and Georgina Rumbellow at Ordovas, Mike Crawford at Lighthouse Darkroom, Jane England at England and Co, John Riddy, Alison Owen, Celia Paul, Sophie de Stempel, Jane Ewart, Leah Kharibian, Jeni Cook, Jake Auerbach and Lizzie McInnerny, Lesley Bell, Matthew Hamilton at the Hamilton Agency and Rebecca Nicolson for introducing us, and Antoinette at the Oughterard Heritage Group for the photograph of Haile Selassie with my great uncles Ronald and Noel Stevens.

Thanks also to my husband Mark Pearce for his unconditional love and constant support, to my son Vincent, to Alex and Anna and Finn Allan Pearce Golightly and to my daughter Stella for her encouragement and understanding.

And joyful gratitude to Lucy Astor and all my other inspirational friends and their children and grandchildren.

Not to mention Esther Freud for her wise guidance, and to Annie Freud, Annabel Freud, Bella Freud, Susie Boyt, Isobel Boyt, Kai Boyt, Ali Boyt, Frank Paul, Frances, Lucy and Alice Costelloe and all my other beloved brothers and sisters and nieces and nephews – I can't thank you enough.